Data Collecting Methods and Experiences

Data Collecting Methods and Experiences

A Guide for Social Researchers

Edited by
Manohar Pawar

NEW DAWN PRESS, INC.
USA • UK • INDIA

NEW DAWN PRESS GROUP

Published by New Dawn Press Group
New Dawn Press, Inc., 244 South Randall Rd # 90, Elgin, IL 60123
e-mail: sales@newdawnpress.com

New Dawn Press, 2 Tintern Close, Slough, Berkshire, SL1-2TB, UK
e-mail : ndpuk@mail.newdawnpress.com

New Dawn Press (An Imprint of Sterling Publishers (P) Ltd.)
A-59, Okhla Industrial Area, Phase-II, New Delhi-110020
e-mail: sales@sterlingpublishers.com
ghai@nde.vsnl.net.in

Data Collecting Methods and Experiences: A Guide for Social Researchers
Copyright © 2004 by Manohar Pawar (Ed.)
ISBN 1 932705 03 1

All rights are reserved. No part of this publication may be reproduced, stored in a retrieval system or transmitted, in any form or by any means, mechanical, photocopying, recording or otherwise, without prior written permission of the original publisher.

PRINTED IN INDIA

Preface

When I was collecting data, I read a book, *The Field Worker and the Field* (Srinivas *et al*, 1979*), that inspired me to work on the present title. In many respects this book is unique. First, it focuses on popular survey research data collecting experiences, which very few researchers have documented and disseminated. Many available books on field experiences and the field workers mostly deal with anthropological, ethnographic or qualitative research. Second, while many books on field experiences just discuss various authors' field experiences in a narrative form, this book uniquely combines data collecting methods and strategies, and data collecting experiences. In addition, it clearly points out lessons we can learn from other researchers' experiences. Third, most of the data collecting experiences presented here are from the distinguished authors' own doctoral research data collecting experiences. Thus they are coming straight from the horse's mouth. Fourth, the book covers both Indian and overseas researchers' data collecting experiences, an overseas researcher's experience of collecting data in India and an Indian researcher's experience of collecting data overseas. Finally, the content of the book is organised and presented in such a way that both new and experienced researchers can use it before, during and after research data collection.

The major thrust of this book is data collection methods and experiences. It is organised in six parts with a separate introduction and conclusion. In part I, the first chapter presents a pluralistic

---

* Reference details on page 129

approach to data collecting methods. The second chapter looks at issues relating to several research and data collecting methods, and strategies with a brief discussion on their strengths, limitations, purpose and utilisation skills. At the end, an annotated bibliography is provided for further reading. In part II, four researchers present their experiences of collecting data on sensitive issues such as bankruptcy, ethnicity, development of children and the accused in the criminal justice system. Part III shares three researchers' experiences of collecting data from rural and indigenous communities. In part IV, two researchers narrate their experiences of gathering data on and from non-government organisations. Part V shows what a researcher gains and loses by collecting data from computerised sets. The last part, the concluding chapter, draws lessons from the various data collecting experiences and shows a direction towards developing better data collecting knowledge and skills. It is hoped that social science researchers, research methodology students and teachers, and MPhil and Ph.D. scholars will find the book interesting and useful, and will creatively think about answers to the questions this book raise. Although I have edited the book, the authors are responsible for the views expressed in the respective chapters.

Acknowledgements

This book, in its present shape, would not have come out without contributions of distinguished scholars (names and details appear under Note on Contributors) who have honestly and frankly presented their unique data collecting experiences. I profusely thank them for their cooperation, understanding and patience in finalising the chapters and publishing the book. I am grateful to blind referees for going through the chapters and offering valuable comments and suggestions. My colleagues, Professor Margaret Alston, Director of the Centre for Rural Social Research, Professor Tony Thomson and Professor Frank Vanclay, provided helpful comments on the drafts of the book. I really appreciate them for the valuable time they spared. I thank Bill Anscombe, Wendy Bowles, Jenny McKinnon and Karen Bell for their support. I would like to thank Gail Robinson and Gail Commens who have typed most of the chapters. I wish to thank New Dawn Press for publishing the book. Any research and writing cannot be completed without denying well deserved time to the most loved ones. My wife Jaya and our recently arrived baby, Neel, have accommodated my absence from their company. I appreciate their support to my involvement in research, teaching and other academic pursuits.

Manohar Pawar

Contents

Preface v
Acknowledgment vii
Introduction xi

PART I
Data Collecting Methods and Strategies

Chapter 1: A Pluralistic Approach to Data Collecting Methods — *Manohar Pawar*   3

Chapter 2: Data Collecting Methods and Strategies — *Manohar Pawar*   17

PART II
Gathering Data on Sensitive Issues

Chapter 3: Interviewing the Stigmatised: Experiences of Collecting Data from Consumer Bankrupts in Australia — *Martin Ryan*   61

Chapter 4: Research Design: An Intricacy of Data Collection — *Ranu Jain*   79

Chapter 5: Data Collection: Multifaceted Experiences in Day Care — *Rajani M. Konantambigi*   93

Chapter 6: Searching for Data in the Criminal Justice System — *Manohar Pawar*   110

Part III
Gathering Data from Rural and Indigenous Communities

Chapter 7: The Stranger with a Shoulder Bag: Reflections on Field Research — *Lakshmi Lingam*   133

Chapter 8: An Approach for Data Collection in Tribal Areas — *I.U.B. Reddy*   142

Chapter 9: Reflections on Collecting Data from a Rural Development District in Kerala — *M.E. Thomas*   156

Part IV
Gathering Data on and from Non-Government Organisations

Chapter 10: An 'Outsider's' Tale: Experiences of Collecting Data on Voluntary Agencies in India — *Simon Combe*   175

Chapter 11: The Research Climate in NGOs: My Experience in Data Collection — *Swapan Garain*   200

Part V
Making Sense of the Available Data

Chapter 12: Social Research Using Computerised Data Sets — *Joseph M. Chandy*   223

Part VI
Conclusion

Chapter 13: Learning from Data Collecting Methods and Experiences: Moving Closer to Reality — *Manohar Pawar*   237

Note on Contributors   261

Manohar Pawar

Introduction

The main objective of this book is to critically discuss data collecting methods and strategies and present social researchers' first-hand data collecting experiences with a view that readers of these experiences may be able to choose appropriate data collecting methods, follow effective strategies to collect high quality data and enhance the understanding of research issues for the benefit of the whole society.

The book is organised in six parts with a separate introduction and conclusion. In part I, the first chapter presents a pluralistic approach to data collecting methods. It highlights the significance of data collecting methods in the research process and raises several questions which will help researchers at the initial stages of research problem formulation. By pointing out some limitations of conventional ways of choosing research and data collecting methods, it suggests strengths of a pluralistic approach to data collecting methods. The second chapter presents several data collecting methods and strategies, and concisely analyses each method's strengths, limitations and purposes. Further, it indicates basic skills required to use these methods. At the end, it provides an annotated bibliography for further reading. It is hoped that many research teachers and students will find this chapter handy, both in the classroom and the field.

The second part of the book looks at the four researchers' data collecting experiences from sensitive respondents and settings such as bankrupts, women, children, day care centres, the accused and the criminal justice system. To understand the perceptions and experiences of bankrupts in Melbourne, Australia, Martin Ryan had undertaken the very challenging and daunting task of interviewing bankrupts. Ryan reports that bankrupts are the most reluctant interviewees as the subject matter of the interview is so sensitive and personal to them. Ryan succinctly discusses his experiences of collecting data from the stigmatised through a structured interview schedule and insights gained from such experiences. In addition to providing useful hints for interviewers, Ryan suggests his own 'theory of action' for data collection. His analysis underscores the need to study sensitive topics, particularly, by human service professionals.

An equally interesting study was undertaken by Ranu Jain. Jain was interested in understanding ethnicity in plural societies with particular reference to Jain Oswals in Kolkata. To address the question – how an ethnic group constructs its own meaning of ethnicity and maintains boundary around itself – Jain collected data from observation, case study, informal unstructured interviews, analysis of genealogies and secondary data and 'oral history'. Jain discusses how she progressed in the field and encountered and overcame several data collecting problems. Based on her first hand experience, Jain makes thought provoking arguments, which, I am sure many researchers will find useful.

Rajani Konantambigi's research involved collecting data from young children (3 to 6 years), their mothers and day care centres in Bangalore, India. Konantambigi employed an interview schedule, several psychological scales and observation method to collect the needed data. The aim of the research was to find out the influence of family and environmental factors on the development of children. Particularly, Konantambigi looked at family environment and day care centres and their contribution to children's development. Konantambigi's data collecting experiences make us think about the limits of psychological scales, particularly, when they are used to collect data from young children. Konantambigi discusses several data collecting problems and how they affect the quality of research. To Konantambigi the data collecting experience was a test of her wits and patience.

Pawar's paper presents experiences of gathering data from the criminal justice system. His research design followed observation and survey method. To understand the working of the magisterial courts in Mumbai, Pawar collected data from multiple sources. First, he undertook an observation study of court working. Second, a sample of case files were followed up over a period of ten months to examine the pace of their progress. Third, during the same period, by employing an interview schedule, he interviewed the accused to ascertain their views on their processing in the criminal justice system. Fourth, Pawar approached lawyers and public prosecutors several times and asked them to complete a questionnaire and provide their views on the working of the judiciary and delay in deciding cases. The paper brings out difficulties encountered and strategies employed to overcome such difficulties while collecting the data. Most importantly, it implicitly questions the usefulness of such methods, particularly when they are used to collect data from sensitive settings such as the criminal justice system.

In the third part of the book, three researchers enthusiastically share their experiences of collecting data from rural and indigenous communities. To examine the relationship between agro-ecological differences and social structure, and its influence on women's role and position, Lakshmi Lingam studied two villages in East Godavari district of Andhra Pradesh, India. Lingam employed three sets of schedules to gather village data, household data and women-specific data. Based on her field experiences, Lingam points out important factors that matter in collecting data from villages and shows how she changed data collecting approaches according to field realities. Lingam's reflections show that data collecting from Indian villages is as challenging as interesting. To Lingam the analysis of casual experiences and observations was more thrilling than a prosaic activity of filling up an interview schedule.

I.U.B. Reddy selected Semliguda block in Koraput district of Orissa, India, a typical tribal area, to formulate a micro level plan for its development. First, Reddy discusses five broad development parameters and data needed to analyse those parameters. Then he lists several difficulties he encountered in collecting such data from the tribal area. Reddy's field experiences provide useful suggestions for development researchers.

In the last chapter of the third part of the book, M. E. Thomas takes us to Manathavady and Sultan's Battery development blocks in the district of Wayanad in Kerala, India. Motivated by his grassroots level work with a voluntary agency, Thomas decided to study dynamics of rural development in the two blocks. The study had several objectives and dimensions. Thomas was keen to understand the felt needs of communities and available resources to meet those needs, development policies and programmes and their implementation process, the involvement of development functionaries, people's participation strategies and impact of development programmes. Thomas approached the field with a set of interview schedules to collect data from programme beneficiaries and non-beneficiaries, opinion leaders and development functionaries. In addition, data were collected through secondary sources and observation method. Although Thomas faced several difficulties and inconveniences while collecting data, to him the unique field "restructured his experience, modified his perceptual reality and provided richness and meaning to the problem under study". In hindsight, Thomas makes ten important points, which any researcher will find useful.

The fourth part of the book looks at the two researchers' experiences of collecting data on and from voluntary agencies. Simon Combe's article shows how he was drawn into the subject of voluntary agencies in India. Combe was mainly interested in understanding the Indian voluntary sector and in constructing a definition of voluntary agency. His main source of data was available documents, interviews and conversations and observations. Combe honestly and frankly tells us how his research interest changed over a period and how he selected the topic he researched in India. Combe has constructively reflected on his data collecting experiences both at personal and professional levels. Without any reservations and in a most interesting manner Combe shares with us the difficulties he encountered, where he went wrong, and how he learnt from his own trial and error approaches. Many foreign researchers and Indian scholars, I am sure, will find this chapter interesting and educative. Being an insider, Swapan Garain did not have fewer problems in researching non-government organisations (NGOs). Garain undertook a kind of pioneering work in understanding organisational effectiveness in NGOs. Realising that theories and models developed for formal organisations in government and industry cannot be applied for NGOs, Garain tried to adapt and develop research instruments to collect data. One was used to collect data on NGOs and another one consisting of several scales was used to collect data from NGOs' staff. In hindsight, Garain tells us his anxious moments and how he was oscillating with research methods and how the research methods evolved as he grew in his research work. Garain thoroughly discusses his experiences of visiting NGOs' projects and personnel in Maharashtra and West Bengal, India, how he established rapport and gained cooperation of respondents and how he failed to do so in respect to a few NGOs. There are many lessons that we can learn from Garain's experiences. In addition, his analysis helps us to gain an understanding of research climate in NGOs and to take effective steps to conduct research on similar issues.

In the fifth part of the book, Joseph Chandy takes us away from the field. Chandy discusses his experiences of researching by using computerised data sets. Chandy was deeply involved in understanding and analysing resiliency factors that help vulnerable populations to function normally. The study mainly involved the analysis of available data that were drawn from an Adolescent Health Survey, which was conducted in Minnesota, USA. Thus Chandy's 'field experience' was mainly limited to computer data-sets, computers and SPSS statistical procedures. Chandy succinctly discusses some of the advantages and disadvantages of a research approach he followed and what he gained and lost by not going to the field.

The concluding part analyses the researchers' data collecting experiences, suggests strategies to minimise data collecting problems and raises several critical questions which have implications on the way we construct, understand and apply research methodology and research methods. Do social science researchers need to develop alternative research methodology and methods to better understand ourselves and the reality surrounding us? It also underscores the need to become a reflective field researcher.

PART I

Data Collecting Methods and Strategies

1

MANOHAR PAWAR

A Pluralistic Approach to Data Collecting Methods

Introduction

This chapter discusses the importance and relevance of data collecting methods and strategies, and the place of data collecting methods in a whole research enterprise. It briefly outlines approaches to selecting research methods and suggests a pluralistic approach to data collecting methods.

Importance and Relevance of Data Collecting Methods and the Research Process

No research can be undertaken without data. All social science researchers look for the data which help them answer their research questions and achieve their research objectives. Often the quality, quantity, adequacy and appropriateness of the data determines the quality of research. To a great extent the data collecting methods affect the quality, quantity, adequacy and appropriateness of data. Since there are several data collecting methods, generally researchers attempt to employ the most appropriate data collecting method(s) in their research projects, though they are not free to choose a method which they like. Researchers' selection of data collecting methods are often dictated by practical considerations such as the nature of the research problem, cost in terms of time and money and availability of data and access to it. Sometimes, researchers select a particular method or methods simply because they like them and they have used them earlier, irrespective of whether or not such chosen methods are most appropriate to the research problem.

In fact, there appears to prevail an unconducive research culture in which many young researchers are groomed to mechanically pick up any issue, undertake ceremonial literature review, blindly prepare instruments, often questionnaires or interview schedules, by looking at a few earlier research instruments and complete the instruments in the field with several difficulties and limitations. Then without much consideration, they subject the data to statistical tests and write a report in a ritualistic manner. I think there is a need to cease this kind of research culture.

Are researchers free to choose research and data collecting methods according to their own liking? No. Researchers have no choice in selecting research and data collecting methods. These methods are merely instruments of the problem which they have selected to study. Indeed it is the nature of the research problem which should determine the choice of research design and data collecting methods. Although the subject of this chapter is data collecting methods, it cannot be discussed without referring to certain important stages of research as these stages are interconnected and flow from one to another.

Before jumping to data collecting methods and instruments, researchers should identify an unambiguous and specific issue, clearly formulate the problem and then establish familiarity with it by reviewing relevant literature. The literature review is not the summarisation of earlier research studies. Many novice researchers have the tendency to fall back to this style. Instead of merely summarising the earlier studies, the literature review should address the following questions:

- What is the established knowledge?
- What are the gaps in the knowledge?
- What research questions have been addressed?
- What research questions need to be addressed?

Next, the objectives of the research should flow from this analysis of research gaps and questions. The researcher may not be able to address all the identified research gaps and questions. Thus objectives should reflect the delimitation of the problem and what specific issues will be addressed in the research. Following the objectives, depending upon the nature of the research problem, hypotheses and research questions are framed in unambiguous terms. Although it is not essential to have explicit hypotheses and research questions in every piece of research, we need to be conscious that researchers have some implicit hypotheses and research questions in their minds. Researchers may not be able to spell out what is going on in their minds, because the debate continues and causal relationships and questions are still in the process of being developed towards achieving clarity. Often researchers themselves are not sure what is happening in their minds, but something is certainly bothering them. Otherwise, they would not be researching. Ongoing awareness of the researcher's 'inside mind' phenomenon is vital as such reflection will provide fundamental leads to the researcher.

Any well-planned research will then involve the development of clear concepts and independent and dependent variables. If some researchers do not identify and develop them in the beginning, they cannot escape from dealing with them in the course of their research.

Depending upon the nature of the problem, almost simultaneously or in a coordinated manner, researchers will consider and develop a research design. Generally, the development of the research design involves the selection of the research method or methods, sampling method(s), determination of the sample size, data collecting methods and the development of instruments, and data collection, analysis and presentation plan. Any well-prepared researcher would recognise and appreciate that the nature of the research problem, objectives, implicit or explicit hypotheses and research questions, the selection of research and sampling methods, the determination of sample size, data collecting methods and instruments, and data collection and analysis are logically interconnected. Thus every research design should be coherent.

However, researchers are often thrown into a 'research

methodology jungle', more so in the case of beginning researchers. Not only do they try to identify and understand the research problem, but also grapple with several research methods, sampling methods, data collecting methods and data analysis techniques.

Although there are three broad types of research – exploratory, descriptive and explanatory – Sarantakos' (1998) research methodology textbook lists 12 other types of research. These are: quantitative research, basic research, applied research, longitudinal research, qualitative research, classification research, comparative research, causal research, theory-testing research, theory-building research, action research and participatory action research. Other research methodology books discuss observation, case study, focus group, survey and experiment research methods (Yin, 1989; Mark, 1996). Feminist research could be added as another research method.

Of these, quantitative and qualitative research methods appear to be the two major umbrella categories often used and debated by researchers. Research methodology books show that quantitative research uses standardised measures, bases on limited number of predetermined responses, facilitates comparison and statistical aggression of data, generalises set of findings, and focuses on the measuring instrument. On the other hand, qualitative research dwells in depth and detail, does not use predetermined categories of analysis, increases understanding of cases and situations, reduces generalisability and focuses more on the researcher as her/his skills and competence are crucial to the research (Patton, 1990). Does this kind of quantitative and qualitative compartmentalised researching make any sense? For research purposes, can we in this way divide the phenomenon that logically constitutes both quantitative and qualitative aspects? We must raise these and similar questions. I think we need to change this quantitative and qualitative divisive research culture.

Many research methodology and statistics textbooks discuss probability and non-probability sampling methods. Probability sampling methods include simple random sampling, systematic sampling, stratified random sampling, cluster sampling, multi-stage sampling, area sampling, multi-phase sampling and spatial sampling. Non-probability sampling methods include accidental sampling, purposive sampling, quota sampling and snowball sampling (Sarantakos, 1998; Alston and Bowles, 1998).

Several data collecting methods include observation, case study, questionnaire, interview schedule, semi structured/unstructured interview schedule, interview guidelines, telephone interviews, in-depth interviews, experiments, treatment and its results, focus group discussion and primary or secondary data proforma. Sometimes, data collecting aids such as the field diary, video and cassette recorder and camera are employed to facilitate the data collection process.

Data analysis methods include a number of quantitative and qualitative techniques such as single frequency, central tendency and dispersion, several tests of associations and significance, narrative analysis, developing themes and content analysis.

Thus a wide range of methods, though independent, are logically interconnected in the research design (Figure 1). The nature of research problems, research objectives, hypotheses and questions with the objective and subjective influence of the researcher will lead to the selection of a particular research method or methods. The selected research methods suggest suitable sampling methods. All the three together suggest appropriate data collecting methods. The selected research problem, sampling and data collecting methods and the collected data determine appropriate data analysis methods. In other words, the choice and employment of the data collecting methods depend upon the research problem, objectives, hypotheses and questions, and the chosen research and sampling methods. The choice and the employment of the data analysis methods depend upon the research problem, sampling procedures, the data collecting methods and the data.

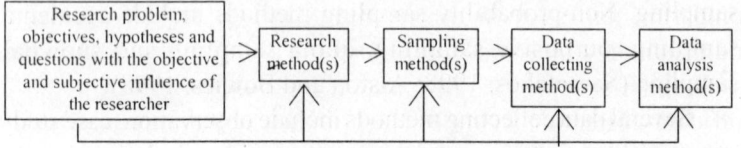

Figure 1: Interconnectedness of data collecting methods with the other methods within the research design

Research methodology students and prospective researchers not only have to understand a wide range of research, sampling, data collecting and data analysis methods, but also have to learn to choose the most appropriate methods which are convincing to oneself and reasonably acceptable to other researchers. Sometimes, this choosing process may become formidable, confusing and contestable. Researchers should note that any research process and its outcome are often contestable and they should not get bogged down by research methodology and the research methods. It is important to pause and raise the following questions, and reflect on the underlying philosophy of the research methods.

- What is the fundamental aim of my research?
- What am I trying to discover?
- Why have I chosen the methods (research, sampling, data collecting) I have chosen?
- Do these methods help or hinder my efforts towards understanding reality?
- Are there any alternative methods to understand the phenomenon I am trying to understand?
- Do these categories of methods make any sense in understanding the reality?

Choosing Research Methods

There are two approaches to choosing appropriate research methods (Figure 2). The first approach is somewhat traditional and hierarchical, which is dated and has been seriously challenged, though there is some wisdom to gain from such an approach. The second approach is pluralistic, which differs substantially from the first one since it does not view research methods in a compartmentalised and hierarchical manner and it allows the mix and match of various methods.

In the first approach, the research methods, thus the sampling and data collecting methods, are placed in a continuum on a hierarchical basis. In a progressive manner, the hierarchy moves from explorative to descriptive to explanatory in terms of the research methods. In the same vein, in terms of research strategies, it moves from observation, case study, survey to experiments. The basis of the hierarchy is knowledge. That is, if the existing knowledge is very little or nil and the gaps in the knowledge are very high, researchers begin exploring the problem by using observation and case study methods. Therefore, such researches are branded exploratory.

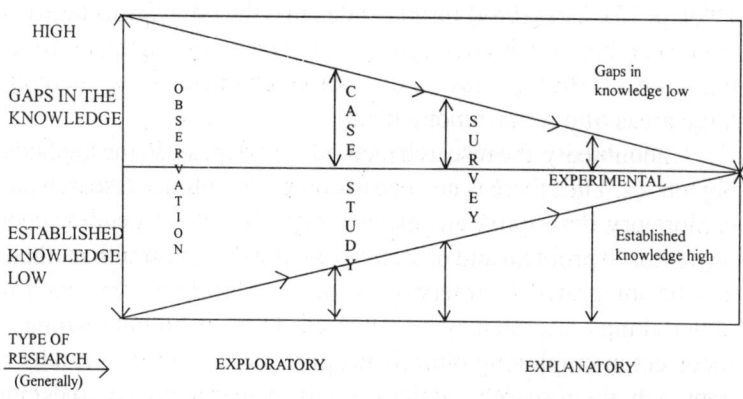

Figure 2: An approach to choosing the research and data collecting methods

If the established knowledge and the gaps in the knowledge are moderate, researchers generally undertake descriptive or explanatory research and employ survey research methods. Therefore, such researches are branded descriptive or explanatory.

If the available knowledge is very high and the gaps in the knowledge are very low, researchers generally follow the explanatory research method in which experiments are conducted and variables are controlled and manipulated to ascertain causal relationships.

Although the above approach was popular at one time and is useful to examine the available knowledge and gaps in it, the approach has been increasingly questioned and rejected simply because that kind of compartmentalisation and the hierarchy of research methods was not helping to understand the reality. Many researchers now agree that teaching of this approach to research methodology students is incorrect. In addition, some researchers have become very critical of a positivistic framework and survey research methods and their results, at least in some social sciences.

While comparing case studies with other research strategies, Yin (1989) notes that some of the best and most famous case studies have been both descriptive (for example, *Whyte's Street Corner Society*, 1943) and explanatory (see Allison's *Essence of Decision Making: Explaining the Cuban Missile Crisis*, 1971) cited in Yin, 1989, p. 15). Yin (1989) further states that the boundaries between the research methods (strategies) are not clear and sharp, and even though each strategy has its distinctive characteristics, there are large areas of overlap among them.

Undoubtedly, the research methods overlap, so do the methods' objectives. Thus there is no need to compartmentalise research into exploratory, descriptive and explanatory research. Depending upon the research problem and objectives, all the three research methods can be integrated or interwoven, and a pluralistic approach to undertaking research may be followed. There is nothing wrong or incorrect in employing pluralistic approach. Under the pluralistic approach, the research problem and the researcher have to decide whether to restrict the research at exploratory, descriptive or explanatory levels, or combine all the three. Reflecting back on Figure 2, now we might raise a question: If a lot of exploration and description has already been made on a particular issue and some hypotheses can be made in regard to what causes what, why should the researchers waste their valuable resources on repetitious exercise of exploration and description? In such a case, researchers should test their hypotheses, experiment and explain. For example, in psychology and medical science often explanatory researches are conducted, where it is possible to play with cause and effect (independent and dependent) variables by controlling and manipulating them.

However, most of the social sciences, social issues, and human services areas do not readily tune with the so-called positivistic and experimental framework (natural science research method), which has been imposed on them under the influence of positivism. We now know that positivism in social sciences has generally failed to achieve 'grand theories', or even paradigms which enhance our understanding of social problems and alleviation. It may have sound generalisations, but all these cannot hold ground in all the places and all the time. Here, I am not advocating the abandoning of positivism. I would like researchers to take the best out of it and at the same time challenge its shortcomings.

Rowan and Reason (1981) have systematically listed 18 points that show some of the negative outcomes of the practice of positivism. Through the positivistic framework, people may be treated as robots in research, they may be trivialised and manipulated according to the design of the research. When information is reduced into variables, categories and numbers, researchers may not know persons, groups, communities as such, since people are turned into things. The application of determinism on variables is unidirectional, thus there is an element of coercion of independent variables on dependent variables. Positivistic research may produce statistically significant results, but these are humanly insignificant. Standardised instruments/scales are culturally biased and often used in unfair ways. Researchers may unnecessarily withhold information. Debriefing may not help people overcome bad experiences in research. Large messages or broad generalisations are often made from small samples and unrepresentative bases. Detachment from the phenomenon keeps away researchers from knowing. It may be used to maintain status quo in favour of the rich and powerful. Sometimes research may be designed and results may be obtained just to confirm the decisions already taken. Many people may not understand the language of research due to the technical nature of presentation (Rowan and Reason, 1981).

Although many social issues like unemployment, drugs, freedom movements, disability, human rights, poverty, development, displaced people, indigenous people, social disorganisation in various forms, etc., occur worldwide, we cannot generalise and build unidirectional and universal grand theories by gathering data in only one corner of the world. History and the developmental context of issues and their solutions differ from place to place and time to time. This is one great limitation of research in social sciences as they follow the framework of positivism (natural science method).

In addition, we need to go beyond the framework of positivism to challenge some of its outcomes. According to Popper (1965), the purpose of research is to falsify with certainty and universality. Although in social research universality has some problems, contextually falsifying with certainty is a useful approach. With varied data collecting methods it may be possible to falsify. McKenzie (1997) rightly observes that "Modern social research seeks to develop claims which are eternal and immutable. In contrast, we need to be aware of the transient and contingent nature of our understanding" (p. 17) and make it explicit in our research. Questioning the unified scientific approach to research, McKenzie draws on Kuhn's work (1962, 1974) and elaborates that science itself is a social process in which scientists solve puzzles posed by the dominant methodology of the particular scientific community in which they participate. Since every community has its own way of thinking, research tradition, 'coloured glass', its research outcome will be full of that dominant colour. For example, predominance of survey research method and the use of questionnaires and interview schedules in social science research, and policies guided by national statistical averages and rates (gross/national/domestic product, per capita income, unemployment, literacy, etc.) ignore significant pockets and high rates of unemployment, ill-health, illiteracy, homeless youth, poverty, etc. According to Kuhn (1962, 1974), progress in understanding and dealing with the issues can only be achieved if existing paradigms are destroyed.

> Because it demands large-scale paradigm destruction and major shifts in the problems and techniques of normal science, the emergence of new theories is generally preceded by a period of

pronounced professional insecurity. As one might expect, insecurity is generated by the persistent failure of the puzzles of normal science to come as they should. Failure of existing rules is the prelude to search for new ones (p. 67-68).

In my view, a creative and pluralistic approach (Figure 3) to data collecting methods can facilitate the search for new rules and ultimately the destruction of problematic paradigms. The pluralistic

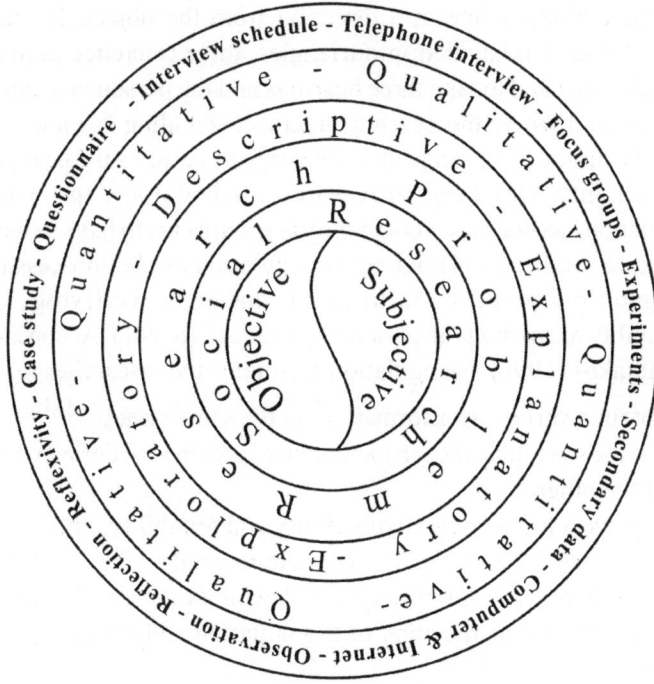

Figure 3: A pluralistic approach to data collecting methods

approach provides the researcher a wide range of research and data collecting methods and allows the researcher to develop his or her own needed permutations and combinations of research and data collecting methods in the light of research problem. It views varieties of research methods in unison without any hierarchy. It also does not demarcate between quantitative and qualitative approaches, and objectivity and subjectivity dilemmas. In addition, it does not aim to discover one single reality.

The pluralistic approach is somewhat like a triangulation approach, but it is not exactly the same. The word 'triangulation' does not exist in *Oxford Advanced Learner's Dictionary* (Cowie, 1989). I think it originates from the word 'triangular', which means a situation involving three people, ideas, opinions, etc. It appears that the term 'triangulation' is taken from geographical survey methods. The use of one object on the ground locates the person somewhere along a line in a direction from the object. In land surveys the area is divided into triangles, three reference points/ landmarks are used to take three bearings and the person is located on the ground where the bearings intersect (Fielding & Fielding, 1986). Accuracy of bearings to known objects narrows the triangle of uncertainty. However, in research methodology, the word triangulation has been used commonly and it appears to have gained acceptance. Stake (1994) defines triangulation as the "process of using multiple perceptions to clarify meaning, verifying the repeatability of an observation or interpretation" (p. 241). According to Sarantakos (1998), triangulation facilitates the researcher to:

- obtain a variety of information on the same issue;
- use the strengths of each method to overcome the deficiencies of the other;
- achieve a higher degree of validity and reliability; and
- overcome the deficiencies of single-method studies (p. 169).

In his book, *The Limitations of Social Research,* Shipman (1997) simplifies the meaning of triangulation and critiques it as follows.

> In everyday life we crosscheck, believe that two heads are better than one, seek second opinions and others' points of view. In social research this is labelled triangulation. It has been further elaborated into time, space, person, respondent, data source, researcher, theoretical/ methodological/ partnership/ team, multi-disciplinary, reflexive, and no doubt many other triangulations (see, for example, Denzin, 1970 cited in Shipman, 1997). These are all ways of reducing dependence on the one-person, one-model, one-method collection of evidence.

Triangulation is a reflection of the difficulties faced by social research in producing valid and reliable evidence. If the aim is to change the world rather than to study it, the sole view can be confidently stated. But triangulation is an acknowledgment that social research is rarely decisive and the confidence is best established by collecting and presenting a number of viewpoints (pp. 105-106).

Although triangulation is useful to check the credibility of evidence, it neither ensures reliability and validity nor objectivity (Shipman, 1997).

The triangulation approach has been criticised by employing the yardsticks of positivistic framework. As stated earlier, the pluralistic approach is not exactly the same as triangulation because it is based on the following premises.

- The pluralistic approach aims to discover more than one reality, multiple realities.
- This approach admits that it is nearly impossible to remain absolutely objective in social research. Thus the pluralistic approach recognises and includes both objective and subjective aspects of reality.
- Instead of separating, it integrates qualitative and quantitative research dichotomy.
- The pluralistic approach rejects methodological barriers to understanding reality.

Appreciating this pluralistic perspective, the next chapter looks at various data collecting methods.

References

1. Alston M. and Wendy Bowles (1998). *Research for Social Workers*. Sydney: Allen and Unwin.
2. Cowie A.P. (1989). *Oxford Advanced Learner's Dictionary*. Oxford: Oxford University Press.
3. Kuhn T. (1962, 1974). *The Structure of Scientific Revolution* (2nd edn). Chicago: University of Chicago Press.
4. Fielding N.G. and Fielding J.L. (1986), *Linking Data*. London: Sage.
5. Mark R. (1996). *Research Made Simple*. London: Sage.

6. McKenzie G. (1997). 'The Age of Reason or the Age of Innocence' In: McKenzie G., Powell J. and Usher R., *Understanding Social Research: Perspectives on Methodology and Practice*. London: The Falmer Press.
7. Patton M. Q. (1990). *Qualitative Evaluation and Research Methods*. Newbury Park, CA: Sage.
8. Popper K. (1965). *The Logic of Scientific Discovery*. New York: Harper and Row.
9. Rowan J. and Reason P. (1981), Foreword. in: Reason P. and Rowan J. *Human Inquiry: A Source of New Paradigm Research* (ed.), Chichester: John Wiley and Sons.
10. Sarantakos S. (1998), *Social Research*, Melbourne: Macmillan.
11. Shipman M. (1997), *The Limitations of Social Research*, London: Longman.
12. Stake, R. E. (1994), Case Studies, in: N. K. Denzin and Y. S. Lincoln (ed), *Handbook of Qualitative Research* (pp. 236-247), Thousand Oaks, CA: Sage.
13. Yin R. K. (1989), *Case Study Research: Design and Methods*, London: Sage.

2
Manohar Pawar

Data Collecting Methods and Strategies

Introduction

This chapter provides an overview of six data collecting methods in terms of their meaning, strengths, limitations and handy hints to effectively employ them. These are observation, case study, questionnaire, interview/interview schedule, focus groups and secondary data.

Observation

This method involves collecting data by observing observable phenomena. Historically this method was generally popular with ethnographic researchers, though recently other social researchers have been increasingly using it. The observation method has been further delineated into four categories:

- Structured observation (requires systematic planning and clearly defined obversion categories).
- Unstructured observation (requires purposeful, open and flexible approach).
- Participant observation (requires the observer to participate in the observed phenomena and to interact with the researched, with informed consent. Lack of consent raises ethical issues).
- Non-participant observation (requires passive observation by remaining outside the phenomena being observed).

The following are six tips on doing the first observations and writing field jottings and logs (Ely *et al*, 1991).
- Observe deeply on the first visit. Be quiet – silence is golden now – and record your observations seriously. Ask people no questions yet. Be patient and watch the setting unfold itself.
- If any one asks you about the nature of your assignment, tell them you are observing how the programme, class, job, or person operates as part of a homework assignment. Be honest but not so specific that people begin to 'act' for you.
- Describe your observations without evaluations. Even if what you see is not agreeable to you, it needs to be described in the log as such. It has helped me to cite my judgements during log analysis, not during the initial description of the setting.
- Do write about your feelings and the questions you pose as you observe.
- If your participants seem persistently uncomfortable when they see your notepad, and you cannot convince them of your benign presence, then allay their fears by putting the notepad away.
- Some researchers take frequent trips to the water fountain, rest room, or their parked cars so they can record some key words and phrases.

As soon as possible after leaving the field, find a private place and the time to expand your field jottings into the log narrative and to think about it. Then make for yourself some directions for the next observations (pp. 71 -72).

Strengths: In terms of strengths, the observation method helps to overcome some of the limitations of other data collecting methods such as interview, questionnaire and focus group discussion. The method helps collect rich and insightful data in natural settings with relatively less cost and less inconvenience to the researched.

Limitations: Some of the important limitations are subjectivity, lack of generalisability, selectivity, interpretation and bias. In addition, it cannot be applied for large groups and events. It is helpful to study only the present. It is demanding in terms of the observer's time. It is difficult to observe everything at a time.

Purpose: Although observation method was originally used in ethnographic studies and case studies, in my view, it can be employed to undertake exploratory, descriptive, explanatory, social action and feminist research.

Utilisation Skills: Effective utilisation of the method calls for professional training and a lot of practice, flexibility, patience, the awareness of the self and researched, inclusion of both subjective and objective elements, careful exclusion of some observations and retention of observations (through log/diary, audio-video equipments and memory) and writing of the observed matter according to the design of the study.

There is a lot of confusion and controversy over the observation method and the four types of observation. A number of research methodology books list observation method under qualitative methods and criticise it by applying the limitations of qualitative research. In my view, the observation method is much broader than how it has been used so far. Observation is not merely seeing or visually noticing. Observation is essentially making sense by using some or all of the five sources of the sense perceptions. These are: eyes (seeing), ears (hearing), nose (smell), tongue (taste) and skin (touch). In addition, observation involves interpretation and meaningful construction. Observation is fundamental in both social and natural research. We not only observe when we use observation method, but also when we employ other data collecting methods such as interviews, focus group discussions and experiments. Thus observation method cuts across various other data collecting methods and qualitative and quantitative dichotomy.

Case Study

Case study is one of the important data collecting methods in social research. In research methodology, the phrase, 'case study', is in use both as a research design and data collecting method. The concept of case study is somewhat confusing to at least some researchers since it is used as an independent research design and data collecting method, as well as along with other research and data collecting methods. For example, some researchers use observation, interviews and surveys within a case study. Case study is a study of a single case by employing a data collecting method or a combination of varied data collecting methods and such a case may include an individual, family, a group, an organisation, community, a small town or village, an event and an issue. According to Yin (1989), "Case study investigates a contemporary phenomenon within its real-life context; when the boundaries between phenomenon and context are not clearly evident; and in which multiple sources of evidence are used (p. 23)."

Stake (1994) classifies case studies into three types. These are:

Intrinsic – purpose is to gain deeper understanding of an individual case by describing, not to build a theory or to understand a broad social issue.

Instrumental – purpose is to elaborate a theory and to gain a deeper understanding of a social issue.

Collective – purpose is to understand group of people or an issue by conducting several case studies.

Strengths: Case studies include detailed, deep and rich information on various aspects of a case, and identify unique features. Generally, the researcher's involvement is intensive. Case studies often make an impact and can be used in planning an effective intervention in the respective case.

Limitations: Depending upon the type of case study, generalisation would be limited to the case. Some case studies may take a long period and may be lengthy in terms of implementing and writing. Case studies are often more demanding and take time for organising and articulating the data. They may not provide a comprehensive perspective and may distract (entice) the reader.

Purpose: The case study method may be employed to undertake exploratory, descriptive and explanatory research.

Utilisation Skills: Generally, utilisation skills require professional training, reading of some good case studies, observing, listening and interviewing skills, establishing clear boundaries, periodic debriefing with experienced supervisor, frequent checks to keep on the track, and meaningfully relating data to the objectives. Researchers should make necessary field preparations (gaining entry, interview/observation guidelines) and build sufficient evidence. They also should have the skills of periodically reviewing the data, analysis and interpretation, and of writing the report in an engaging manner.

Questionnaire

Questionnaire is one of the most popular data collecting methods within the survey research method. It has become popular perhaps because it appears easy, though technically it is not. Some researchers use questionnaire and interview schedule interchangeably or synonymously, which is incorrect. Questionnaires and interview schedules are two different data collecting methods which should be clearly understood and used separately. A questionnaire is a document consisting of closed (forced choice) and/or open-ended structured questions covering research objectives, questions and variables. It may cover ordinal and/or nominal and independent, dependent and intervening variables, depending upon the research objectives, questions and hypotheses. It may also include scales consisting of several questions/statements (items) which require validity and reliability tests, and we have consciously excluded discussion on such statistical measures. The questionnaire is completed or filled by the respondent her/himself. Here there is no role for the interviewer. In other words, when you employ a questionnaire as the data collecting method, you do not need an interviewer.

Those who employ questionnaire method should address two important strategies. First, the construction of a questionnaire and second, administering it. The construction of a questionnaire involves the following steps:

a. Constructing questions
b. Designing appropriate lay out
c. Preparing effective cover letters, informed consent forms and instructions
d. Developing a complete questionnaire for trial
e. Pretesting or piloting the questionnaire
f. In the light of pretesting and/or piloting, revising the questionnaire

Several guidelines are available to develop an appropriate questionnaire. de Vaus (1995) provides a checklist of 16 questions to avoid the most obvious problems with preparing questions. These are:

1. Is the language simple?
2. Can the questions be shortened?
3. Is the question double-barreled?
4. Is the question leading?
5. Is the question negative?
6. Is the respondent likely to have the necessary knowledge?
7. Will the words have the same meaning for everyone?
8. Is there a prestige bias?
9. Is the question ambiguous?
10. Do you need a direct or indirect question?
11. Is the frame of reference for the question sufficiently clear?
12. Does the question artificially create opinions?
13. Is personal or impersonal wording preferable?
14. Is the question wording unnecessarily detailed or objectionable?
15. Does the question have dangling alternative?
16. Is the question likely to produce a response set?

For detailed discussion on these questions, please see de Vaus's (1995) chapter 6, 'Constructing Questionnaires'. Careful attention to these questions will help any researcher to prepare good questions.

By referring to relevant sources, Foddy (1993) has formulated seven broad guidelines to construct questions. These are:

1. Make sure that the topic has been clearly defined.
2. Be clear both about the information that is required on the topic and the reason for wanting this information.
3. Make sure that the topic has been defined properly for the respondents by:
   − avoiding the use of 'blab' words (i.e. words that are so abstract or general that they lack specific empirical reference)

- avoiding words that are unlikely to be understood by all respondents either because they are rarely used in everyday life, or are specialist words (i.e. jargon)
4. Make sure the question is relevant to respondents by:
    - using an appropriate filter, e.g. undecided, unsure, do not know, etc. (According to Foddy (1993), a question or question component that is explicitly offered to a respondent, either to establish the relevance of the question to the respondent, or to emphasise that it is acceptable for the respondent not to answer the question, is generally referred to as a 'filter'.)
    - avoiding asking for information respondents are likely to have forgotten
    - avoiding hypothetical issues
5. Make sure that the question is not biased by:
    - ensuring balance in the introduction to the question (e.g. some people like X, and some people dislike X. Do you like X or dislike X?)
    - ensuring that sets of response options are complete
    - ensuring that sets of response options are balanced
    - avoiding using words that are likely to invoke stereotypical reactions
6. Eliminate complexities that prevent respondents from easily assimilating the meaning of the question by:
    - avoiding asking two or more questions at once
    - avoiding the use of words that have several meanings
    - checking whether the question has been worded as simply as possible
    - avoiding the use of too many 'meaningful' words in one question
    - avoiding the use of qualifying clauses and phrases and the addition of complicating instruction which cause respondents to start to answer, before they have been exposed to the whole question.

If qualifying clauses and phrases have to be used, they should be placed at the beginning rather than at the end of the question,

making sure that question is as short as possible, avoiding the use of both negatives and double negatives.
7. Ensure that respondents understand what kind of answer is required by:
   - setting the question in context
   - informing respondents why the question is being asked
   - informing respondents what will be done with the information they give and
   - specifying the perspective that respondents should adopt

Lay out of questions and questionnaire is very important. It should facilitate respondents' involvement and responses, and avoid monotony. Alston and Bowles (1998) recommend paying attention to the following aspects:
   - Use different fonts to distinguish between instructions and questions
   - Filter questions and instructions about where to go in the questionnaire should be seen at a glance
   - Appropriately space the questions
   - Provide adequate room for answers to open-ended questions
   - Leave a column on one side of the page for computer coding
   - Type of envelopes and colour of the paper should be appropriate
   - Print only one side of each page

Preparing effective cover letters, informed consent forms and instructions

Simple, clear and effective cover letter, informed consent form and instructions are essential elements of a good questionnaire. As these elements often influence responses and overall response rate, researchers need to carefully draft them. Alston and Bowles (1998) provide useful hints to prepare cover letters, informed consent forms and instructions. According to them the cover letter should not be more than one page and should include the following points.
   - Official letterhead of sponsoring organisation.
   - Introduction to yourself and your role in the study.

- What the survey is for and why it is important.
- How the person was chosen and why their response is important.
- Measures to protect confidentiality or anonymity (explain the identifying number if using).
- Right to refuse.
- General information about the research procedure (whether they will be contacted again, who will interview them, reply dates etc).
- Contact phone numbers for further questions.

Many of the above elements are integral part of the informed consent form. Generally, in the informed consent form, the respondent signs a statement which states that she/he has been explained about the research, the respondent's participation is voluntary and one can withdraw from the participation at any time. It should also include confidentiality clause and further contact details. In some surveys, the cover letter is also used as a consent form and return of a completed questionnaire is assumed as consent of the respondent. In my view, it is better to use a separate informed consent form due to ethical considerations.

The questionnaire should have simple, clear and accurate instructions. These appear to influence the quality of response and the response rate. Wrong and confusing instructions will lead to wrong responses. Alston and Bowles (1998) and de Vaus (1995) suggest that instruction should state:

General instructions
- Who should complete the survey?
- How you want the questions answered and in what order.
- How to return the questionnaire and by what date.
- Instructions which introduce different parts.
- Provide section introductions, if necessary.
- Thank at the end.
- Provide contact details for further questions or information, if possible.

Specific instructions
- Provide specific guidelines to answering different questions.
- Clearly direct through lines and arrows to answer filter or contingency questions.

Completion of the above three steps will result into the fourth step, developing a complete questionnaire for trialling. The completeness of the questionnaire should ensure that it covers:
- all the research objectives
- all the research questions and hypotheses
- all the independent and dependent and intervening variables
- simple, clear and accurate instructions and
- a cover letter and informed consent form

It also should ensure that questions are well sequenced and there is a logical flow. Researchers should check these to make sure the completeness of the questionnaire.

Pretesting or Piloting and Revising the Questionnaire

Some researchers distinguish between pretesting and piloting of the questionnaire. While the former is done in somewhat informal way, the latter is more formal in which the questionnaire is tested under the same conditions of actual survey. However, the purpose of pretesting or piloting is to improve the questionnaire. Thus researchers should look for the following while testing the questionnaire.
- Variation in responses
- Understanding of the intended meaning of questions
- Duplication of questions
- Unnecessary items in a scale or index
- Non-response pattern
- The tendency of some respondents to agree with the statement, regardless of the question content (Acquiescent response set)
- Flow
- Question skips
- Timing
- Respondent interest and attention (see de Vaus, 1995)

Researchers also should look for any questions that made the respondent uncomfortable; questions that had to be repeated; questions that appeared to be misinterpreted; questions that were difficult to read or questions the interviewer came to particularly dislike; sections that dragged; and sections where the respondent seemed to want to say more [Converse and Presser, 1976, p. 72, cited in de Vaus (1995)].

The questionnaire should be revised in light of the above analysis.

Once the final version of the questionnaire is ready, the second strategy, administering the questionnaire, needs to be addressed. The questionnaire can be administered by employing any of the or a combination of the following methods.

- Mailing the questionnaire to respondents' address and follow up through phone calls and letters.
- Administering the questionnaire to large groups in classrooms or conference halls.
- Personally distributing the questionnaire to respondents on certain occasions or certain locations and collecting it back then and there.

Questionnaires can be administered through computers, provided both the researcher and the respondent have access to computers and have the skills to use it. Some researchers include this method in the interview category (Sarantakos, 1998) as they perceive that computer replaces the interviewer and performs the functions of interviewer. This is an incorrect perception. When questions are administered through computer by using well-developed software programmes, it more resembles a questionnaire rather than an interview. In a questionnaire the respondent sees question on the paper, when computer is used, he/she sees the same on the computer screen. Only difference is that it might mechanically check inconsistent responses and warn/guide the respondent what to do. Although efficient, this method calls for additional developmental cost and computer literacy/skills. There is also risk that computer system might breakdown or fail.

I have not included face-to-face and telephone interviews as questionnaire administering methods, though some researchers discuss these as such (Alston and Bowles, 1998; de Vaus 1995). Once the interviewer is involved, whether face-to-face or through telephone, I would prefer to treat the instrument as interview schedule rather than questionnaire. (Face-to-face and telephone interviews will be discussed in the next section.)

While choosing the above stated three methods, researchers need to consider response rate, maintaining the representative sample, quality of response, speed and cost of administering it.

Strengths: Questionnaire method is cost effective. Researchers can reach large geographical areas. Respondents can complete the questions according to their own time and pace. It is possible to maintain the highest level of anonymity and confidentiality. The questionnaire data are free from interviewers' bias and influences. The data obtained through questionnaires are easy to analyse and produce quick results.

Limitations: The questionnaire method has a number of limitations. A major one is that it cannot be used for those who cannot read and write. It requires motivated respondents. Sometimes, questionnaire may not be completed by the right respondent. Some questions may go unanswered as further probing, prompting and clarification of questions is not possible. Some respondents may not follow the order of questions. Overall response rate may be less. Shipman (1997) notes that "What is said may not tally with what was actually done. Beliefs and opinions change rapidly, minor changes in wording produce major changes in response, questions are misinterpreted, answers are affected by questions asked earlier, the order of questions affects answers, opinions are expressed even where nothing is known about the subjects" (Foddy, 1993). Feminist researchers have criticised predetermined, prestructured questioning as manipulative and authoritarian (Harding, 1986, cited in Shipman, 1997).

No response, do not know, cannot recall, cannot say, etc., have more meaning to them than what we think. Restricted predetermined responses may not fit respondents' views. Respondents may guess and lie. Scales and tests used in the questionnaire can pose other limitations. Shipman (1997) states that "their face validity, whether they look convincing, can be suspect. Content validity can be challenged if items are meaningless to those being tested. Concurrent validity can be challenged because no two tests will be focused on identical attributes. Construct validity, actual behaviour for comparison, can be frustrating because the latter can be inconsistent. Finally predictive validity is often low" (p. 84). All these limitations pose problems in relation to the reality we are trying to understand.

Purpose: It can be employed for explorative, descriptive and explanatory research.

Utilisation Skills: It calls for some professional training in survey research methodology and preparing questions under the supervision of experienced survey researchers, at least in the beginning.

Interview/Interview Schedule

Like questionnaire, interview is another very popular method of data collection. In interview method, two persons – interviewer and respondent – directly (face-to-face) or indirectly (over telephone) purposefully interact, the interviewer asks questions and the respondent provides responses. In turn the interviewer records the responses by using various aids (memory, pen and paper, cassette recorder, etc). The questions can range from highly structured to highly unstructured pattern, which can be viewed as two extreme approaches in the same interview continuum. There are as many as 28 types of interviews (Sarantakos, 1998), though with some overlapping. In my view, interviews can be broadly categorised into three types (Table 1) in the one continuum.

Structured interviews are conducted by employing an interview schedule. The interview schedule consists of a set of structured questions. It is almost like a questionnaire and the same above discussed guidelines/hints apply for preparing questions in the interview schedule. But we should be aware of two fundamental differences between the questionnaire and interview schedule. First, the questionnaire is self administered and completed/ filled by the respondent, and the interview schedule is completed / filled by the interviewer by asking questions to and writing responses of the respondent. Second, all the instructions in the questionnaire refer to the respondent, whereas in the interview schedule some instructions refer to the interviewer.

As the name indicates, in structured interviews, the interviewer must adhere to the instructions and follow the set pattern of questions without any flexibility. The interviewer cannot change the content, wording and order of questions. Sarantakos (1998) aptly states that in the structured interview (at least in its extreme form) the interviewer is expected to perform like a 'robot', acting in a neutral manner, keeping the same style, appearance, prompts, probes, etc., and showing no initiative, spontaneity or personal interest in the research topic (p. 247).

However, at the end, the interviewer can write his/her observations about the interview. Some interview schedules provide space for such observations.

Table 1: Types of interviews

Type	Structured	Semi structured	Unstructured
Instruments	Interview schedule (IS)	Semi structured IS	Interview guidelines Open interviews
Mode	Face-to-face, telephone and other electronic means with observation		

Semi structured interview schedule, as the name indicates, is somewhat structured. The degree of structured and unstructuredness differs from one research project to another. In the interview continuum, some semi structured interviews may lean more towards structured interview and some towards unstructured interview, and some may incorporate elements of both in a somewhat equal way. Semi structured interviews allow the interviewer to ask other relevant questions, appropriately probe further, and seek needed additional information. Essentially, the interviewer can depart from or modify the structured questions and raise additional related questions which are relevant to the objectives of the research. A semi structured interview ensures some basic information according

to the structured questions and provides scope for gathering additional relevant information, which would have otherwise missed if the structured interview was followed. To conduct semi structured interviews, interviewers must have the following knowledge and skills:
- Knowledge of the research topic and objectives.
- Controlled non-directive probing.
- Appropriate prompting.
- Manoeuvering the interview to bring back the respondent to the semi structured questions, if the respondent leaves the track of the interview.

Unstructured interviews do not have preset structured questions, order, sequence or a pattern. There are no strict or rigid procedures and instructions to conduct the interview. However, interviewers may use interview guidelines to make sure that they cover all the research areas in the interview. In unstructured interviews, interviewers often ask open-ended questions and enter into a dialogue with the respondent in almost a natural or informal setting. Interviews and themes can go forward and backward, and can end or change abruptly. Respondents play an active role in the interview, though interviewer carefully directs it. The approach is one of "I do not know anything and you know everything", that is placing the respondent on an equal footing or above the interviewer. According to Ely *et al* (1991), the major purpose of an in-depth ethnographic interview is to learn to see the world from the eyes of the person being interviewed. Thus unstructured interviews are ideal for conducting in-depth or narrative interviews. Researchers need to be proficient in conducting interviews and they must have the following knowledge and skills:
- Thorough knowledge of the research topic and objectives
- Knowledge of the underlying philosophy of placing the respondent above the ladder
- Active listening and comprehending skills
- In-depth probing and appropriate prompting
- Keeping the interview/dialogue as open, flexible, and natural as possible and relevant to the objectives of research

Preparing answers for the following questions will help researchers plan the interview well (Ely, 1991).
- What do I know about the interviewee? What should I know?
- How will I gain access? What explanations will I give? What assurances of anonymity can I provide?
- How will I begin my questions? (Rule of thumb: start with questions that the respondent will feel comfortable answering).
- How will I be able to influence the choice of the physical setting for the interview? Will there be sufficient privacy?
- How much time should I request?
- How will I record responses? (Memory, paper, pen and tape recorder. Obtain permission by describing my efforts to protect confidentiality and anonymity. Mention sharing of transcript, if this is reasonable. Tell this person where to reach me.)
- How will I conclude the interview? What opportunity will I provide for clarification? How do I make arrangements for a follow up interview (p. 59)?

Irrespective of whether the interview is structured, semi structured or unstructured, interviewers need to follow certain steps to ensure that useful data are collected. The following steps and strategies may help them effectively achieve that objective.

STEP 1: *Preparing for the Interview and Arranging the Interview*

- Prepare yourself for conducting the interview. If necessary, complete a relevant training programme or practise research interviewing skills.
- Review books and relevant literature relating to the process and techniques of research interviewing.
- Seek guidance from experienced research interviewers and discuss with peer interviewers.
- Pilot test the interviews.
- Plan recording method and practise.
- Introduce yourself and the research project, explain the purpose of the contact and interview either through a letter, phone call or direct visit.

- Obtain formal or informal consent depending upon the ethical requirements to make contact and interview.
- According to the respondent's convenience determine place, time, and approximate length of the interview.
- Determine the place by keeping in mind the need for privacy and least interruptions during the interview.
- If the respondent refuses or is not cooperative, please do not force.

Step 2: *Beginning the Interview*

- Greet in a culturally appropriate manner and reintroduce yourself and the purpose of the visit/interview.
- Initiate rapport building process by asking simple and interesting questions. This is most commonly accomplished by giving information about what will transpire, what is expected of the respondent and inviting the respondent to join with the interviewer in the process.
- Encourage the respondent to begin by describing present experiences or activities of a non-controversial nature to help create rapport and a reference point for other questions.
- Complete formalities such as signing informed consent form and clarifying and confirming response-recording method (taking notes, tape recorder, video, etc).
- Please note that in some developing countries and cultures signing formal consent form may lead to complications and refusal to interview. If you think there is informal consent, it may be accepted. The reason for this conclusion should be recorded.
- Dress in a culturally appropriate manner.

Step 3: *During the Interview*

- Ask one question at a time with a single idea in each question.
- Get into the habit of asking open-ended, neutral/ non-judgemental questions worded in a language that the respondent understands, and can easily relate to.

- Keep background and demographic questions to a minimum and collect this information near the end of the interview rather than at the beginning.
- It is important that the interviewer finds ways to demonstrate that he/she is listening carefully. Use brief verbal cues that he/she is interested in, and follow what the respondent is saying. Asking clarifying questions from time to time and using neutral but encouraging phrases provides feedback about the progress of the interview.
- Allow sufficient time to respondents to organise their thoughts.
- Be mindful of your own cultural norms and considerate of other peoples' cultural norms, values, beliefs, and learning styles.
- Place difficult or potentially sensitive questions in the middle of the interview so that there is time to deal with any repercussions before the end of the interview time.
- Have some open-ended questions, prompts and problems prepared in case of semi and unstructured interviews.
  For example:
  What did you mean by ... ?
  You said ... Tell me a bit more about that, please.
  You told me you ... Why is that so?
- Do not upset or cause distress to the respondent.
- When the respondent does become overwhelmed with emotion:
  - It is best for you to sit quietly and wait for him or her to regain some composure.
  - You might ask, "Is it all right to go on?" before continuing or
  - Indicate your understanding, stating something like, "It's been very hard on you."
  - Be prepared to call a halt to an interview if it appears that the respondent is becoming too upset to continue.
  - Please do not step out of the role as researcher/ interviewer and inappropriately take on the role of a "social work practitioner" or "friend".

Data Collecting Methods and Strategies 35

STEP 4: *Closing the Interview*

- As the time scheduled for the interview draws to a close, it is helpful to signal about 10 minutes beforehand that the interview is coming to an end.
- Ask if there is anything more the respondent wishes to convey.
- If possible, ask the respondents for feedback on how the interview went for them, and if there are any suggestions they would make to help you prepare for your next interview with another respondent.
- Clarify permission for follow-up procedures, further interviews, callbacks, etc., if needed.
- Inform how the respondent can contact the researcher for more information, or anything further s/he wishes to say.
- Do not make promises you cannot keep.
- Thank the respondent.

STEP 5: *Reflecting in and on Action about the Interview*

Reflecting involves reviewing and analysing the interview process. It is important to reflect during (in) the interview and after (on) the interview. The following and similar questions may be employed to reflect in and on the interview.

During the interview
- Is this information really needed for my study?
- Is the information good enough to be used in my study?

After the interview
- Am I getting the kinds of data that are relevant for my study?
- Was this interview too structured?
- What should I do to get more in-depth information on a pattern that seems to be emerging?
- Is the respondent withholding something – and what should I do about it?
- What impact could my race, social status, gender, ethnicity, or political beliefs have on my study, or the respondent?
- Did what the respondent say ring true – did s/he want to please me, look good, idealise a situation, or push a particular agenda?

- Why am I feeling so stressed after this particular interview?
- What assumption did I make when I asked a particular question to the respondent?

(Adapted from Alston & Bowles, 1998;
Tutty, Rothery & Grinnell, 1996.)

A Few Words and Tips on Telephone Interviews

According to Sarantakos (1998), telephone interviewing is employed when the interviews are simple and brief, when quick and inexpensive results are sought, when it is not required to approach the respondent face-to-face and when sampling inaccuracies (e.g. non-subscribes and unlisted numbers) are not considered important. Telephone interviewing has the same elements as standard interviewing, except that it is not conducted in a face-to-face context. This context has some implications for collecting data. Although interviewers will not be able to make non-verbal observations, they need to be sensitive to the respondent's pause, voice, tone, consistency and frequency of errors in providing responses. In addition, telephone interviewing calls for a special preparation. Telephone interviewers should develop and practise an introductory spiel (statement) that covers the following points.

- An introductory spiel with enough information to reduce as much as possible any nervousness on the part of the person answering the telephone who hears that a stranger is calling to conduct a telephone survey.
- In most of the surveys it is unnecessary, and thus inadvisable, to devise an introductory spiel that contains a detailed explanation of what the survey is about.
- Identification of the interviewer, the interviewer's affiliation, and survey's sponsor.
- A brief explanation of the purpose of the survey and its sampling area (or target population).
- Some positively worded phrase to encourage cooperation.
- Verification of the telephone number dialled by the interviewer.

(Adapted from Lavrakas, 1993)

About one-third of the telephone survey respondents are likely to ask back some substantive questions about the survey prior to the start of the interview. Some frequently asked questions, as under may be noted and effective responses should be prepared to such questions so that the data can be successfully collected from the respondents.

- What is the purpose of the survey and how will the findings be used?
- How did you get my telephone number?
- Who is conducting/sponsoring this survey?
- Why cannot someone else in my household participate?

Material incentives (money, a chance to win a prize or offering to send a research report) and psychological or sociological incentives (expressing one's own opinion, helping policy making, helping society, altruism, etc.) may be employed to seek respondents' cooperation. If material incentives are used, this should be stated in the introductory spiel.

(Adapted from Lavrakas, 1993)

Strengths: Advantages of telephone interviews are: It is cost effective; covers large samples; produces quick results, facilitates relatively open communication; reduces some biases, and it is relatively anonymous.

Limitations: High refusal rate, difficulty in verifying the right respondent, lack of control on the interview and the exclusion of some category of respondents are some of the limitations of the interview method (Sarantokos, 1998).

Tips on Recording

Although tape recording can capture the richness and subtleties of the speech of the respondent and can provide a means of self-monitoring and improvement for the interviewer, it may be intrusive and a barrier to full disclosure. Also note that the tape record is not a substitute to note taking. The notes can serve as a back up or safeguard against mechanical difficulties (breakdown, changing batteries, etc).

However, be aware as some people may react negatively to your taking notes during the interview; they may feel that you are evaluating or judging them in some way. If you sense that taking notes has an effect on the interview, it would be preferable to wait to write a summary until afterwards.

If you decide to record the responses after the interview, Neuman's (1994) recommendations may be followed to ensure quality and complete data.

- Record your notes as soon as possible after each interview, and do not talk with others until your observations are recorded.
- Begin the record of each interview with a new page, with the data and time noted.
- Use jotted notes only as a temporary memory aid, with key words or terms, or the first and last things said.
- Use wide margins to make it easy to add to notes at any time. Go back and add to the notes if you remember something later.
- Record events in the order in which they occurred, and note how long they last (e.g., a 15-minute wait, a one-hour ride).
- Make notes as concrete, complete and comprehensible as possible.
- Frequently make paragraphs and use quotation marks. Exact recall of phrases is best, with double quotes; use single quotes for paraphrasing.
- Record small talk or routines that do not appear to be significant at the time; they may become important later.
- "Let your fingers flow" and write quickly without worrying about spelling or "wild ideas".
- Never substitute tape recordings completely for note taking.
- Include diagrams or maps of the setting, and outline your own movements and those of others during the interview.
- Include your own words and behaviours in the notes. Also record emotional feelings and private thoughts in a separate section.

- Avoid evaluative and summarising words. Instead of "The sink looked disgusting," say, "The sink was rust-stained and looked as it had not been cleaned for a long time. Pieces of food and dirty dishes which looked several days old piled into it."
- Reread notes periodically and record ideas generated by the rereading.
- Always make one or more backup copies, keep them in a locked location, and store the copies in different places in case of fire.

Strengths: Semi-and unstructured interviews are flexible, interviewers can clarify, verify, probe deep and adjust to circumstances. Through interviews, data can be collected from illiterate respondents. Since interviews are held face to face, it is possible to observe verbal and non-verbal communication, identify problems or misunderstandings and, if possible, sort them out. Interviewer and the respondent can mutually constructively use the control on the interview situation to complete the interview to their satisfaction (Sarantokos, 1998). Through in-depth interviews, understanding of the phenomenon can be enhanced.

Limitations: Asking questions and seeking responses involves several steps and at each step can pose several problems or limitations in collecting data. Based on the symbolic interactionist perspective, Foddy (1993) notes that humans negotiate shared definitions of their situations as they communicate and identifies four steps to asking questions and seeking responses. These steps are: The researcher must encode a clear question, the respondent must decode it as the researcher intended and then encode the answer containing the information required. Finally, the researcher must decode this information as the respondent intended. At each step, there is potential for communication breakdown (Shipman, 1997). This, I think, is the greatest limitation of this method.

In addition, compared to the questionnaire method, the interview method is costly and time consuming, more inconvenient and less anonymous. To some extent, interviews are affected by interviewer and his/her biases and by other unexpected adverse circumstances, if any. Discussion of sensitive issues may pose some limitations (Sarantokos, 1998). The method of recording respondents' responses has potential to cause some limitations to the data collecting process. If recorded (interview schedule, note pad or tape recorder) during the interview, it affects the responses. If recorded after the interview, memory has its own shortcomings. The real question is, to what extent the reality is reduced or reconstructed according to the perception of the interviewer.

Purpose: As discussed above, although there is a great variation in interviewing methods, interview method can be employed to undertake exploratory, descriptive and explanatory research. This method also cuts across other data collecting methods such as observation, case study and focus group discussion.

Utilisation Skills: Although interviewing is a general data collecting method, within that structured, semi-and unstructured and telephone interviews have some specific skill requirements. Thus interviewers need to be well trained in general interviewing skills and specific interviewing skills depending upon the type of interview. Shipman (1997) argues that training and careful preparation can raise both validity and reliability. Practice under the supervision of experienced interviewers is highly recommended. Basic knowledge of survey research methodology would be helpful.

Focus Groups

Data collecting through focus groups is becoming increasingly popular (Kitzinger and Barbour, 1999; Stewart and Shamdasani, 1990). By employing questionnaire and interview methods data are collected from individuals; similarly, by employing the focus group method data are collected from groups. Like the interview method includes different types of interviews, the focus group method includes different types of groups. The use of different types of groups has created some confusion among researchers as to what is focus group and what is not. I think this confusion emerges due to the use of different terms with different purposes. Thus it is important to look at different types of groups and how they are worded. Table 2 lists a wide range of groups and their purpose and features.

Table 2: Types of groups, their purpose and features

Types of Groups	Purpose and Features
Group interviews	To identify preliminary research questions in a new area of inquiry. To test new research and clinical techniques. Focuses on a specific topic. The introduction of a stimulus by the interviewer. Relative freedom for the respondent. Opportunities for increased information.
Group discussion	To collect information about breadth and variation of opinions on a set of issues. Used for personnel assessment and recruitment. Employs discussion in a non-standardised form and observation at its sources. The discussion includes more than one person at a time.
Nominal group	Specially convened and often includes ranking exercises to establish participants' priorities and concerns. Members may not gather at one place. No spontaneous interaction. May not interact directly. Responses of each member are shared with others. Helps to avoid the influence of group opinion and of dominant group members. Useful when the group conflict is likely to be high. Useful to bring out dissenting opinions. Suitable for specialised groups like scientists, senior government and business executives and international participants.
Delphi groups	To develop forecasts of future events and trends. Requires panel of experts, the design of the set of questions, summarisation of individual input. May not meet face-to-face.
Consensus panels	To develop agreed professional principles or protocols.
Brainstorming sessions and	To generate new ideas and encourage creative expression. Quantity of ideas is important. Not to be critical of any ideas. Brainstorming may not have a designated moderator.
Synectics	It follows a structured approach. Presence of trained moderator. Groups view problems, needs or actions from new perspective. Looking for unconventional and innovative solutions.

Leaderless discussion groups	Used for personnel assessment and recruitment. No moderator. The group is given instructions. The group and the pattern of interaction are observed.
Group work	A social work method to enhance the social functioning of group members. Social worker works as group facilitator. Often research is not the purpose of the group activity, but it can be.
Electronic media	Teleconference, video-conference, E-mail and Internet forum may be employed to conduct some of the above focus groups. Purpose and features may vary depending upon the type of group, focus of discussion and the media used.

(See Kitzinger and Barbour, 1999; Stewart and Shamdasani, 1990; Sarantokos, 1998; Mark, 1996).

I think, first, the confusion between group interviews and group discussion should be clarified. A number of research methodology textbooks (Sarantakos, 1998; Alston and Bowles, 1998; Mark, 1996; Stewart and Shamdasani, 1990) appear to make no distinction between the two. It appears that group interviews and group discussion are used interchangeably, which is incorrect and confusing. In group interviews, each person is asked questions on a particular topic and responses are recorded. According to Kitzinger and Barbour (1999), in focus group discussion, researchers encourage participants to interact with each other: asking questions, commenting on each other's experiences and point of views. They further argue that: "Focus group research is not the same as work involving 'Delphi groups' or 'consensus panels' where these are employed simply to facilitate an *outcome* of an agreed response rather than to observe the *process* of prioritisation and decision-making. However, any group discussion may be called a 'focus group' as long as the researcher is actively encouraging of, and attentive to, the group interaction" (p 4-5).

To Sarantokos (1998), "Focus groups involve persons specially selected owing to their particular interest, expertise or position in the community in an attempt to collect information on a number of issues, as well as to brainstorm a variety of solutions, and ultimately facilitate group discussion as a tool of data collection and possibly policy construction" (p 180-181).

Based on the available literature and my research experience, I have identified 10 elements of a focus group. I hope these elements help distinguish between the focus group and other group activities and discussion. These elements should also help include or exclude other varieties of groups from the focus group method. In my view, any focus group that does not have these elements may not be considered as focus group for data collecting purposes.

Basic Elements of a Focus Group

1. Addresses the specific research questions to achieve research objectives.
2. Explores a specific set of issues.
3. Purposeful composition of groups.
4. Involves Collective activity (e.g. debating a set of questions, viewing a video, etc.)
5. Occurrence of group discussion.
6. Intragroup interaction in a face to face to environment.
7. Facilitation by moderator/researcher in the light of research objectives and questions.
8. Participants talk to each other.
9. Moderator/researcher encourages group to interactively address a specific set of issues.
10. Recording of the content and/or process of group discussion by employing appropriate methods.

To collect data from focus groups, researchers need to employ the following strategies.

Composition and Recruitment of Group Members, and Selection of a Venue

The size of the group varies and some suggest up to 20 members. In market research the size of group may be 8 to 12 members. In sociological research a smaller number is preferred, maybe 6 to 8. I think the size of the group should depend upon the nature and urgency of the issue, kind of participants, and practical

circumstances, though these should not compromise the research objective.
- Avoid extreme homogeneity and heterogeneity of group members.
- It is good to have members having some shared experiences and some differences.
- The group members may be strangers or known to each other, but the discussion should not result into coopting (members may implicitly develop a kind of consensus in regard to an idea, opinion or the topic in question that may not be conducive for an open and healthy discussion).
- Avoid members having hierarchical relationships. Subordinates may not be able to frankly express views in the presence of their officers or dominating leaders.
- Develop clear plans to access and recruit group members.
- If you are not directly accessing group members and are taking the help of some kind of gatekeepers such as community leaders, teachers or managers, be careful in case gatekeepers suggest 'handpicked' members, whose views may be one-sided.
- Clearly state the purpose and topic of discussion to the members (if the research method permits) and obtain informed consent as part of the recruitment process.
- In anticipation of dropouts, recruit several more members than are actually needed.
- To facilitate members' presence in discussions, travel expenses may be reimbursed or payment may be offered.
- If possible, focus group meetings may be arranged during established meeting slots such as staff meeting, training and special gatherings.
- Arrange discussion venue that is convenient to most of the members. A venue familiar to members should be preferred.
- The focus group meeting room needs to be quiet and comfortable, free from interruptions and protected from observation by those not participating in the research.

Data Collecting Methods and Strategies

- Sometimes, when such a perfect room is not available, focus group researchers need to be flexible to use the available venue.

Preparation for Conducting Focus Groups

- Prepare a clear introductory statement and rehearse it.
- Depending upon the type of research, the focus group facilitator should prepare basic outline of key questions or discussion guidelines.
- Plan and collect all the necessary material and take these to the venue. (Flip chart, pens and pencils, leaflets, cartoons, newspaper clippings, current relevant issues, small group games, warm up exercises, etc.)
- Plan some statements and interventions which can be politely employed if the discussion diverts from the research objective.
- Prepare a thanking statement and rehearse it.
- Plan recording method and take recording aids. Please do not totally depend upon electric or electronic recording aids.

Conducting Focus Group Sessions

- Conducting focus group sessions calls for effective facilitation skills.
- If inexperienced, try to develop facilitation skills by conducting pilot group discussions.
- Do not present yourself as an expert.
- Be non-judgmental.
- Do not make assumptions which close off exploration.
- Should know when to remain silent and when to intervene.
- Be alert, clarify ambiguous statements, facilitate the completion of the sentences/ideas.
- Encourage everyone's participation and interaction among the participants.
- There is no need to control the discussion or the group, as long as the focus group discussion progresses and revolves around the objectives of the research.
- If the facilitator's and participants' culture and language are different, additional preparation and skills are required.

- It is good to be aware of the facilitator's potential influences on participants.
- The length of the discussion should be about one to two hours, depending on the research issue.

Recording Focus Group Discussion

Focus group researchers may need to choose a combination of the following recording methods.
- Note taking.
- Use of a flip chart (researcher and participants may list different ideas or to summarise points).
- Tape record.
- Video-recording.
- The facilitator's memory, observation and reflective note after the focus group discussion.
- Collection of the outcome of group exercises, if they are written or drawn.

Strengths: This method helps to generate data quickly at less cost. Direct clarification of issues and responses among the participants and between the facilitator and participants is possible. Availability of large and rich amounts of data in the members' own words can react with and build upon the responses of other group members. Focus groups are flexible. Through this method, data can be obtained from illiterates. May provide sound bases for larger studies.

Limitations: Focus group as a data collecting method has some limitations. Sometimes, members may not express their genuine opinion. Some members may dominate and some members may not participate in the discussion. The discussion may be unduly influenced by the facilitator. There are problems in recording the discussion, particularly, when a number of participants speak at a time. Participants may coopt the discussion. Sometimes, discussion may go off the track.

Purpose: The focus group method is generally used for exploratory studies, particularly, to elicit people's experiences, opinions, wishes and concerns. Kitzinger and Barbour (1999) state that this method is particularly useful for allowing participants to generate their own questions, frames and concepts and to pursue their own priorities on their own terms, in their own vocabulary. It can help prepare the main study. Useful for interpreting previously obtained quantitative results.

Utilisation Skills: Basic knowledge of 'focus group' as research and data collecting method is essential. Group discussion facilitation, observation, note taking skills are needed.

Secondary Data

Meaningful research can be equally undertaken by collecting the secondary data. In fact, in most of the research studies, some data are collected from secondary sources and used as bases for collecting primary data (through observation, questionnaire, interview and focus groups). Some researches are entirely based on secondary sources. More often than not primary and secondary data are used in a complementary way. According to Stewart and Kamins (1993), secondary sources of data consist of information collected by others and archived in some form. These sources are books, journals, newspapers, letters, E-mails, diaries, government documents and reports, census reports, non-government organisations' reports, archived data sets, data stored in electronic form, etc. Like primary sources of data (for example, observing a community or phenomenon, interviewing group of people). Some of the secondary sources of data are so huge that researchers need to decide what exactly they are looking for in the secondary data and what sense they want to make from them. The following strategies may help researchers effectively collect data from secondary sources.

- Be clear about research objectives, questions and hypotheses.
- Clearly identify independent and dependent variables, or topics, contents and themes.
- Acquire the knowledge of the existence of secondary data and means for accessing them.
- Obtain permission to access data, if necessary.
- If desired or required, employ relevant sampling procedures to delimit the data (for example, deciding about a particular

period, or days, or particular columns in newspaper, or particular content of the document).
- Have a glance at the selected secondary data to examine what is available and what is not available, and in what order and from the data is available.

Address the following questions (from Stewart and Kamins, 1993) to examine the data.
1. What was the purpose of the study? Why was the information collected?
2. Who was responsible for collecting the information? What qualifications, resources, and potential biases are represented in the conduct of the study?
3. What information was actually collected? How were units and concepts defined? How direct were the measures used? How complete was the information? Are there any differences in the quality of different variables?
4. When was the information collected? Is the information still current, or have events made the information obsolete? Were there specific events occurring at the time the data were collected that may have produced the particular results obtained?
5. How was the information obtained? What methodology was employed in obtaining the data?
6. How consistent is the information obtained from one source with information available from other sources?

On the basis of this overview, develop a flexible secondary data collecting proforma that allows to reduce or extend the proforma, if you encounter new relevant information in the data. Use the proforma to collect data from selected secondary resources

Strengths: Secondary data take relatively less time and are less expensive. If there are time pressures to answer research questions, secondary data sources offer practical alternatives. These data provide a useful starting point for additional research. Secondary data help to understand gaps in the existing knowledge and new research questions. They also provide a base for comparing the new data. Depending upon the data, it is possible to find out whether or not the new information is representative of a population. Sometimes secondary data may be the only source of information (Stewart and Kamins, 1993; Sarantokos, 1998). If the material is in the public domain, access and approval processes are less problematic.

Limitations: Some of the secondary data such as government documents, private letters, diaries, etc., are not easily accessible. Some documents may be incomplete. It may be difficult to categorise or code some secondary data. The secondary data may produce deliberate or unintended bias. Interpreters of the data may arrive at different and conflicting conclusions. If original purpose of the data and the purpose at hand are different, researchers may need to deal with issues relating to category definitions, particular measures or treatment effects (Stewart and Kamins, 1993; Sarantokos, 1998). If a huge amount of data are collected without clarity and purpose, researchers may find it difficult to use it.

Purpose: Secondary data are useful to undertake exploratory, descriptive and explanatory research. On the basis of secondary data, researchers may formulate the problem and design a new research project. Some secondary data help understand what is already known and what remains to be known, about a particular issue. It can be used to compare new data.

Utilisation Skills: Basic knowledge of research methodology is necessary. One should have the knowledge of the existence of the secondary data and the means for accessing them. Depending upon the type of data, knowledge and skills of data organisation and categorisation, qualitative and quantitative analysis are needed.

Obtaining/Choosing Instruments Designed by Others: A Word of Caution

Many researchers look at instruments – observation/interview guidelines, questionnaires, interview schedules, secondary proforma – developed by others and some simply copy them without much thought to conduct their own research. In some instances these will be a very good source of instruments which have a history of validation and documentation of psychometric properties. Even if the research being undertaken amounts to a replication, the instrument is tested further. If proper attention is paid to considering and reporting carefully changes in its use, e.g., difference in sample, population or context, it may further strengthen the value of the instrument as well as the research outcome. One should always look at other research studies and their method of investigation, but the blind use of instruments, particularly questionnaires and scales, developed by other researchers may lead to a lot of problems and may frustrate the researcher. By uncritically using readily available instruments researchers may collect invalid and unreliable data, get perturbed in the process of data collection that the instrument is not working, suggest findings which may not be useful and may not be relevant to the research, collect data that may not be needed to achieve the research objectives and waste their own and the respondent's resources (time and money).

Researchers need not reinvent the wheel every time. They should choose the approach which is ethical, efficient and effective for their study. It is a good practice to study how other researches have been conducted. However, when they decide to use other researchers' instruments, they must critically examine each question/item, see whether it is relevant to their own research objectives, whether it will help answer research questions and achieve the research objectives. In this respect, Corcoran's (1988) guidelines may be of use to determine, locate and evaluate measuring instruments. Based on this critical examination, researchers may modify the instrument to make it suitable for the research objectives and the respondent's culture, and for answering specific research questions. If translation of the instrument is required, translate it well to ensure that the intended meaning is captured in both the languages. Test it to make sure that it helps you collect accurate (valid and reliable) data. On the whole, researchers must clearly understand and appreciate benefits and shortcomings of the use of instruments developed by others and where necessary, carefully adapt them with due acknowledgment of their origin.

The data collecting methods and strategies discussed in this chapter are in a summary form and are prepared for quick reference and direction. Those interested in detailed information may refer to the annotated bibliography below for further reading.

Annotated Bibliography

Alston M. and Wendy Bowles (1998). Research for social workers (Chapter 6). Sydney: Allen and Unwin. This chapter succinctly discusses various steps involved in constructing a questionnaire and three types of interviews. It provides four handy hints for interviewers. It includes clear illustrations which help beginning researchers easily understand the concepts. It also analyses main features of mail survey, telephone survey and face-to-face interview.

Berg B. L. (1989). Qualitative research method for the social sciences (Chapter 2). Needham Heights, MA: Allyn and Bacon. The chapter discusses different types of interviews, types of questions and common problematic questions. Further, it describes the roles of the interviewer and ways to overcoming common problems when conducting research interviews.

Corcoran K. J. (1988). Selecting a measuring instrument (Chapter 7). In Grinnell R. M., *Social Work Research and Evaluation* (3rd edition), Illinois: F. E. Peacock Publishers. In this chapter, the author provides guidelines in regard to how to choose and use instruments designed by others. First, he discusses six questions to determine measurement need: 1. Why will the measurement occur? 2. What will be measured? 3. Who is appropriate for making the most direct observations? 4. Which type of format is acceptable? 5. Where will the measurement occur? 6. When will the measurement occur? Second, the author provides a useful list of sources where several instruments can be located. The third section suggests to answer twenty-four questions to evaluate the instrument and to select the most appropriate one.

Creswell J. W. (1998). *Qualitative Inquiry and Research Design: Choosing among Five Traditions*. London: Sage. This is an excellent book on qualitative research. It mainly discusses five qualitative research methods: A biography; a phenomenological study; a grounded theory study; an ethnography; and a case study. Besides discussing philosophical and theoretical frameworks, the author comparatively discusses the five methods and presents the analyses in tables which are easy to understand. Chapter seven deals with the issue of data collection.

de Vaus D. A. (1995). Surveys in social research (Chapter 6 and 7). Sydney: Allen and Unwin. These two chapters provide a number of useful hints for constructing and administering questionnaires. Several questions have been raised to aid the checking of the wording of questions. Types of questions, telephone questionnaire, lay out, pilot test, relative advantages and disadvantages of questionnaires and interviews, tips for maximising the response rate and smooth implementation of surveys have been thoroughly discussed.

Ely M., Anzul M., Friedman T., Garner D. and Steinmetz A. M. (1991). Doing qualitative research: Circles within circles (Chapter 3). Bristol: The Falmer Press. This chapter discusses in brief about interviewing and informal and formal interviews. It raises several questions to help researchers prepare well for interviews, such as: What do I know about the interviewee? How will I gain access? How will I begin my questions? How will I conclude my interview? It also gives hints to keep the interview in tune with the interviewee and to prevent inappropriate probing. In addition to questioning, the chapter suggests that researchers must attend to rhythm, form and impact of questions.

Erlandson D., Harris E., Skipper B. and Allen S. (1993). Doing naturalistic inquiry: A guide to methods (Chapter 5). Newbury Park, CA: Sage. The chapter discusses the purpose of interview, question construction, active listening and proper recording, which are important elements of a successful interview. It emphasises on respect for research participants and provides practical steps to prepare for and conducting the interview.

Foddy W. (1993). *Constructing Questions for Interviews and Questionnaires.* Melbourne: Cambridge University Press. As the title of the book indicates, it gives thorough treatment to various aspects of constructing questions for interviews and questionnaires. The author delineates fundamental communication problems in interviews and questionnaires and suggests several guidelines to reduce communication problems between the researcher and the respondent. I think this is an excellent book on constructing questions.

Fontana A. and Frey J. (1994). Interviewing: The art of science. In: N. K. Denzin and Y. Lincoln (ed), *Handbook of qualitative research* (pp. 361 -376). Newbury Park, CA: Sage. This chapter discusses structured, unstructured and group interviews with their advantages and disadvantages, and skills required to use them. It covers some common issues relating to gaining access, understanding local language and culture, self presentation, key informants, gaining trust and building rapport. Further, it discusses the impact of gender in interviews, methods of recording and ethical concerns.

Glesne C. and Peshkin A (1992). Becoming qualitative researchers: An introduction (Chapter 4). White Plains, NY: Longman. The chapter discusses the importance of creating useful questions and location, the length and recording of the interview. It looks at the interviewer's five attributes: Preparedness, rapport building skill, openness to learning, being analytical and patience. The chapter also discusses problems of dealing with resistant individuals and nonstop talkers in interviews.

Lavrakas P. J. (1993). *Telephone Survey Methods.* London: Sage. This book looks at various aspects of the telephone survey process. Mainly, it looks at sampling, respondent selection and supervision. Although it does not discuss how to develop good questionnaires, it provides practical hints on how to select respondents and secure cooperation and how to effectively supervise interviewers.

McKenzie G., Powell J. and Usher R. (1997). *Understanding Social Research: Perspectives on Methodology and Practice*. London: The Falmer Press. This is an edited volume consisting 16 articles and three parts. The first part deals with the nature of enquiry, the second, the nature of disciplines and the third part looks at research practice. Several authors have critically reflected on theoretical and philosophical bases of research methodology and particularly examined social work research, qualitative approaches, grounded theory, action research and observation.

Patton M. Q. (1990). Qualitative evaluation and research methods (Chapter 7). Newbury Park, CA: Sage. The chapter discusses (1) the informational-conversational interview, (2) the general interview guide approach, and (3) the standardised open-ended interview. Strengths and limitations of each interview approach are comparatively presented. Then it looks at posing, sequencing and wording of questions. Other aspects discussed in the chapter are: the use of probes, follow-up questions and data recording.

Rosaline S. Barbour and Jenny Kitzinger (ed.) (1999). *Developing Focus Group Research*. London: Sage. This is an excellent edited book on focus groups. The first chapter provides a comprehensive introduction to the book and discusses the concept of focus groups, when and how to use them and how to combine focus groups with qualitative and quantitative research. Based on the first hand experience of many researchers the book suggests strategies for sampling, group composition, recruiting group members, preparing materials, facilitators and recording group sessions.

Sarantakos S. (1998). *Social Research*. Melbourne: Macmillan. This is a widely referred textbook on social research. Chapter 7 to 13 of this book comprehensively discuss various data collecting methods. The author analyses relative advantages and disadvantages of each method and discusses when and how to use them. In addition, historical development and philosophical bases of data collecting methods have been included, though in brief.

Shipman M. (1997). *The Limitations of Social Research*. London: Longman. This book has run into the fourth edition, which shows its usefulness and popularity. Part two of the book looks at techniques for collecting information. It points out several limitations of data collecting methods and raises a fundamental question: Does the evidence reflect the reality under investigation? The author's arguments and observations are based on several research studies conducted by scholars from varied disciplines.

Stewart D.W. and Kamins M.A. (1993). *Secondary Research: Information Sources and Methods*. London: Sage. This book is very useful for any researcher who is interested in conducting research that is based on secondary data. The authors discuss advantages, disadvantages and sources of secondary data. The second chapter helps to evaluate the appropriateness of secondary data. Then it dwells into government and non-government organisations' data, CD-ROM technology and how to integrate secondary data.

Stewart D.W. and Shamdasani P. N. (1990). *Focus groups*. London: Sage. In the introduction, the book deals with uses of focus groups, advantages and limitations, steps in the design of focus groups and other types of groups. The remaining chapters look at design and conduct of focus groups and the role of a group facilitator, and analysis and interpretation of the focus group data.

Tutty L.M., Rothery M. and Grinnell R.M. (1996). *Qualitative Research for Social Workers*. Boston: Allyn and Bacon. Phase two of this book provides a thorough treatment to the data collecting process. Particularly, it looks at the qualitative research interview, types of interviews, problems and approaches in qualitative interviewing, and five steps in interviewing.

Yin R.K. (1989). *Case Study Research: Design and Methods*. London: Sage. In this book, Yin discusses case study as a research strategy and compares case study with other research strategies. The author rightly argues that each strategy can be employed for exploratory, descriptive and explanatory purposes. Other topics discussed in the book are preparing for data collection, collecting evidence, analysis and preparing the case study report

References

1. Alston M. and Wendy Bowles (1998). *Research for Social Workers*. Sydney: Allen and Unwin.
2. Berg B.L. (1989). *Qualitative Research Method for the Social Sciences*. Needham Heights, MA: Allyn and Bacon.
3. Corcoran K. J. (1988). 'Selecting a measuring instrument' (Chapter 7). In: Grinnell R.M., *Social Work Research and Evaluation* (3rd edn), Illinois: F. E. Peacock Publishers.
4. Creswell J. W. (1998). *Qualitative and Research Design: Choosing Among the Five Traditions*. California: Sage.
5. de Vaus D. A. (1995). *Surveys in Social Research*. Sydney: Allen and Unwin.
6. Ely M., Anzul M., Friedman T., Garner D. and Steinmetz A.M. (1991). *Doing Qualitative Research: Circles within Circles*. Bristol: The Falmer Press.
7. Erlandson D., Harris E., Skipper B. and Allen S. (1993). *Doing Naturalistic Inquiry: A Guide to Methods*. Newbury Park, CA: Sage.
8. Foddy W. (1993). *Constructing Questions for Interviews and Questionnaires*. Melbourne: Cambridge University Press.
9. Fontana A. and Frey J. (1994). 'Interviewing: The art of Science'. In: N.K. Denzin and Y. Lincoln (ed.), *Handbook of Qualitative Research*. Newbury Park, CA: Sage.
10. Glesne C. and Peshkin A. (1992). *Becoming Qualitative Researchers: An Introduction*. White Plains, NY: Longman.
11. Kitzinger J. and Barbour R. S. (1999). 'Introduction : The Challenge and promise of focus groups'. In: Rosaline S. Barbour and Jenny Kitzinger (ed), *Developing Focus Group Research*. London: Sage.

12. Lavrakas P. J. (1993). *Telephone Survey Methods*. London: Sage.
13. Mark R. (1996). *Research Made Simple*. London: Sage.
14. Neuman W. L. (1994). *Social Research Methods: Qualitative and Quantitative Approaches* (2nd edn). Needham Heights, MA: Allyn & Bacon.
15. Patton M. Q. (1990). *Qualitative Evaluation and Research Methods*. Newbury Park, CA: Sage.
16. Sarantakos S. (1998). *Social Research*. Melbourne: Macmillan.
17. Shipman M. (1997). *The Limitations of Social Research*. London: Longman.
18. Stake, R. E. (1994). 'Case Studies'. In: N.K. Denzin and Y. S. Lincoln (ed.), *Handbook of Qualitative research* (pp. 236-247). Thousand Oaks, CA: Sage.
19. Stewart D.W. and Kamins M.A. (1993). *Secondary Research: Information Sources and Methods*. London: Sage.
20. Stewart D.W. and Shamdasani P.N. (1990). *Focus Groups*. London: Sage.
21. Tutty L.M., Rothery M. and Grinnell R.M. (1996). *Qualitative Research for Social Workers*. Boston: Allyn and Bacon.
22. Yin R.K. (1989). *Case Study Research: Design and Methods*. London: Sage.
23. Weiss R.S. (1994). *Learning from Strangers: The Art and Method of Qualitative Studies*. New York: Free Press.

PART II

Gathering Data on Sensitive Issues

3
MARTIN RYAN

Interviewing the Stigmatised: Experiences of Collecting Data from Consumer Bankrupts in Australia

Introduction

The rise of consumer credit, particularly in major developed countries, brings with it many benefits. But it can also result in debt and overcommitment which manifest themselves in a range of problems from marital discord and break-up, physical and emotional health problems through to homelessness. This chapter focuses on data collection in a study of those most overcommitted – those who petitioned to be declared legally bankrupt in Melbourne, Australia.

Bankruptcy is an unknown concept in many countries. In Australia, the term signifies the legal procedure in which a debtor gives up certain assets (apart from necessary items and exempt assets) and hands over control of their financial affairs for a three-year period to a trustee (appointed official). In return, the debtor receives protection from further legal action and creditors' demands and then is totally released from debts at the end of the bankruptcy period. Amongst the drawbacks of bankruptcy, one is that it becomes a matter of public knowledge (having to appear in an official government gazette); bankruptcy is generally thought to be stigmatising and embarrassing for a person, in that, it publicly signifies that they are unable to pay their debts.

The numbers of those petitioning for bankruptcy has increased markedly in the last 15 years in Australia, particularly for those involved in business. The peak was reached in 1991-92 with 16,780 bankruptcy proceedings being recorded with two-thirds of these being of a non-business nature (Annual report on the operation of the *Bankruptcy Act 1966*, 1991-92).

Despite this increasing occurrence, there was little Australian empirical research on bankruptcy and in the general area of consumer indebtedness. In particular, there was very little known about bankrupts other than what was provided in the official statistics in the annual reports on the operation of the *Bankruptcy Act 1966*.

Given that no researcher had previously sought to actually interview Australian bankrupts in an appreciable way, I set out to do just that in my study (1989). (The study's results have subsequently been reported in Ryan, 1992a; 1992b; 1993a; 1993b; 1993c; 1995.) The general aim of this study was to examine the perceptions and experiences of a sample of undischarged (those still in their three year bankruptcy period), non-business voluntary bankrupts in Melbourne (the capital city of the southern state of Victoria, Australia) regarding their own bankruptcies. The important element of the study was that it was to be an exploration of the subjective, qualitative nature of the bankrupt's experience.

The remainder of this chapter will, first, outline the design and methodology used in the study, then describe the reality of the data collection process, and conclude with some general lessons for researchers based on my experience in this study.

Design and Methodology of the Study

The study's objectives were to obtain: a basic demographic and social profile of consumer bankrupts in Melbourne; a picture of the perceived causes of the bankruptcy and the events leading up to the debtor's petition for bankruptcy; and an account of the nature of the experience of bankruptcy from the perspective of the bankrupts themselves. It also sought to examine the role of creditor harassment in the decision of the debtor to petition for bankruptcy and to explore the relevance of the concept of stigma to this sample of bankrupts. Finally, it examined the views and attitudes of others involved in the bankruptcy process towards bankrupts.

Research Design

The research study had two stages, with the first stage involving interviews with a random sample of consumer bankrupts about their bankruptcies. There were interviews with a sample of 76 undischarged bankrupts, of which 31 were males, 29 female and 16 were joint bankrupts. Their names had been randomly sampled from the Melbourne newspaper which regularly published the names and addresses of bankrupts at the time of petition. The sample was drawn from those who went bankrupt in this category in a particular year. Letters requesting an interview were sent to a total of 242 bankrupts. The 76 respondents were a 31 per cent sample of this population and so were considered representative of the population.

The sample was interviewed on an average 17 months after their petition for bankruptcy which was designed to ensure that they had a clear memory of the events leading up to the bankruptcy, and were likely to have adequate experience and knowledge of what being an undischarged bankrupt meant to them subjectively, emotionally and financially.

The mean time for each of these interviews was 115 minutes and was conducted at a place chosen by the respondent, generally their own home. Interviews were conducted over a 10-month period.

The structured interview schedule consisted of both open - and close-ended questions and covered the events leading up to the bankruptcy petition, the debts involved and the nature of the experience of being an undischarged bankrupt. Responses were recorded on the schedule forms for later coding.

The second stage of the study consisted of interviews with a range of other personnel involved in the bankruptcy process including bankruptcy officials, financial counsellors, solicitors and credit providers. Thirty-four respondents were interviewed in total for this second stage of the study to obtain a description of their views and attitudes towards consumer bankruptcy and bankrupts.

(These interviews are not covered in this chapter. For further details on them, see Ryan, 1995, pp. 189-203).

In the first stage of the study, the aim was to interview a sample size of one-tenth of the population involved. This was based on the convention that a sample of one-tenth of the size of the population will give reasonable control over sampling error. This proportion also applies to various categories of the population, i.e. one-tenth of each category can be sampled (Hays and Winkler, 1971, pp. 333-335; Seaburg, 1981, p. 90).

The type of sample employed for this stage of the study was a stratified random sample with a uniform sampling fraction (proportionate stratified sample) (Moser and Kalton, 1973, pp. 85-92). This meant that particular strata (layers) of the population were selected, e.g. it could have been on the gender basis or income, and then a random sample drawn from each stratum. This is done to ensure the precision of the sample and that different stratification factors are represented in a design. The sample was stratified into gender combined with the type of bankruptcy to form a stratum broken sole male bankruptcies, sole female bankruptcies and joint bankruptcies. My reason for stratifying the sample was to ensure that the sample was representative of the population, thereby preventing the sample consisting overwhelmingly of one type of bankruptcy such as mainly sole female bankrupts and ensuring that the three different types of bankruptcies were represented in the sample.

The instrument employed in the first stage of the study was a structured interview schedule which was developed after a review of previous interview schedules in this area, including those by Jacob (1969), Caplovitz (1974), Puckett (1978). It also included questions developed by the author. The schedule was pretested and it was generally found to have utility and applicability. Problem areas in the schedule were identified and corrected.

Contact was made with the sampled bankrupts initially by letter requesting their participation in the research study by agreeing to be interviewed. Previous researchers such as Siporin (1967), Stanley and Girth (1971), Caplovitz (1974) and Puckett (1978) have found defaulting debtors and bankrupts as a group very reluctant to be interviewed. Response rates were of the order of 20 to 60 per cent. People who have defaulted on debts are likely to be mobile as they may have rent arrears and may move elsewhere to avoid their creditors. It was anticipated that mobility would not present such a problem with bankrupts, given the legal requirement that they notify their trustee of any change of address.

Prior to letters being sent, no contact had been made with any of the bankrupts in the sample about the proposed research study. Confidentiality and suppression of actual names was guaranteed to all respondents.

Each respondent was asked to make records of the debts involved in their bankruptcy, if any, available at the interview, if possible. This was done at the time they agreed to do the interview when an appointment for the interview was also made. At the conclusion of the interview, each interviewee was asked if they would be willing to sign an authorisation form providing the researcher with access to their official receiver's office file for comparison purposes.

Prior to interview, all close-ended (forced choice) questions were pre-coded. With open-ended questions in the schedule, these were postcoded after 26 interviews had been completed, based on the responses of these subjects. A list of these people's responses to these questions was made and coding categories were developed from these lists. At the completion of data collection, all schedules were then coded prior to computer analysis utilising the SPSS-X package (Statistical Package for the Social Sciences) (SPSS Inc., 1986).

Experiences in Collecting Data

This section will address a number of issues that arose in the course of collecting data for this research study. These are: (i) the problems of interviewing people about the sensitive subject of their finances and more particularly what could be perceived as their failure in financial matters, i.e. their petitioning for bankruptcy; (ii) overcoming the problem of systematic bias in interviewing bankrupts about their situation in that they may have distorted the "facts" to present themselves in a more favourable way. Finally, utilising Schon's approach (1983), I will outline my own "theory in use" on data collection based on conducting this study.

Interviewing People about Finances and Bankruptcy

I spent a year preparing a detailed research proposal prior to beginning the data collection. A major concern I had was whether people would actually be prepared to speak to me about their bankruptcy, given the sensitivity of the topic.

As Lee and Renzetti (1993) point out in their book on research sensitive topics: "... it is probably possible for *any* topic, depending on context, to be a sensitive one" (p. 6). They go on to write that experience tends to suggest that there are a number of areas in which research is more likely to be perceived as threatening than others. Among these are "... where research intrudes into the private sphere or delves into some deeply personal experience" (p. 6). They acknowledge that topics and activities seen as private vary across cultures and situations, but that commonly "... areas of social life concerned with sexual or financial matters remain shielded from the eyes of 'non-intimates'" (p. 6).

To illustrate this sensitivity to discussing financial matters, Singh (1997) begins her book on the meaning of money in marriage by quoting Ian, a 72-year-old retired air force officer for whom: "Talking about money and banking is a bit like talking to your children about where babies come from." (Notice that Ian connects both the areas mentioned by Lee and Renzetti (1993) in this quote – the financial and the sexual). Singh herself, in contemplating her research, points out her own concerns and fears in attempting to research this area: "I also feared the study would be aborted for as an Indian-born Malaysian, I would not be able to access the very private Anglo-Celtic domain of marriage and money. But perhaps more than anything else, I resisted the changed focus because money was a troubled issue in my marriage." (p. 31).

Discussing the intimacies of a person's finances and their debts was not new to me. I had worked for two years as a debt counsellor at the beginning of my professional social work career (Ryan, 1996b). But speaking to people who seek your help as a client, often in a stressed and distressed state, was quite different from asking perfect strangers to discuss the private details of their finances.

This concern was exacerbated by the fact that I would be delving into another area that Lee and Renzetti (1993) identified as being particularly threatening – "the investigation of deviant activities" (p. 6). They suggest that: "... those studied are likely to fear being identified, stigmatised, or incriminated in some way" (p. 6). Clearly, these sentiments applied to the bankrupts I intended to interview. Whilst bankruptcy is not illegal in Australia, it is a signal of deviancy (i.e. being unable to pay one's debts) and brings into play a whole set of legal apparatus and administration (Ryan, 1995, pp. 6-19).

The nature of the stigmatisation involved in being bankrupt was to become clear in the course of the study itself. I found that the bankrupts perceived that they were likely to be stigmatised by others and they themselves felt looked down upon or felt different (characterised as felt the stigma) because of their bankruptcy, but at the same time were unlikely to experience any stigma. When stigma was experienced by them, it was likely to come from immediate family and friends (Ryan, 1992b).

How was this sensitivity addressed in actually collecting the data? Letters requesting an interview were sent out to potential respondents to the address that they used at the time of their petition. If there had been no response from the bankrupt within a week of receiving this letter, I would attempt follow-up contact with them. Firstly, this would be by telephone (if their number was listed in the telephone book) and secondly, if no telephone was listed, by visiting them personally, normally in the evening on a weekday. This often necessitated driving long distances around Melbourne's suburbs at dusk and long into the night.

I took great care in both telephone contacts and personal visits to ensure that no one, other than the bankrupt or bankrupts (if joint) themselves, was informed of the person's bankruptcy, unless they made it clear they were aware of the person's bankruptcy. This was deliberately done to ensure confidentiality and to avoid any unnecessary embarrassment to the bankrupt. In the initial letter requesting the interview and at the interview itself, confidentiality and suppression of actual names was guaranteed to all respondents.

In attempting to persuade people to agree to an interview, I had to tread a fine line between being determined, assertive and having the opportunity to realistically assuage their fears and yet being respectful of their right to refuse to participate. I would usually ask them what their particular concerns were after they had initially refused to participate and then would attempt to reassure them, e.g. they may have been worried about protecting their anonymity. I often emphasised to people that I was keen to hear *their* side of the events that lead to bankruptcy.

The 76 people interviewed represented only 31 per cent of those sent letters (242), meaning 166 (69%) were not interviewed. The non-respondents were not simply those that refused – 74 (30%) could not be traced, 15 (6%) were found to be business bankruptcies and therefore ineligible for the study, one was in prison and another terminally ill. Those that refused actually constituted 31 per cent (75). Most of these 75 did not offer an explanation as to why they refused to be interviewed. Thirty-seven people did have at least some reason, although 23 said simply they were "not interested" in giving the interview. Seven said their bankruptcy was too painful or traumatic an experience to talk about in an interview. Another five expressed the view that their bankruptcy was a private matter that they did not want to discuss with an outsider and that even being contacted by me as a researcher was an unnecessary invasion of privacy. One person was advised by another party not to consent to the interview and another said they had "too many worries at the moment." Overall, it appears that for a significant number, the interview touched upon a topic too sensitive for them to be comfortable enough to give consent.

But 76 people did agree to be interviewed, with the majority (65 or 85 %) of these I rated as producing responses of "good quality". It seemed to me that once people committed themselves to speak to me, they tended to be cooperative and frank in the interview. The criteria for judging that a person's response was of "good quality" was that the respondent was clearly and genuinely interested in the interview and the research study it formed part of. Such a respondent actively participated in the interview by trying to recall details required, by having relevant documentation available or by being ready to locate such documentation during the interview.

In order to put the person completely at ease and to ensure maximum privacy, they were free to choose the location for the interview. The vast majority (64) were therefore interviewed in their own home. The remainder were interviewed in a range of locations chosen by the respondents in order to make them feel at ease. These included: at my home (3); at the home of a relative of the bankrupt (2); at the bankrupt's work place (2); at a hotel (2); at a community health/welfare facility (2); and at city shopping mall (1).

As other researchers have pointed out (Finch, 1984; Kennedy Bergen, 1993), people, particularly women, are able to establish a particular sort of interaction when interviews are conducted in the privacy of their homes because they feel comfortable and in control of the situation. This seemed to be the case in this study.

The use of an interview schedule with both open and close-ended questions also proved to be appropriate. In structuring the schedule for the first stage of the study, it seemed to be important that the questions followed a chronological sequence, i.e. from the events leading to their bankruptcy, then to the bankruptcy itself and on to the post-bankruptcy events. This then served to closely approximate the natural narrative of their bankruptcy.

I had made a conscious decision prior to commencing interviewing not to audiotape the interviews, instead recording responses verbatim on to the interview schedule again with the aim of maximising the comfort people would feel in the interview. I thought that the use of a tape-recorder may be inhibiting.

In terms of my manner in the interview, based on my experience of having worked as a debt counsellor and as a social worker, I felt confident that I could establish rapport with most of those that I interviewed by displaying warmth, empathy, friendliness and being interested in what they had to tell me. As Singh (1997) writes: "Perhaps it was more acceptable to talk about money to an informed and academically vouched-for stranger than it was to talk about money with friends and family" (p. 37). I met the criterion of being informed, as I had worked as a debt counsellor and as such had assisted a number of people to petition for bankruptcy.

I also met the second criterion in that I was from a university (La Trobe University) – the initial letter was on its letterhead – so I had academic bona fides as well. Whilst I tried to establish rapport and empathy in the interviews, they were also marked by distance and difference. Singh (1997) uses both these concepts in her work which influenced my thinking on these issues. Most were from a different class from me – I was middle class and they were mainly working class. There was no desire for an ongoing relationship on either of our parts and it was unlikely I would share their social and family networks. (Interestingly, I was to encounter a respondent after I had interviewed him in a work situation. We handled this by waving to each other in a friendly way, but both chose not to speak to each other; it was clear that neither of us wished to do so.)

Rapport and connection seemed to be established with most of those I interviewed. Respondents often asked additional questions at the conclusion of their interview about the study and bankruptcy in general. A number of them commented that they appreciated the opportunity to talk about their bankruptcy. Some of these people had never discussed their bankruptcy with anyone, or at least, with anyone outside their immediate family. The research interview appeared to act as a debriefing and as a means of emotional ventilation for such respondents.

In conclusion to this section, I learnt a number of lessons from this study about interviewing people on sensitive topics like bankruptcy. These included: taking particular care to guard the respondent's right to confidentiality and privacy; allowing the respondent to choose the location for the interview – their own home may well be where they feel most at ease and in control; being prepared not to audiotape the interview if it enhances your chances of being granted an interview and having a respondent who feels at ease; and endeavouring to be connected to your respondents by being informed and having appropriate credentials and authorisation.

Overcoming the Bias in Interviewing only Bankrupts and Ensuring the Validity of the Data

Whilst this study did incorporate interviews with creditors, they did not speak about the same events as the bankrupts addressed. Therefore the argument of presenting a one-sided picture could not be levelled at it, nevertheless, the possible charge of systematic bias, in that "... respondents might have distorted the truth to present themselves in a more favourable light" (Caplovitz, 1974, p. 315) could be made about the study. This became an issue that needed to be addressed in the data collection and subsequent analysis. In particular, this could allegedly be the case with debtors who blamed creditors entirely for their financial difficulties and their petition for bankruptcy. In fact, the research found this was not the case. For example, when asked about the most important reasons for their financial difficulties, 76 per cent of the sample mentioned that they were poor debt managers or blamed their circumstances, whereas only seven per cent blamed creditors. There were many opportunities, to use Caplovitz's words "... far less than truthful, self serving answers" (1974, p. 318) and these opportunities were not often taken by respondents.

Some of Caplovitz's methods of preventing and determining bias were applicable to this study and will be discussed in turn as they apply to it.

1. *The plausible pattern,* which refers to patterns found in previous research or widely held beliefs, was confirmed in this study. There were many examples of such plausible patterns in the present study. For example, the fact that debt default was more due to changes in circumstances than to wilful default was confirmed by the findings. Another was that low-income people tend to use high-interest finance companies as sources of credit rather than comparatively low-interest banks and credit unions. Again, the data confirmed this. All these points gave plausibility to the interview data.

2. *Testimony of multiple witnesses,* refers to there being multiple sources of corroborating evidence for the bankrupts' viewpoint, i.e. themselves. Caplovitz points out that these

witnesses are free of collusion for they do not know each other (1974, p. 320) This was particularly apparent in the respondents' accounts of their treatment by bankruptcy officials and also in their reports of the collection methods of particular credit-providers.

3. *Official records*, were also used as a comparison with respondents' accounts. These official records were able to supply details of the debts involved in the bankruptcy, including names of creditors, when the debt was contracted and the amount owed. The files in the Official Receiver's office also recorded the bankrupt's income and its source, as well as their version of the cause of the bankruptcy. Most accounts (91%) were found to be at least substantially accurate when compared to official records.

In combination, these factors strongly supported the contention that valid interview data was collected in the course of the study.

A "Theory of Action" for Data Collection

I have found the "reflection-in-action" model of Argyris and Schon (1974) and Schon (1983) useful in thinking and reflecting on my research. (See Ryan, 1996a for my attempt at applying this approach in reflecting on longitudinal research). In Argyris and Schon's terms (1974), there may be a marked difference between the theoretical assumptions a person may articulate in a conscious way ("espoused theory") and the theory typically implicit in a person's actions ("theory-in-use"), from these two can then emerge a "theory of action" that is the person's own. In this section of the chapter, I will outline my theory of action for data collection, based on my experience in this study, in a series of numbered points.

POINT 1 *Pick a data collection method you are comfortable with and confident about using, of course, it should go well with the research problem.*

The espoused theory of data collection tends to emphasise that it is something that proceeds in a logical, linear way from formulating a research problem, reviewing the relevant literature and developing research questions and hypotheses to be answered or tested in the field. The data collection methods and procedure will be chosen after careful thought about what is most appropriate. Alston and Bowles (1998), in their book on social work research, quote Sarantakos (1993, p. 157) who wrote: "... for the social scientist, methods are the tools of trade and each method is used where and when it proves to be suitable." Alston and Bowles go on to suggest that: "We should ... choose methods that are the best ways of obtaining the information required" (p. 68).

The key term in the above quote are the words "best ways" which is presumably decided after a cold, hard weighing up of the pros and cons of a particular method and its applicability to your particular study. In my case, there were elements of this type of thinking. The literature revealed that little had been heard in Australia from bankrupts themselves, so it seemed to me to be important to communicate with them directly about their perceptions of their own bankruptcies. This could be done in a number of ways, e.g. a survey questionnaire, focus group interviews or individual interviews (face-to-face or telephone). I opted for a face-to-face interview rather than a mailed questionnaire because it was likely to increase what would be a low response rate in any case. It was also more "personal" and it would not have all the problems associated with it of trying to gather people together for a focus group, e.g. finding a convenient time and place and encouraging people to talk to strangers about something as intimate and potentially embarrassing as their bankruptcy. It was also a method that I, as a social worker, felt comfortable with. In addition, it gave me the opportunity to actually meet bankrupts and, hopefully, gained some idea of their lifestyle by being invited into their homes for the interviews. The latter point proved to be accurate.

POINT 2 *Follow up of potential respondents needs to be done in a determined and assertive fashion, but mindful of treating people in a respectful fashion and conscious of their right to refuse to participate.*

I could have been relatively reactive in trying to get people to interview, i.e. send out the initial letter and wait for them to contact me, agreeing to be interviewed. I quickly discovered that this rarely happened and, that when it did, it was only in a handful of cases. The fact that only 13 per cent of all contacts with potential respondents were initiated by them after receiving the initial letter testifies to this fact. Fifty-one of the 76 interviews (67%) came about as a result of me either visiting the respondent (33 interviews) or telephoning the potential respondent (18 interviews). Just under one-third of those interviewed (25) contacted me themselves after receiving the initial letter. It quickly emerged that it was important to do direct follow-up of potential respondents after a letter requesting an interview was sent to them. Despite this active follow-up, only 31 per cent (76) of those sent letters were actually interviewed. Again this fact emphasises the degree of difficulty in interviewing defaulting debtors and bankrupts which has previously been noted by Stanley and Girth (1971) and Caplovitz (1974). It also emphasises to all those who intend to attempt research with such groups in the future, the importance of exhaustive, persistent follow-up of potential respondents in order to achieve a sample of reasonable proportions. (My determination may have gone beyond what was required or needed on the occasion when I was bitten by an Alsatian dog after I decided to ignore the "Beware of the dog" sign on a bankrupt's gate in my attempt to get to the doorbell to ring it!)

POINT 3 *The best motivation to sustain you through a piece of research is that it is driven by curiosity.*

Part of my determination was driven by curiosity. I genuinely wanted to find out the answers to questions that I had about bankrupts' lives. Allan Kellehear (Professor of Palliative Care at La Trobe University) has coined the term "curiosity-driven research" and that for me must be ultimately what research, and the data collection it involves, is about.

Satisfying my curiosity applied particularly in this study when it came to the question of creditor harassment and its influence on a person's decision to petition for bankruptcy. Based on my own practice experience as a debt counsellor, I had noticed that for some of my clients, who were insolvent, it was the pressure from creditors (often in the form of persistent phone calls and visits) that was the major precipitant for them to petition for bankruptcy as a direct means of stopping these demands from creditors. (The interview data was to support this contention, with the most direct evidence coming from the fact that 59 per cent of the respondents thought that pressure from creditors played a significant or crucial part in their decision to petition for bankruptcy.)

POINT 4 *In researching people, especially on a sensitive subject with potentially stigmatised people, you need to ensure that you "win" people over.*

Once a person has agreed to be interviewed as part of a research study, it is important that they be engaged in the process. Rapport needs to be established, at least in a temporary sense, between the researched and the researcher for a genuine, informative encounter to take place. This may involve sharing experiences, as Singh (1997) did, e.g. discussing shared holiday destinations, worries about children and the problems of migration. She cites Riddell (1989) in saying that some of this shared experience can become "manipulative" in the interview context which, at times, I think I was guilty of.

Conclusion

Trying to interview stigmatised people, like bankrupts, is clearly challenging, even a daunting task, but not an insurmountable one. In this chapter, I have discussed some of the problems that I faced and the ways I attempted to address and overcome. Brewer (1997) has encapsulated my approach when he points out that a researcher studying a sensitive topic needs to bring a tough, single-minded, tenacious but pragmatic attitude to the task. I would also add that such an attitude needs sensitivity.

There is no doubt in my mind that sensitive topics need to be studied, particularly by social work researchers advocating on behalf of the oppressed and the voiceless. As Sieber and Stanley (1988, p. 55) eloquently write: "Sensitive research addresses some of society's most pressing social issues and policy questions ... shying away from controversial topics, simply because they are controversial, is also an avoidance of responsibility."

References

1. Alston, M. and Bowles, W. (1998). *Research for Social Workers: An Introduction to Methods*. St. Leonards, N.S.W. Allen & Unwin.
2. *Annual Reports on the Operation of the Bankruptcy Act 1966* (1991-92). Canberra: Australian Government Publishing Service.
3. Argyris, C. and Schon, D. (1974). *Theory in Practice: Increasing Professional Effectiveness*. San Francisco: Jossey-Bass.
4. Brewer, J. (1997). 'Sensitivity as a Problem in Field Research: A Study of Routine Policing in Northern Ireland,' in Renzetti, C. and Lee, R. (ed) *Researching Sensitive Topics*. Newbury Park, CA.: Sage, pp. 125-145.
5. Caplovitz, D. (1974). *Consumers in Trouble: A Study of Debtors in Default*. New York: The Free Press.
6. Finch, J. (1984). 'It's great to have someone to talk to: The ethics and politics of interviewing women,' in: Bell, C. & Roberts, H. (ed) *Social Researching: Politics, Problems and Practice*. London: Routledge & Kegan Paul.
7. Hays, W. and Winkler, R. (1971). *Statistics: Probability, Inference and Decision*. New York: Holt, Rinehart and Winston.
8. Kennedy Bergen, R. (1993). 'Interviewing Survivors of Marital Rape: Doing Sensitive Research on Sensitive Topics,' in: Renzetti, C. and Lee, R. (ed) *Researching Sensitive Topics*. Newbury Park, CA.: Sage, pp. 197-211.
9. Jacob, H. (1969). *Debtors in Court: The Consumption of Government Services*. Chicago: Rand McNally and Company.
10. Lee, R. and Renzetti, C. (1993). 'The Problems of Researching Sensitive Topics: An Overview and Introduction,' in: Renzetti, C. & Lee, R. (ed) *Researching Sensitive Topics*. Newbury Park, CA.: Sage, pp. 3-13.
11. Moser, C. and Kalton, G. (1973). *Survey Methods in Social Investigation*. 2nd edn. London: Heinemann Educational Books.

12. Puckett, T. (1978). 'Credit Casualties: A Study of Wage Garnishment in Ontario,' *University of Toronto Law Journal*, 28, pp. 95-194.
13. Riddell, S. (1989). 'Exploiting the exploited? The Ethics of Feminist Educational Research,' in: Burgess, R. (ed) *The Ethics of Educational Research*. London: Falmer Press, pp. 77-99.
14. Ryan, M. (1989). *The Last Resort: An Empirical Study of Non - Business Voluntary Undischarged Bankrupts in Melbourne, Australia*. Unpublished Ph.D thesis, La Trobe University, Melbourne.
15. Ryan, M. (1992a). 'Consumer Credit, Debt Poverty and Counselling: The Australian Experience,' *International Social Work*, 35, 2, April, pp. 217-227.
16. Ryan, M. (1992b). 'The Stigma of Bankruptcy', *Socio-Legal Bulletin*. 7, Spring, pp. 6-10.
17. Ryan, M. (1993a). 'Consumer bankrupts in Melbourne,' *Australian Journal of Social Issues*, 28, 1, February, pp. 34-49.
18. Ryan, M. (1993b). 'Consumer bankruptcy: Is there a link between creditor harassment and consumer bankruptcy?' *Alternative Law Journal*, 18, 4, August, pp. 158-162.
19. Ryan, M. (1993c). 'Inequality and Low-Income Debtors: Towards a Better Deal,' in: *Theory and Practice in Australian Social Policy: Rethinking the Fundamentals*. Proceedings of the National Social Policy Conference, Sydney, July 14-16, 1993. Ed. P. Saunders and S. Shaver. Volume 3: Contributed Papers, pp. 121-132.
20. Ryan, M. (1995). *The Last Resort: A Study of Consumer Bankrupts*. Aldershot: Avebury.
21. Ryan, M. (1996a). 'Doing Longitudinal Research: A Personal Reflection,' in: Fook, J. (ed.) *The Reflective Researcher: Social Workers' Experiences with Practice Research*. Sydney: Allen & Unwin, pp. 111-124.
22. Ryan, M. (1996b). *Social Work and Debt Problems*. Aldershot: Avebury.

23. Schon, D. (1983). *The Reflective Practitioner*. New York: Basic Books.
24. Seaburg, J. (1981). 'Sampling procedures and techniques,' in: Grinnell, R. (ed.) *Social Work Research and Evaluation*. Itasca, Illinois: F.E. Peacock Publishers.
25. Sieber, J. and Stanley, B. (1988). 'Ethical and Professional Dimensions of Socially Sensitive Research,' *American Psychologist*, 43, pp. 49-55.
26. Singh, S. (1997). *Marriage Money: The Social Shaping of Money in Marriage and Banking*. St. Leonards, N.S.W.: Allen & Unwin.
27. Siporin, M. (1967). 'Bankrupt Debtors and their Families' *Social Work*. July, pp. 51-63.
28. SPSS Inc. (1986). *SPSS-X User's Guide*, 2nd edn., Chicago: SPSS Inc.
29. Stanley, D. & Girth, M. (1971). *Bankruptcy: Problem, Process, Reform*. Washington, D.C.: Brookings Institute.

4

RANU JAIN

Research Design: An Intricacy of Data Collection

Introduction

Social science research, in general, develops through certain stages, which can be sequentially arranged. In the initial stage, researchers are expected to review existing literature on the area under investigation and formulate a theoretical base along with a research design for the study. The next phase takes them to the field where they test their interview schedules, questionnaires or research guides in a short pilot study. Once the changes advised through the pilot study are incorporated in the research tools, field work begins. The last phase of research consists of desk work which includes the processes of data analysis and report writing.

Such compartmentalisation, many a time, results in an incomplete understanding of the phenomenon under study. More specifically, when the research field has been adequately explored and the variables properly deciphered, it is conducive to go to the field with a compact research design; the same practice may not be useful in exploratory studies. It is highly probable that a pre-planned research design would not cover all the relevant aspects of a social phenomenon mainly because the researcher, at the time of developing the design, might not be aware of these aspects. In fact, many a time, interesting and important dimensions of the phenomenon have been discovered during the process of data collection. These dimensions are generally ignored by the researchers while following a pre-planned research design, as it remains important for such researchers to implement the prescribed methodology. This results in an incomplete coverage of the phenomenon under study.

The need, I feel, is to keep contact with one's field while designing the research. However, can the process of designing a research continue along with the exploration of the field or, more specifically, with the process of data collection in exploratory studies?

Attempts will be made to address this question on the basis of my experience of data collection during the field work.

The Study

The topic of my research was, 'Ethnicity in Plural Societies with Special Reference to the Jain Oswals in Kolkata'. The objectives of the research were:
- to examine the dynamic nature of ethnicity with reference to the process of boundary maintenance, and
- to understand the concept of an ethnic group.

The nature of research was exploratory. The method was Case Study and the research techniques employed for the purpose were multiple, namely, observation, informal unstructured interviews, and analysis of genealogies and secondary data. In the absence of relevant authentic documents, the method of 'oral history' was used for acquiring a historical perspective on the process of migration and settlement of the selected community in West Bengal, especially in Kolkata.

'Marwari Jain Oswal' of Kolkata, was the community selected for the study. The family was the unit for analysis. More than a hundred families from the Oswal caste and its social atmosphere comprising Gujarati and non-Oswal Marwari Jains, Hindu Marwaris and Bengalis, were covered. The field work was spread over a period of two years (Jain, 1987; Jain, 1991).

The Initial Research Design

In the initial stage, the research questions under study were:
- Why and how does an ethnic group persist in a plural milieu?
- How does the process of acculturation[1] affect an ethnic group?

The study of this nature did not seem feasible through methods like the survey method. This made me employ the Case Study method and the Marwari community of Kolkata was selected for the purpose. The initial plan was to conduct the field work in two phases. In the first stage, identity profile and the interaction pattern of the 'ethnic group' were to be explored, while in the second stage, emphasis was to be laid on the 'culture' of the group. For the pilot study, an unstructured interview guide was prepared and 25 cases from Gujarati, Bengali and Marwari communities were interviewed, which lasted for approximately 15 days.

The result of the pilot study was thought-provoking. I found that going by the definition of an ethnic group[2], the 'Marwari' community could not be accepted as one. Not all individuals falling within the boundary of the primordial category of 'Marwari' identified themselves as 'Marwari'. Definite divisions within the said population were persistently apparent.

The finding was not very disturbing as, being a wide regional category, the 'Marwaris' comprised various primordial units like, castes and religions. All of these units had potential for creating a base for the emergence of an ethnic group. Thus, I planned to delimit the selected group to a smaller social unit. An attempt was made to locate that smaller unit, within the category of 'Marwari', which might not be further divided on a primordial basis. In this regard, the social unit of the Marwari Jain Oswal (MJO) group, appeared as the most appropriate one as, at that time, I felt that this unit could not be further divided on an ascriptive basis. People falling

---

1. Acculturation refers to 'the assimilation by one group of the culture of another which modifies the existing culture and so changes group identity' (Abercrombie, Hill and Turner, 1984).
2. For practical purposes, ethnic groups can be described as those groups that are based on ascriptive criterion, maintain their cohesiveness on cultural grounds and enjoy a conscious self and alters identification with the group.

within its boundary, followed the Jain religion and belonged to the Oswal caste. Further, cultural homogeneity within the unit could be assumed to some extent as, in general, all the members of the unit traced themselves to the Marwar region of Rajasthan. However, experience of the initial exposure to the field made me defer the actual process of data collection by a week. I planned to conduct a random exploration of the selected population as I felt it could reveal hitherto unexplored dimensions of the said population which, in turn, would help me in assessing the adequacy of my research design. My research supervisor also advised the same. He felt that, at least in the initial stage, I should just observe and probe into the intricacies of the field. Detailed and in-depth talks with the senior members of the community was felt to be a good method for understanding important, yet undeciphered, dimensions of the selected population.

The findings of these seven days, virtually jeopardised my theoretical base, hence the research design. I found a lack of consensus in the identification pattern of the population selected for the study. This made me realise the necessity for an in-depth study of the field, which would reveal hitherto unexplored aspects of ethnic dynamics and would make significant contribution to the debate whether ethnic groups are primarily primordial or political units?

Now the focus of the study became:
1. What is an ethnic group? Can a cultural category be considered synonymous to an ethnic group or is it an assertion of primordiality for certain situation-specific objectives?
2. In case of an ethnic group being an 'effect' of primordiality, how and why does a specific primordial base get asserted to generate an ethnic group? How does the group project and maintain its boundary?

Getting Ahead

On the basis of the field experience gathered so far, I did not attempt to revise my research design. Rather, I planned to get into the field, see what was there to be studied, come back to my books and search relevant tools for conducting the required study.

Further, I planned to explore the field from the perspective of a 'lay person' rather than an 'elite' or leader of the community. This decision was relevant, because I was trying to understand the dynamics of an ethnic identity and the process of boundary maintenance in an ethnic group. Impressed with the contemporary ethnic politics of India, leaders might have projected a superficial homogeneity across groups in order to command stronger numerical front. More specifically, they might have tried to lead me to believe that the MJO could be considered as one ethnic group. However, as the elite also formed an integral part of the social reality, I covered them at a later stage of the study.

This new approach made the research, issue-oriented. Issues, as has already been stated, were picked from the field, and I tried to deal with one issue at a time.

My initial exploration of the field had already made me aware of the existence of three ethnic groups in the MJO community of Kolkata. I also knew that these ethnic groups had emerged due to the exposure of the community members to varying situations during the process of migration and the settlement in West Bengal. Hence, it became necessary to understand not only the history of migration and the settlement pattern of the community in West Bengal, but also the context in which the groups survived. Above all, what I really had to understand was the adaptive strategies used by the groups, as these strategies were supposed to have left a lasting impact on the boundary of the groups.

The task was formidable and became even more so when I discovered the absence of relevant, authentic historical data. The community was not very important for the historians whose attention, in general, remain focussed on the power structure. The important position that the community held in the Indian economy during the eighteenth and nineteenth centuries, had resulted in some mention of it in the historical documents. However, such information was not adequate to draw a comprehensive view of the history of migration and settlement of the community in West Bengal. Besides, it was important for the study, not only to trace the identity profile of the community in the last two and a half centuries, but also to understand the 'whys' and 'hows' of this profile. I wanted to focus not on the 'facts' as narrated by the historians, but on the 'social reality' as existing in the minds of the people, for it is not the facts but its perception, interpretation and memory, which helps in the assertion of an identity.

Thus, without hesitation, absence of relevant historical data was compensated with 'oral history'[3]. In order to counter a subjective bias and memory lapse (to the extent possible) of the informants, I cross-checked the data collected through gossip sessions with other informants as well as written documents wherever available. These strategies gave me a fairly good idea of the selective nature of information provided by the informants. Besides, comparison of the data collected through oral history with that collected through documents, revealed the nature and extent of maneuvering of facts, and the importance of this maneuvering for the projection and maintenance of the group boundary.

Further to the above-mentioned techniques, the strategy of making people, especially the senior members of the community, relate their and their forefathers' life situations (to the extent remembered), was adopted. The most significant problem faced in this context, was the difficulty in confining narrations to the specified nature of the data required. In general, informants used to narrate about maximum one or two famous (well-recognised in the community) ancestors of their families. As a result, at times, the entire discussion used to centre around impressing me with the 'greatness' of their forefathers. I attempted to counter this situation by tracing genealogies of their families on paper. The idea was to start a discussion about the first person mentioned in the genealogy, to find out, how and why he/she came to Bengal; who helped in his/her coming; where did he/she stay; what did he/she do; where did he/she study; who formed his/her social context, and so on.

---

3. Dixon and Swanton (cited from Jan, 1965: 9) maintain that the reliability of oral tradition can be considered if the information it contains is in line with evidence derived from archaeology, linguistics, physical anthropology and ethnology.

Analysis of genealogies proved more useful than was expected in the initial stage. It facilitated frequent meetings with the informants and helped in getting minute details from them as well as in understanding changes in the socioeconomic profile of the family over generations. It also kept a check on the possibility of manipulation of the information by the informants. They had to discuss each person mentioned in the genealogies, generation-wise.

After tracing a couple of genealogies, I started insisting upon details on educational, occupational, marital and residential status of the members mentioned in the genealogies. The task was difficult. Informants, though cooperative, found the process exhaustive and time consuming. I tried to keep their interest alive by allowing them to get into their favourite topics and slowly bringing them back to the information required. In general, I found it difficult to get the data on women. While narrating exhaustively long genealogies (some genealogies extended to six generations), people of a patrilineal society felt justified in not providing information on the daughters of the families. Besides, it used to get difficult for them to remember details of the families of the daughters with whom interactions used to lessen over generations. A note of caution is important here. Such memory lapses and the possibility of under- and over-reporting by the respondents, make it necessary to be extra careful while drawing inferences on the basis of genealogies.

Once a comprehensive impression of the history of migration and settlement of the MJO community in West Bengal was acquired, need was felt to understand the processes of projection and the maintenance of groups' boundary. The historical data collected so far, had thrown some light on the said processes; yet, the understanding was not adequate.

Having had a formal training in sociology, I knew that the understanding of the above nature, necessitates an exploration of 'norms' and 'values' prevalent in a group. It was also felt necessary to understand the processes through which these norms and values get inculcated. I attempted to cover, not only the processes per se, but also the mechanisms like ideology, social rituals, gossip, conscious prescription of code of conduct through community panchayats and voluntary organisations, that directly or indirectly facilitated the processes.

The method of participant observation was used for collecting abstract information of the above mentioned nature. Being an 'insider'[4], it was possible for me to 'hang around' the community members keeping my eyes and ears open. I observed social rituals, participated in community ceremonies, chatted with community members, and many times, used my family members for collecting relevant information. Besides these, I listened to the 'gossip'[5] of the community members and through these deciphered what was valued in the group and what was condemned. Comparing the notes of the gossip sessions of the three ethnic groups, the presence of variegated life patterns in the three groups was revealed. It also gave an idea of the interrelationships prevailing among the three groups.

Here, it is important to mention that, in general, information collected from gossip sessions was further probed into and verified through different sources, mainly with the help of certain 'key informants', with whom I had established a good rapport. Exposure to the field had made me realise the significance of these 'key informants' for an exploratory study. These informants were those community members who had a high degree of social awareness and information, and who, by being present in the field, were well-acquainted with its intricacies, and who were accessible.

The strength of using gossip sessions, as a research tool, was the spontaneous nature of the available data, while the weakness was difficulty in recording this rich data. Use of paper and pen during the sessions was out of question. Despite recording the data at the earliest, I often found conspicuous gaps in the recordings, especially of names and dates. In order to solve the problem, I acquired a tape recorder, but found it difficult to use it on occasions like public ceremonies. Further, in certain interviews, people

---

4. I belong to the Srimal caste. Srimals, over the years, have developed close contacts with the Oswals. As a result, I had many kith and kin ties with the members of the Oswal caste. This resulted in my being considered an 'insider' by the group under study.
5. Informal conversation among people on various issues and people.

objected to its use. However, it is interesting to note, that while on certain occasions tape recorder invoked resistance, on others, it made people more vocal and forthcoming with information.

The above-mentioned methods and tools, helped me not only in acquiring an intricate understanding of the field, but also in recording the relevant data, at least to some extent. However, just like other researchers involved in exploratory studies, I too found that it was difficult to 'substantiate' the impressions thus gathered, for the purpose of report writing. Nevertheless, this shortcoming of the exploratory studies had to be accepted. I tried to tackle this problem by making careful, detailed and honest recording of the available data.

Problems Encountered

Further to the difficulties faced in the formulation of the research design and selection of tools for studying the research design, like any other researcher, I faced problems at almost every step of data collection. It was found impossible to locate the 'universe' of the community selected for the study. The population of MJO was found to be dispersed all over Kolkata. As census reports in India do not record community/caste-based information after the 1960s, no comprehensive list of the MJO community members of Kolkata was available to draw samples from. The lists available with the Kolkata Corporation office were also of not much use, as many names of the MJO community members were found similar to those of the Hindu Marwaris and Gujaratis. The lacunae made it necessary to use a sample design drawn, somewhat in line with 'snow-ball sampling'. Although the strategy helped in locating different categories of selected population, it did not ensure complete coverage of the 'universe'. The problem was solved by using two entry points into the field. In the initial stage, I started with the non-elite informants from the MJO community, with whom I had contacts prior to the research. Once it was felt that the information collected likewise had been exhausted, attempts were made to enter the field from the second entry point. In this phase, the 'elites' or the 'leaders' of the community were covered. Only when I failed to acquire new information on the issues under study, I considered the field explored. The strategy undoubtedly was not foolproof; however, it provided an assurance of maximum coverage of the field in the said circumstances.

The second major problem that I encountered, was of establishing a rapport with the informants. As has already been mentioned, I did not start my exploration with the 'elites' and hence, could not be introduced to the community members on a common platform. Besides, the MJOs were found to be dispersed all over Kolkata. Thus, I had to introduce myself to almost each and every informant. An introduction generally extended over the phone by informants, was adequate for acquiring access to the other informants but was not sufficient for rapport building or for breaking ice, enough to make the respondents know the 'purpose' behind my visit and to start talking on the relevant issues. However, despite the extra hours lost in covering long distance and introducing myself to each and every person, in general, I found people cooperative. One reason behind this cooperation might be that I was a 'good friend' or 'relative' of their near relatives or friends who introduced me to them. However, I had my share of negative experiences. I still find it difficult not to flinch when remembering how one woman closed the door on my face, as the 'men of the family' were not around and she did not want a girl who 'behaves like a man' to enter the house in the absence of the 'men'. Out of a sense of privacy, snobbishness, vanity and other such sentiments, a few people refused to cooperate.

Assuring cooperation of the informants is a problem that social scientists, especially those who do not have a sanction from the government or a higher authority, generally face. Having been influenced by the materialistic values of the capitalist world, many of the potential informants do not understand the 'importance' of research on social issues and thus, do not cooperate. Not much is gained by forcing information from reluctant individuals as, in such cases, reliability of information cannot be ensured. Hence, I did not use any coercive strategy for collecting data. Appeal for cooperation was the only technique employed for establishing rapport with the informants. As suggested by my research supervisor, I used to 'drop' any informant who was reluctant to give me information. Some informants were 'reserved'. Although willing to give information, these informants wanted specific questions to which 'to the point' answers could be provided. This necessitated making detailed questionnaires with open-ended questions. Although consulted frequently, these questionnaires were administered very sparingly and flexibly and were frequently changed with the changing enquiry. I did not reject or ignore a willing speaker. The underlying notion was, that 'any information is better than no information'. Nevertheless, my main strategy was to concentrate on talkative and 'not very busy' individuals, not only because they were ready to give time, but also because I could collect many 'important' and 'unexpected' pieces of information from them during 'unguarded' moments in conversations.

The process of establishing a rapport included overcoming resistance of the informants. In order to avoid controversies and to encourage people to speak, I used to follow the principle that 'the informant is always correct'. It is important to mention here, that this strategy cannot be implemented indiscriminately. I remember an incident, when I was collecting data on intercaste marriages. The informant had a negative opinion and not to put him on the defensive, I agreed with his opinions. The interview was proceeding smoothly, till another informant entered the room. He was 'pro-intercaste marriages' and I had agreed with him on an earlier occasion. The situation was embarrassing and it required a blunt revelation of the strategy for avoiding a 'misunderstanding'.

Another problem that I faced related to communicating to my informants, was that I was working on the Jain Oswal community and not on Jain religion. One question most frequently raised by the informants was: what is there to study about the community? Till this date many informants think that I have worked on 'Jainism'. Convinced that the community can be studied only through religion, my informants used to emphasise upon 'Jainism'. Invariably, I had to go through long lectures on Jain philosophy. In the beginning many of the interviews used to end abruptly as and when the respondents realised that I did not have much knowledge on Jainism. I solved the problem, by deferring the field work for a couple of months in order to study 'Jainism'. The study helped me in understanding the ideological background and certain behaviour patterns of the Jains. It also helped in understanding how religion could be manipulated for the purpose of boundary maintenance. On the whole the study was useful.

Many of my questions were considered redundant by the respondents, as being a 'Jain' I should have 'known' the answers. I solved this problem by telling them that 'being basically a student involved in school and college studies, I have not been much in contact with the Jain community and thus would they mind explaining ...' Fortunately, the strategy was effective as almost all of them 'knew' that people who studied were not very 'social' and, thus, did not know much about their communities.

The last mentionable problem, that I faced, emerged due to conventional gender specification. Even when not exactly 'obstructing' my work, the status of 'woman' did slacken its pace. I was literally treated as a 'conventional' Jain woman. I did not get evening appointments which effectively reduced my days to hours. Many times, I had to wait for weekends for getting appointments. However, the status of 'woman' had its advantages too. I did find it easier to gain access to the 'houses' of the informants, as, in general, the women of the houses used to 'trust' me.

The Status of an Insider

Although I was not exactly an 'insider', I enjoyed the status of an 'insider' because of rich interpersonal relations prevalent between the castes – Oswal and Srimal. If the status of an insider was a hindrance on certain occasions, it was a boon on others especially when it provided me with an excuse to linger around the community members and to collect data, which might otherwise have been difficult for an 'outsider' to collect. I did enjoy an easier 'access' to the internal world of my informants. However, familiarity with the culture obscured registering and recording of certain 'obvious' (to me) information. I realised the extent of this problem, when I was asked to give a note on 'specificities' of the MJOs of Kolkata. It was only when I went to Jodhpur (Rajasthan) and observed the

MJOs there that I could understand and record the differences between the two communities and specificities of the MJOs of Kolkata.

The status of an insider must have coloured my understanding and interpretation of data to a large extent, not only because I might have been exposed to a specific set of data, but also because I might have been unable to record structural patterns with which I was very 'familiar'. However, I have no regrets in conveying a 'Jain point of view' as both, the etic and the emic, approaches are required for acquiring a holistic picture of a phenomenon.

Conclusion

As already mentioned in the introduction, the paper attempts to reveal the intricacies of research. It attempts to show that research is not a compartmentalised activity, where one draws a research design in the beginning, goes for data collection and then writes a report. Such clear stages may be relevant for a survey method or for experimental designs, where both the field and the variables remain adequately specified. The above method is inappropriate for exploratory studies, where a pre-planned research design may result in compromising with the quest of knowledge. Such researches may end with an incomplete exploration.

An exploratory research requires building of a dialogue between the text and the context. Literature survey is essential for acquiring initial understanding of the field; however, research design should not be developed without prior acquaintance with the field. I found that the ideal approach is to understand objectives of the study and then to plunge into the field. Appropriate methods and tools can be used only when the researcher gets acquainted with the 'unique' features of the field.

Further, I learnt that research is an insightful activity. For useful contribution, a researcher should be aware not only of the intricacies of his/her field but also of the particular vantage point (like insider/ outsider or male/female) from which he/she is operating. He/she should be aware of the advantages and biases resulting from this vantage point and their probable impact on the interpretation of data. Social science research means knowing the uniqueness of both, the field and one's position in the field and to use both to their utmost advantage. Only through the understanding of this 'uniqueness' would one be able to make a meaningful contribution in the comprehension of social reality.

Acknowledgement

I sincerely acknowledge the contribution of Prof. Surajit C. Sinha, supervisor of my research, who had taken keen interest in the dissertation, especially its methodology.

This article has appeared in the *Indian Journal of Social Work,* vol. 60, issue 4, pp. 525-537. It has been reproduced with the kind permission from the Department of Publications, the Tata Institute of Social Sciences.

References

1. Abercrombie, N., Hill, S. and Turner, B.S. (1984). *The Penguin Dictionary of Sociology*. England: Penguin Books Ltd.
2. Jain, R. (1987). "Jain Oswals of Calcutta as an 'Ethnic Group': A Socio-Historical Perspective", *Man in India*. 67(4), 137-149.
3. Jain, R. (1991). *Ethnicity in Plural Societies with Special Reference to the Jain Oswals in Kolkata*. Unpublished Ph.D. Dissertation, Kolkata: University of Calcutta.
4. Jan, V. (1965). *Oral History : A Study in Historical Methodology*. London: Routledge and Kegan Paul.

5
Rajani M. Konantambigi

Data Collection: Multifaceted Experience in Day Care

Introduction

This paper is an account of my field experiences relating to a study on day care and home environment on the development of children. The respondents involved parents, caregivers and children. I employed survey and observation methods to conduct the study. To confound the problem, an assessment of the children between the ages of 3 and 6 had to be undertaken. The focus of the paper is on the problems faced in the field at various stages of the study and its implications for the study. Problems in acquiring the necessary permission to collect data, interviewing, observing and testing the respondents and sample acquisition are the main topics of narration and discussion in the paper. Before I commence to discuss these issues and problems, the rationale and objectives of the study are presented in brief.

With increasing industrialisation, as elsewhere in the world, the contexts of child care socialisation have been undergoing changes in India too (Kagan, 1984; Sinha, 1984; Gore 1970). In addition to the family, the neighbourhood, abodes of friends and relatives, the nursery schools, play centres and day care centres or creches have emerged, especially in the urban areas, as alternative settings for child care and socialisation (Naidu, 1987; Nakhate 1987a, 1987b; Gopal, 1983).

The changing contexts of child socialisation which imply adjustment for the child, as well as her/his family are sources of anxiety for the parent and issues of concern for the psychologists and child development professionals. For more than half a decade, the latter have been studying the impact of changing contexts of child socialisation (or different substitute care forms) on various aspects of children's development. Some of the findings are varied and certain issues are controversial. Research studies conducted during the decades 1940 to 1960 blamed maternal employment as the factor adversely influencing the development of children. Subsequently it was realised that the stress that the family was experiencing and satisfaction in non-mothering roles were the factors determining development. Researches after 1970 till date have focussed on the developmental differences between children of employed and non-employed mothers, children attending day care and those not attending day care and on the quality of day care centres. The claimed adverse effects of maternal employment or of day care attendance *per se* on the development of children have not been proved by research. The results are not consistent in either direction of effects. The finding vis-a-vis the quality of day care is that higher the quality of care the higher the development. Taking stock of day care research and applying this ecological perspective to understanding development Bronfenbrenner (1986) emphasised one of the primary milieu of child development, i.e., the family as playing a more crucial role. Gamble and Zigler (1986) in particular proposed a model with the combined effects of the quality of family care and day care in which, if one is of poor quality, it is compensated for by the other.

Objectives

The main objectives of the study were:
  − To determine the extent of contribution of the home and day care in the development of children and to test the premise that there are no developmental differences between children in day care and those not in day care.
  − To verify the Gamble and Zigler's (1986) model.

The Initial Exploration

The initial exploration for the study was undertaken in Bangalore city. Although day care centres were becoming a feature of urban, especially, metropolitan India, I wanted to be sure that I would find an adequate number of care centres and centres with varying quality. I felt that it was possible in Bangalore. The choice of Bangalore was also made keeping in mind my fluency with the regional language, Kannada. To my dismay I found that Tamil, Telugu and Malayalam were also the languages in use, and my sample would be very mixed. This situation was no different from the one I would have encountered in Mumbai. I decided to collect data in Bangalore because the caregivers, parents and children that I encountered were fluent in Kannada, and at that time there was no study on the day care centres at Bangalore, while Mumbai had. I visited about eight day care centres, obtained information that there were about 20 in all, and felt assured that my sampling would comprise of day care centres with varying qualities. The information about the prospective sample helped crystallise my objectives and decide the mode of data collection. Although I had decided to assess the psychological environment of the home and day care, I could not lay my hands on the relevant ready made tools. I did have parent-child, caregiver-child interactions in mind. During the visits to day care centres, the need to study psychological stimulation provided to the child became very salient. In one centre, I observed the caregiver to be sensitive to the child, talking in a pleasant and affectionate manner and conducting a variety of activities for children. In another, contrary behaviour and lack of activities were observed; the caregiver constantly scolded the children in an angry voice, ordered them to be quite all the time, marched up and down the hall which was reminiscent of suppressive pedagogy! I had to go and look for or prepare the appropriate tools. I also started thinking about the tools for child development outcomes, the dependent variable/s in my study.

Design of the Study

Given the objectives of the study, the respondents were to be drawn from two groups. In the day care group there would be preschoolers attending day care, with working mothers. The comparison group would have preschoolers not in day care and mothers who were not employed. The preschoolers were to be in the age group of 3 to 6 years. The mothers of these children and caregivers of the day care centres were also to be the respondents.

Data Collecting Instruments and Requirements

With the help of a preliminary interview schedule the sample was screened to determine whether a family and the child met the research criteria. Maternal employment, absence of family stress, age of the preschool child (3-6 years) and continuous stay of child at the day care centre in question for past year were the criteria for selecting the day care group. In case of the comparison group maternal non-employment, absence of family stress and the age of the child were the criteria. Through the preliminary schedule, socio-economic status (SES) and other family-related information were also obtained.

Bradley and Caldwell's (1979) Home Observation for the Measurement of the Environment Scale (HOMES) was adapted to assess the physical and psychological environment of the home as well as day care. Muralidharan and Kaur's Cognitive Development Test (Muralidharan & Kaur, 1983;1986; see also, Konantambigi, 1990), and Vineland's Social Maturity Scale were used in child assessments. Muralidharan and Kaur's Test was slightly modified to suit the environment of the current sample. The cognitive test comprises of functions like identifying familiar objects and actions by the child, sequential thinking, listening, comprehension language proficiency, knowledge of the environment, familiar body parts and their functions, and Phatak's (1987) Draw-a-Man Test. The test kit with the required pictures and objects had to be made. They were made with the help of artists and a carpenter or at times the items were bought from the market. Phatak's (1987) Draw-a-Man Test was used as a part of the battery of tests. It can also be used independently as it yields percentile and IQ scores. Moreover it has Indian norms. In this study it was used independently also to see its relationship to the dependent variables. Vineland's Social Maturity Scale, is used in clinical settings in India; there are no Indian norms. It comprises of social development and self help/ self reliance items. The respondents for the Vineland's scale are to be the people who live in close contact with the child. It was decided to interview the parents for the purpose. In the original scale to assess home environment all the items required observation. However, I felt that certain information could be more easily elicited by questioning the mother of the child but on the other hand, one cannot do away with the observation method as the psychological stimulation provided to the child was also to be assessed. If there was doubt regarding the authenticity of the response by the mother, it was to be followed up through the observation method.

Bradley and Caldwell's (1979) HOMES was the tool for assessing the quality of the homes and day care. The observation method necessitates rating by at least three researchers. Due to economic and time constraints, it was not possible to employ three researchers. I was aware that my bias could affect the observations and I made efforts to consciously check the bias. I time-sampled the observations. Thus, the observations were conducted three times per child at home with her/his mother and likewise in the day care context with the caregiver. This was done for assuring the consistency of the response. Utilising only the interview technique might have elicited socially acceptable responses from most respondents. Currently multi-method approach is being advocated (Kulkarni and Puhan, 1988, Messick, 1984; Wig, et al, 1983).

Although I had shown the interview schedule and observation formats, the observation format was not discussed in the interest of research. They were not made overtly conscious of it, because it was felt that such knowledge would elicit socially acceptable responses or make them too conscious of their behaviours. Both these occurrences would have defeated the purpose of observation. Keeping the respondents ignorant when some of their behaviours are being observed raises ethical issue which is much debated in the research circles. However, the pursuit of truth in research is held higher especially when the respondents/subjects are observed in their natural settings and where the researcher is permitted to be present. This is one of the greatest dilemmas of this piece of research. If not for this rationale, research by participant observation becomes questionable.

Problems in Sample Acquisition

Concerned authorities cooperated by granting permission for the study, providing the list of creches and asking the concerned caregivers of the day care centres to extend their cooperation. The authorities in the department of Factories and Boilers, Government of Karnataka took their time. Only after a number of telephone calls and three visits to their office did they provide the list. A ready-made list was not available. I had to note down the names as one of the factory inspectors recited the names of the factories where creche facilities were available. Some of the personnel and welfare officers in the factories exhibited a keen interest in the study. This expedited the granting of permission that had to be obtained from the factory authorities.

Even for the pilot visit, I had to seek permission from the concerned authorities – the State Women and Child Welfare Department, the Karnataka State Council for Child Welfare (KSCCW), the Factories and Boilers Department, the Bangalore City Corporation (BCC) and the concerned personnel in factories, etc. By and large, obtaining the necessary permission was not a problem. However, one experience left me befuddled! The following is an anecdote of that experience. I visited the Karnataka State Social Welfare Advisory Board (KSSWAB) to obtain the list of their creches and their permission. They had no objection to my visiting the creche and interviewing the caregiver. The list of creches that I needed, one of the senior office-bearers said, was being compiled and that if I could wait or come back in the afternoon the list would be given to me. I replied that I had an appointment at KSCCW and that if possible I would return in the afternoon, if not, the next morning. At the KSCCW office there was a call for me. I was very surprised because my schedule for the day had not been discussed with anybody as I had no intimate friends there at the time. When I answered the call, a male voice at the other end was asking me for a date! I was shocked and trembled for few seconds. It then struck me that I had let slip to the office bearer at the KSSWAB that I was proceeding to the KSCCW office. Of course I am not certain that the call was from one of the KSSWAB office bearers. However, it sounded logical and convincing at the time and one can well imagine my consternation as I had to visit the person to collect the list of creches. During my prior visit to the KSSWAB I had no such untoward experiences. This incident set me thinking pessimistically: How will I face the man tomorrow? What if he would not give me the list? Would he let me conduct my research in the KSSWAB centres? What if I have more such experiences?

The next day with my heart in my mouth I visited the person. All my fears and anxieties were quelled as he wordlessly handed me the required list of creches! I clutched the sheet of papers tightly and almost fled from the room! Fortunately, I did not have any such unsettling experiences in the later phase of data collection. Once in the creche set-up or in the home, my interactions were mainly with women and children. In situations where men were present, they treated me with dignity and respect whenever they interacted with me.

On obtaining the list from various places, the centres of the Bangalore City Corporation (BCC) had to be excluded from the sample. These centres, nine in number at the time, were not running regularly. Due to problems in securing ration, the nutrition component of the day care programme could not be fulfilled and so the children absented themselves. These centres did have children aged 3 to 6 years, but it was of no avail to me. After excluding the latter, 24 – day care centres were to form the sample. As the study progressed six more had to be dropped as children from these centres were from families with stressful background. Due to severe selection criteria, the size of the target sample reduced. To expand the sample, I would have had to conduct the study in yet other cities. But, due to resource constraints it was not possible.

Locating day care centres was both easy and difficult. Easy when they actually existed, a chase for the mare's nest when they did not! I was driven to exhaustion as I asked directions, kept moving, "left, right, straight, right again and left", was proved wrong; again I go, "right, straight, left, left, right again"! My memory is so vivid that it brings tears of exhaustion in my eyes again! It will be a matter of concern to note here that some of the centres listed and financed by the KSSWAB were the ones that did not exist. This was reported to be true also for the state of Maharashtra in a seminar held at the National Institute for Public Cooperation and Child Development, Bangalore Centre, on 10-11 August 1989, where representatives from different organisations and schools of social work involved in the task of supervision and monitoring of creches were the participants (personal communication).

The study, as mentioned before, involved home visits and these were also very difficult because of my unfamiliarity with Bangalore city. At times, locating addresses in Bangalore can make you feel sorry for yourself. Those familiar to Bangalore's "Mains and Crosses" know what I am referring to! For the lucky people who are not, "Mains" are supposed to the main roads and "Crosses" are the by-lanes. To further compound the problem, the fantastic way in which the numbering of houses is done puts extra icing on the cake! The state of affairs befuddles a Bangalorean, one can well imagine the state of non-Bangalorean researcher, with a satchel full of questionnaires, inventories, and sometimes with a kit heavy with the testing materials, dragging herself along in the summer heat, asking "Is this the 9th Main, 5th Cross?" Whoever said research was a bed of roses! In some cases, in spite of a prior appointment made, respondents were not to be found in their residences. "Last minute changes, could not help it!" would be their response. But they really did feel bad afterwards when they saw all the material I was dragging along. Sometimes respondents gave incorrect address – they were not residing in the address provided. Two respondents refused to cooperate. Such incidences reduced the sample.

After the pilot visit I had hoped to acquire about 125 preschoolers in day care centres. This was not possible. A sample of 72 day care preschoolers was obtained. For the comparison group (preschoolers not attending day care), the sample was halved and the sample size obtained was 36.

The Data Collection Process

I had the task of three observation periods (Patton, 1990) at both the care centre and the home. In the day care setting observations were facilitated by the fact that I had to visit the creche a number of times, once to interview the caregiver, and then to meet parents of the sample children to collect their home addresses. In day care centres for low-income groups, the observation had revealed that there would be no space available to conduct any type of psychological testing. Administering the test for the cognitive development at the child's place was the ideal choice. This enabled the child to be herself/himself as s/he was in familiar surroundings. In the home setting, I created the need to visit at least thrice by giving one of the legitimate reasons, to establish adequate rapport with the child, as an intelligence-like test was to be administered. As mentioned earlier, the respondents were being observed in their natural setting which was not made obvious to them. Both the interview and observation sessions were held during every visit to the home and the creche. The observation period was mostly after the interview when I conversed with the respondents. This was not a problem as I only had to tick whether the responses recorded were consistent. Both the pretesting and the proper testing situation proved that true behaviour manifested themselves shortly after the formal questions had been answered. Schedule of interviews, observations and testing the child were thus planned and executed (Table 1). This was proved at the pretesting itself.

Table 1: The schedule of data collection

Visits	Sessions			
	Nature of Researcher's activity	Respondents	Observations	Situation
First	Preliminary interview	Mothers	First observation	Mother's interaction with the child
Second	Interview for Vineland's Social Maturity Scale	Mothers	Second observation	Mother's interaction with the child
Third	Testing the child's cognitive development and Phatak's Draw-a Man Test	Children	Third observation	Mother's interaction with the child

For the Vineland's Social Maturity Scale the respondents selected were the mothers of the children. According to Vineland, competence of the child is accepted if her/his behaviour/skill in question is exhibited 75 per cent of the time. To judge this the researcher is supposed to ask probing questions. If the respondent exaggerates, it is possible to test this by requesting the child to perform a particular task or by simulating a situation. It was necessary to test some of the claims of some mothers in the pretesting as well as during the research proper. It becomes essential to be alert and highly probing, observing and questioning with a researcher's mind. Moreover, through a pilot visit and pretesting, the unforeseen issues and situations come into focus, they alert and make the data collection proper and efficient process.

The above-mentioned points were more than well proved in the pretesting of Muralidharan and Kaur's (1983; 1986) Cognitive Development Test. The pilot visit revealed that it was not possible to conduct the testing session in the day care. The creches had no privacy to conduct the testing. I had no other choice but to carry on the testing at the child's home. It definitely had the advantage, because it placed the child in highly familiar surroundings in the secure presence of her/his mother. But it also raised issues on controlling the interfering influence of the home environment. To begin with, I told the parents of the child in no uncertain terms that the neighbours had to be kept away and also explained to the neighbours that since this was a kind of test, the child could not be disturbed even by their presence. In the testing situation we closed the door and sometimes even the windows.

The family members too had to be stopped from interfering. This was quite a task when there were too many of them. The testing situation was given as one reason. I had also assured them by saying that their child would do well in the test as it was easy. If the children were younger, the parents were assured that the test was for children aged up to six years and the younger ones were not expected to complete all the items. Finally, they were told that prompting on their part would mean a loss of score for the child which otherwise the child could have gained. In spite of all these instructions, children lost a score here and there. It may not be out of context to note here that parents could be categorised. After the interview sessions and the observations it can be said that there were a set of parents who constantly wanted their child to excel and stimulated their children accordingly. They came through as honest and straightforward. There was another set of parents who would prompt, or tell me that their child actually knew it and was not answering and showed their offspring in a favourable light. They could not help but prompt their child and tried to assure the researcher that their child knew the answer to the particular item. Responding honestly and sincerely to an interview or testing situation, especially in case of adults could be personality trait.

More crucial was the task of contending with the siblings of the target children. This was more so if their age gap was small. When the sibling was younger to the target child, it was not very difficult to keep this child engaged, so that s/he did not interfere with the testing. The competence of the younger child was not a serious interference as the target child was higher up on the development ladder (retarded children or those with any special physical problems were not included in the sample). When the child was older and if s/he was around before the testing began, either s/he was sent out to play or if very naughty and appeared that I could not contend with the child, I administered the test first to this child in private and later to the target child. This situation occurred also in the pretesting session. Though interferences were anticipated I had never thought that I would not be in a position to deal with it. In such situations I had to keep my wits about me and react quickly. However, once the testing had to be postponed as I could not control the sibling and in another case I had to give up the testing session. The previous interview and observations sessions rated were a loss. Contending with the siblings of the comparison group was not a severe problem as I held the testing session when the sibling was in a school.

Testing the Child

Research on children by itself raises a number of issues. The age of the child, establishing rapport with the child, being able to communicate the test questions, sustaining the child's interest, being able to detect if the child is actually responding to the test item or to another stimuli in the environment or a stimuli evoked by the association mechanism and to detect if the child is really failing an item or is it just a case of memory lapse are all important factors to be considered (Messick, 1984; Konantambigi, 1987).

As mentioned earlier, to facilitate rapport with the child, the researcher visited the child at his/her residence twice prior to the testing situation. Visits to the creche also helped in establishing rapport. Some children are friendly by nature. It was easy to establish rapport with such children. However, after being exposed to me at the creche and twice at home, by the time the testing started, even the reserved children accepted me and participated adequately in the testing situation. As stated earlier, the children were 3 to 6 years of age. Thus care had to be taken while communicating with them. I used simple sentences in communicating with them. Children aged 3 to 4½ years are too playful and cannot concentrate on a task for a long time. The researcher's patience was tested most severely. The researcher had to keep repeating questions, had even to ask the child to look at the test item. Some younger children had to be given a break of about 15 minutes during the test period. This break was over and above those given for the child to go to the toilet and to eat and drink.

When working with children everything is not easy. Once during a pretesting session the child answered about three sub-tests, after which he refused to answer any further. No amount of requesting, talking about the attractiveness of the pictures, comparing the picture of the boy with him, and not even bribing (with chocolates) worked. The boy's mother could not do anything either. As a last resort I gave him a colourful beads and blocks of the colour and shape discrimination test, the child just played around with them uttered a response or two and then started throwing the materials around. I could not erase this experience; it was with me. When the situation repeated during the data collection proper I just could not do anything. The sample was lost to me. In a sample of 78, 6 were lost mostly due to the negative responses of the child. The sample loss proportion is 7.7 per cent.

The cognitive test kit used contained coloured picture cards, colourful plastic beads and blocks, and it was attractive to sustain the interest of the children. In the pretesting situation it was observed that the shape discrimination test proved too attractive for children to concentrate on the next test items. It was, therefore, decided to administer this item last. Based on the test items and the responses of children during pretesting, schedule of administering the various sub-tests was decided. Care was taken to sustain the interest of the child and also to see that the child did not tire easily.

The researcher, by being alert during the testing session, could detect if the child was responding to some other stimuli in the environment and not to the test stimuli and also when the child was responding to an association stimuli. However, the parents explained the association stimuli. The children also resorted to describing situations in the test stimuli by their experience. The descriptions did not have any relevance to the test item. However, it was not possible to test whether a child was undergoing memory lapse or whether the child failed on the test item. Whenever the child failed to answer, s/he was given some time and the question was repeated once or twice. In spite of this chance, when the child did not answer, it was considered as failure on the particular item. Since the items had not been scaled, the test was continued till all the items were exhausted.

Summary and Conclusion

Our research methodology text books advocate initial field explorations to polish out research design, to know our sample, to help ascertain the sample size and the kind of anticipated problems in procuring the sample. Pretesting alerts us about possible problems in our interview/observation schedule, in the process of conducting interviews/observations/psychological testing etc. However, pretesting also leads to loss of respondents, which I could not afford as the sample meeting the research criteria was very small to start with. I felt that research is a back and forth process and there is no short cut. Pilot study and pretesting are a must.

In the present research the nature of research study posed certain issues. Controlling for family stress was a delicate issue. People do not generally like to disclose to a stranger the problems that they face. Assessing the home environment which necessitated the observation of psychological stimulation the child received and the mother-child interactions was a complex and difficult task. Assessing the cognitive development of the child is always a herculean task! I had to be highly precautious and had to have my wits about me. The issue was tricky; responses had to be elicited from the child, the child had to be gently coaxed, but s/he could not be forced to respond. Research with children though a fascinating experience, has an equal and opposite force as well. It is a test of one's wits and patience! This task was compounded further as the researcher had to grapple with the problems of sibling and parental interference.

The problem associated with controlling socially acceptable responses, especially on the part of parents and caregivers, necessitated the use of a multi-approach technique in the assessment of the home environment and day care quality. Although the nature of the research topic to a large extent determines the method(s) of data collection, dynamic field realities may suggest to alter these methods and the data collecting process. Accordingly, researchers need to change their data collecting approaches to achieve the objectives of the study. In fact, these data collecting experiences and their analysis have altered my thinking and action in regard to administering scales and conducting quantitative research, helped me question the basic assumptions about "scientific research" and greatly turned my interest towards a new world of qualitative research.

Acknowledgment

The author is grateful to Prof. Usha S. Nayar of Tata Institute of Social Sciences (TISS), Mumbai, under whose supervision the study was completed and to Dr. Ranu Jain also of TISS who critically appraised the manuscript.

References

1. Bradley, R.H. and Caldwell, B.M. (1979). 'Home Observation for the Measurement of Environment: Revision of the Preschool Scale'. *American Journal of Mental Deficiency*. Vol. 84, 235-244.
2. Bronfenbrenner, U. (1986). 'Ecology of the Family as a Context for Human Development: Research Perspectives'. *Developmental Psychology*, 22 (6), 723-742.
3. Gamble, T.J. and Zigler, E. (1986). 'Effects of Infant Day Care: Another Look at the Evidence'. *American Journal of Orthopsychiatry*, 56 (1), January.
4. Gopal, A.K. (1983). *Creches in Plantations*. New Delhi: National Institute of Public Cooperation and Child Development.
5. Gore, M.S. (1970). 'Changes in the Family and the Process of Socialization'. in: E.J.Anthony and C.Colette (ed), *The Child in the Family*, Vol. 5, New York: John Wiley and Sons.

6. Kagan, J. (1984). *The Nature of the Child*. New York: Basic Books Inc., Publishers.
7. Konantambigi, R.M. (1987). *Psychometrics and Children's Behaviour*, nine papers. Unpublished Ph.D. papers. Mumbai: Tata Institute of Social Sciences.
8. Konantambigi, R.M. (1990). *Home Environment, Day Care Quality and Cognitive and Social Development of Preschool Children: A case of India*. Poster presented at the XIII Biennial Meeting of the International Society for the Study of Behavioral Development, Amsterdam, June 28-July 2, 1994.
9. Kulkarni S.S., and Puhan B.N. (1988). 'Psychological Assessment: Its Present and Future Trends'. in : J.Pandey (ed), *Psychology in India: The State of the Art*. Vol. I. New Delhi: Sage.
10. Messick, S. (1984). 'Assessment of Children', in: P.H.Mussen (ed), *Handbook of Child Psychology, History, Theory and Methods*. Vol.2. New York: John Wiley and Sons, Inc.
11. Muralidharan, R. and Kaur, B. (1983). The Impact of an Intervention Programme on the Language and Cognitive Development on Preschool Children from Urban Anganwadis. New Delhi: NCERT. Mimeo.
12. Muralidharan, R. and Kaur, B. (1986). The Impact of an Intervention Programme on the Language and Cognitive Development on Tribal Preschool Children. New Delhi: NCERT. Mimeo.
13. Nakhate, V.S. (1987a). A Report on the Orientation Training Programme for Workers of Private Creches in Greater Mumbai. (March 6-8, 1987), Mimeograph. Mumbai: Tata Institute of Social Sciences.
14. Nakhate, V.S. (1987 b). Family Day Care in Mumbai. Mimeograph. Mumbai: Tata Institute of Social Sciences.
15. Naidu, U.S. (1987). A Survey of Day Care Centres in Mumbai. Mimeograph. Mumbai: Tata Institute of Social Sciences.
16. Patton M. Q. (1990). *Qualitative Evaluation and Research Methods*. Newbury Park: Sage.

17. Phatak, P. (1987). Phatak's Draw-a-Man Test. Pune: Anand Agencies.
18. Sinha, D. (1984). 'Some Recent Changes in the Indian Family and their Implications for Socialization'. *Indian Journal of Social Work*. Vol. XLV, no. 3, October, pp. 271-286.
19. Wig, N.N., Verma, S.K. and Pershod, D. (1983). 'Development of Psychological Tests in India: An Overview of the Current Situation'. *Indian Journal of Clinical Psychology*. Vol. 10, September 83, no. 2.

6
Manohar Pawar
Searching for Data in the Criminal Justice System

Introduction

I was a keen student of criminology and issues related with deviance, crime and justice always interested me. My decision to undertake research on the criminal justice system was a planned one. During my encounters with researchers, I had realised that both the supervisor and the researcher, should be interested in the research topic and the supervisor must have some expertise in it. I had identified a few topics I was interested in researching and consulted a prospective supervisor to determine a mutually interesting research area from the identified topics. Through this consciously planned consultation process, I decided to research on delays in the disposal of criminal cases in the magisterial courts of Mumbai.

A brief literature review of the selected topic suggested that although in the Indian context a couple of studies were conducted on the topic (Mukherjee and Gupta, 1978; Rajan and Khan, 1982;), no systematic research was undertaken on the magisterial courts in Mumbai. Delay in disposal of cases was an important major issue at both state and national levels (Dhawan and Kalpakam, 1978; Dhawan, 1986) and senior judicial officials had frequently raised it in print media and other platforms. But, I was not sure to what extent this is an issue in the magisterial courts of Mumbai. Before

I prepared the research proposal, I was curious to know what is the disposal pattern in these courts and what exactly is the issue to be researched.

To get acquainted with the Metropolitan Magistrate courts and to identify a specific issue, I conducted a pilot survey, which showed that although the institution of IPC (Indian Penal Code) cases was as low as one-fourteenth of total cases, its pendency was as high as one-fifth of the total cases. Disposal of IPC cases through judgement was on average approximately 50 per cent, and without judgement was only four per cent; and total pendency of IPC cases for one year or more was 57 per cent. Some of the courts had negligible number of IPC cases and some predominantly dealt with them. Thus I decided to specifically research delay in the disposal of IPC cases in the magisterial courts.

By visiting leading libraries and by contacting relevant scholars, I intensively reviewed national and international literature that focused on this specific problem. The review showed that by and large research on delay in the disposal of cases in India has been avoided even when the opportunity was offered and research on this issue is much needed. However, studies conducted elsewhere had suggested to look at 'time' factor in courts, court processing in relation to defendants' background characteristics, defendants' perception of the role of the magistrate in a case, the role of the clerk and detailed exploration of solicitor-client contacts (Pawar, 1993). In light of these suggestions and my own insights, I set the following objectives.

Objectives

- To look into the organisation and working of magisterial courts in Mumbai;
- To explain the nature and causes of delay in the disposal of criminal cases;
- To analyse the socio-economic background of the accused and psycho-socio-economic effect on the accused;
- To ascertain the points of view of the accused, the prosecutor and defence counsel on judicial working.

Research Questions

To guide my research step by step, I had formulated the following research questions.
- How is the day-to-day work organised in magisterial courts?
- What is the usual working pattern in courts?
- How far have the courts been effectively managing the working time?
- What is the extent of adequacy of infrastructural facilities?
- What is the amount of time taken in the disposal of various criminal cases?
- What are the factors which contribute to the delay in the disposal of cases?
- What is the socio-economic and legal background of the accused?
- How do the accused persons pass through different stages of justice processing?
- Has the socio-economic background of the accused anything to do with their case progress?
- What is the nature of case progress?
- Are there any stages in case progress which are significantly slow or fast?
- How far does criminal justice processing affect the socio-economic status of the accused?
- What is the experience and perception of the accused of justice processing?
- What is the view of the accused, the prosecutor and the defence counsel on the working of the judiciary?

Research Methods

This research was essentially an exploratory one and it had employed both observation and survey methods. The study required secondary data from court records, annual reports, etc., and primary data from court working, the accused, advocates, police prosecutors and the court staff. Of 48 magistrate courts in Mumbai, 23 courts were selected for the study. It was planned to systematically observe three days' working of each court (i.e. the observation of court working for 69 days) and 2 to 3 cases proceedings on each observation day. From each selected court 10 to 12 newly instituted cases were selected so as to study their progress over a period of time. It was planned to contact and interview one or two accused from each select sample case (i.e. a minimum of 278 interviews). Ten advocates and respective police prosecutors from each court (i.e. 230 advocates and 23 prosecutors) were targeted for the survey.

Research Instruments

Observation Sheet: On the basis of the observation of the working of a few courts and some discussion with the court staff, an observation sheet was developed. The sheet covered items such as timings of court functionaries, time devoted to different court functions, and the role of court officials and others. Other items were included to know how far the court adheres to procedural and legal aspects, attention given to the accused, whether the treatment to the accused differs on the basis of his looks (in shabby cloth, aged, young, illiterate, sex, etc.), examination and cross-examination by the prosecutor and the lawyer, formal and informal interaction among court staff, etc. Part of the observation sheet was also devoted to observe the progress of specific cases.

Case Progress Sheet : Case progress sheet was developed on the basis of case files to study the progress of the case on any given date. It was meant to collect such information as details of the accused, offence, number of adjournments and main stages of criminal justice processing.

Interview Schedule: The schedule aimed to collect information about the socio-economic background of the accused, psycho-socio-economic effect on the accused and attitude of the accused towards law. The questions were mainly on personal characteristics, accused-police interaction, pretrial aspects in custody/on bail, justice processing and impact of justice processing.

Questionnaire: It was developed to know the view of advocates and prosecutors on judicial working. Items were on justice system, advocate-client interaction, bail, justice processing and delay.

A Brief Description of the Study Area

The study covered magisterial courts located in the city of Mumbai. Mumbai is the capital of Maharashtra State and one of the first 10 largest cities in the world. It covers an area of 603 sq km, with 9.9 million population and is one of the fastest growing (at 4.00%) metropolises. It is also considered as industrial and commercial capital of India. One-third of the country's export is done from Mumbai alone. More than 50 per cent of population lives in slums covering a mere 16.66 per cent of the total residential space of the city, which is less than the land occupied by roads (about 25%). "People inevitably live in squatters, thatched houses, rooftops, under flyovers, in dry pipelines, on railway platform and even above public and railway lavatories. Many of its areas are controlled by goondas, crime, corruption, violence, everything is on the increase" (Mayur, 1986). To handle such unlawful behaviour, the city is equipped with a large law enforcement force consisting of more than 4000 police officers and 24160 policemen and 57 police stations. The city has an elaborate system of judiciary having 123 courts of different categories. The study courts were spread over 19 different locations in the city, most of them were in South Mumbai.

Data Collection Process

My knowledge of criminology, crime and justice was mostly gathered from reading and observing. I had not worked in any of the criminal justice systems, except that I had paid some observation visits. So, in a way, I was an outsider, and collecting data from court observations and documents, the accused, prosecutors and lawyers was completely new to me. It was exciting, challenging and sometimes discouraging. While I approached the field quite confidently, new experiences and surprises sometimes shook my confidence and made me find alternatives and change approaches. During the data collection process, I was reading, *The Field Worker and the Field* (Srinivas, *et al*, 1979), that helped me gain strength in the field and inspired me to write about my data collecting experiences. I have organised my field experiences according to the instruments and listed lessons learned from these experiences at the end of the chapter. A study of this kind cannot be conducted without obtaining permission from various authorities. Thus I am presenting my field experiences from this point.

Permission Granted : Being a study of legal systems and its related aspects, seeking formal permission was essential. Towards this an application was submitted to the Registrar of the High Court. After a few reminders, two personal visits and a verification in writing, permission was granted upon the conditions that (1) the data collection should not impede the work of the court, and (2) safety of the record should be ensured.

Although the copy of the permission letter had reached the Chief Metropolitan Magistrate's Office, no action was taken to communicate it to the magistrate courts. This resulted in not getting access to court files in spite of the permission letter. Frequent visits to officials failed to fill in the communication gap. Somehow a clerk having an understanding of official working, some understanding of the place of the present study, took upon himself to expedite the matter. After two days, he and his Office Superintendent together drafted a letter and the clerk pursued it till it was cyclostyled and circulated to 23 court officials.

Since some of the accused were in prison as undertrials, permission from prison authorities was necessary to interview them. The Inspector General Prisons was approached. Visits in person were paid and reminders followed, but in vain. After a period of time they informed that permission was not possible. The Home Secretary and two Under Secretaries of the Government of Maharashtra were approached. Again formal applications were submitted. This was followed by telephonic reminders. Despite all this, it took six long months to receive the permission – with a page full of conditions. But unfortunately by that time most of my respondents were out on bail or were discharged and hardly 10 inmates could be interviewed. The procedure of obtaining official permission was often quite discouraging and frustrating.

Visiting the police stations to get information was not included in the plan of the study as it was not needed. But field situations like the accused continuing in custody or unclear address or difficulty in locating the accused forced the researcher to visit the police station either to interview the accused or to seek some information. All the officials at the police stations visited were helpful without involving any formalities.

Pretesting : Both observation sheet and case proceeding sheet were pretested by observing the courtroom setting and case proceedings. Accordingly necessary modifications were made. Case progress sheet was pretested by studying case files. While studying cases, one of the difficulties was following the writing of the clerk, generally written in abbreviations. Frequently used abbreviations in case files were familiarised by asking the judicial clerk or interpreter. A list of such abbreviations and their explanation was prepared and referred to while studying case files. Pretesting the interview schedule of the accused in judicial lock-up was easy, though it was not convenient. Whereas pretesting the interview schedule of the accused on bail was difficult, locating the accused and convincing him was not simple. Hence, it was planned to approach the accused through their defence counsel, if any. Pretesting the questionnaires of advocates and police prosecutors revealed that they were not readily willing to cooperate, and whoever accepted did not return it on her/his own. At any rate, only a few advocates returned it after repeated reminders. Following this exercise, these instruments were improved, and the data collection through them was launched simultaneously.

Observation of Court Working Days : Using participant or non-participant observation (NPO) method depends upon the nature of study. In this study NPO method was suitable as in courtrooms participant observation was not possible. Besides, the observation work was carried out without the knowledge of their being observed. This was strictly adhered to till the NPO study was completed. A few court officials did know that the researchers had the permission of the High Court to conduct the study, but they were not aware of my observation work. Throughout the study, I lived with an ethical dilemma of collecting data on court actors without their knowledge.

Generally, at the back of the courtroom, accused box was erected where a number of accused persons wait for their case to be heard. Then some benches for the visiting public and litigants were arranged. Next, chairs and tables for advocates and for other court officials were arranged. Then, facing all these categories of people was the magistrate's dais with necessary sitting arrangement to her/his assistants (stenographer and interpreter), and a witness box was arranged left to the dais.

On one of the beginning days, I sat on one of the advocate's chairs and was jotting down observations. This was noticed by a police constable who promptly passed it to the interpreter and the interpreter passed it on to the magistrate. The magistrate said, "Stand up. Who are you?" I replied, "I am a student. I will explain to you my purpose in your chamber." An advocate sitting close by advised not to explain all that. It was a bit confusing. Again the magistrate asked, "Are you a press reporter?" "No", was the reply. He then preferred to ignore the matter. Thereafter, I stopped recording of observations on the spot and started just observing happenings there. This brief experience helped me in many ways to develop my own method to record observations. I would sit or stand (according to the situation) at the back where public and litigants sit. At times, the interpreter noticing me at the back would tell me to sit on an advocate's chair, which I usually declined.

For recording observations, I used a small piece of paper and a short pencil which could be accommodated within the fist. This avoided the undue attention of court officials and others. I tried to remember most of the items of the observation sheet. During observation, points were noted down on a small piece of paper, and at lunch time these were expanded. After reaching my room, the same evening/night, observation points were transferred/ expanded on the observation sheet in detail. A similar procedure was followed in filling case proceeding sheets. At times the main difficulty was not hearing the exact conversation due to the distance, which might have led to missing some points. Out of curiosity, I used to go in front of the crowd in the courtroom. While doing this, in two different courts, I was noticed by the interpreter who informed the magistrate. Consequently, I had to stand inside the witness box, explain what I was doing, and present my identity card and the copy of the High Court permission. I had to tell them that to learn court proceeding I was in the courtroom – omitting to mention that my observation work was in progress. My ethical dilemma continued. Later on, I rationalised that to remain honest to one's work, one has to be at times 'dishonest' to others. Another limitation was that the observation of court working did not fit in the exact sequence of the observation sheet because the court functioned according to the availability of its clients (the accused, witnesses, etc.). Yet another difficulty was that sometimes many actors participated in court proceedings at the same time. In this situation it was difficult to observe even one actor properly. For example, during remand hours, to observe advocate, litigant, police officer, interpreter, magistrate, or peon was a real problem. This resulted in blank items on the observation sheet.

In addition to courtroom proceedings' observation, I also observed and noted other events occurring in the court premises such as lawyers' approaches to their clients and the lawyer-client interaction, the interaction of the accused and their relatives with court officials, etc. These observations helped me in significant ways to understand the working of magisterial courts in Mumbai.

Although it was planned to observe each select court's three working days (total 69 working days), due to the shortage of time it was reduced to observing only two working days (total of 46 working days). Undoubtedly, the observation method generates rich and realistic data, but it is time consuming.

Case Progress through Court Files : Observing the 278 select sample cases in 23 courts was yet another component of the data collection work. From the date of the institution, these cases were continuously followed over a period of 10 months. Any change in these cases was a part of their progress. At every given (adjournment) date what happened in the case was carefully looked into. This was done by observing the case when it was called, and when this was not possible, the same case files were studied from the office and the progress made on the given date was noted down.

To keep track of day-to-day progress of the cases, I had to heavily depend upon court officials particularly the peon. Since the peon was having his own priority to take out case files, he never gave them to me when requested. Sometimes, I had to wait throughout the day and often go back without any success. Asking the court official did not help me to get the cases early as they refused to seriously instruct the peon. Perhaps, all were collaborators in their own 'common endeavour'. Even in a few cases where a court official instructed the peon, he never bothered to pass on the files to me. Perhaps, the peon was not aware of the location of the file at that point of time as sometimes case files were moved to different tables depending upon the work involved. Besides, the case files filing system followed was not the best one, only the court's peon and clerks may follow it. Not getting the cases at the requested time was the main difficulty in studying the case progress. Notwithstanding these difficulties case progress was observed. A list of abbreviations and their explanations was helpful in reading remarks made in case files.

Interviewing the Accused : Interviewing the accused was a sensitive issue (Lee and Renzetti, 1993) as the accused persons' guilt was under question in the court of law, they might have already faced some interrogation by the police and they may be living with fear of punishment. About 40 per cent of the targeted respondents were charged with offence against person, 30 per cent were charged with offence against property, 10 per cent were charged with the offence of accident, mostly involving motor vehicles, and 20 per cent were charged with miscellaneous offences. In addition, some of them were also not-able to distinguish between the police interrogation and the researcher's questions. Due to these complex factors, I faced several field difficulties which have been elaborated below.

The Planned Location of the Interview Failed : I had planned to interview selected accused persons at the court premises. I was keeping track of the progress of 278 cases spread over 23 courts, and I was too naive to assume that on the given date the accused person will appear in the court, and I will meet her/him in the courtroom or in the court premises and request for an interview. I was also aware that the accused in the selected cases may appear in different courts on the same day and I will not be able to cover all of them on the same day. But I thought of tracking those accused persons on the next adjournment date.

However, this idea of meeting the accused in the courtroom as per their adjournment dates and interviewing them there itself did not work. My visit to courts according to adjournment dates would be there. But the problem was that all the accused persons would not come to courts according to their adjournment dates, or else some of them would come but quickly take the next date directly from the interpreter and go away. In some cases the accused would appear in the courtroom, but I would not be in a position to identify them due to overcrowding or the speed of court work. Even when I would 'catch hold' of the accused, they would not be convinced of my introduction and would not cooperate. Hence, only in a negligible number of cases, I could interview the accused at the court premises according to their adjournment dates. Thus the planned location of interview did not work. In hindsight, I realised that the plan of meeting the accused for an interview at the court premises was absolutely flawed one. No accused person may enter the court premises with confidence and comfortable feeling. Most of the accused would be feeling nervous, insecure, fearful of being caught again and would want to run away from the premises immediately as the whole visible court structure – the magistrate with his officers, advocates, police officers on duty – may instil a sense of anxiety in them. If some accused persons were involved in uninvestigated cases, certainly they would keep distance from the structure. Even if the accused agrees for an interview, the court premises is not the right location for conducting free, frank and comfortable interview.

Not finding the accused for interviews, which was an important part of study, became a major problem. As rightly pointed out by Srinivas, *et al.* (1979), "The situations arising in the field have their own dynamics and the field worker is more often their servant than a master", I had to look for alternatives. The alternative I found was to visit/trace the accused according to their addresses as noted by the police on chargesheets. These addresses were spread all over the city and beyond.

Searching the Accused for an Interview: Tracing the accused according to the addresses given by them and noted by the police was not easy. The addresses were ascertained from the chargesheet. As few accused persons would give a correct or complete address, in many cases the effort to trace them remained futile. To exemplify, one whole day I had to walk in a congested slum area after an address. The following morning, when I woke up I was suffering from conjunctivitis. Walking the lanes of Kamatipura (a famous red light area in Mumbai) and in a few *chawls* was far from being pleasant. But there was no alternative. Asking many people in the vicinity and searching by trial and error method was the only way. In some cases I did trace the addresses, only to find that accused had shifted to some other locality. In the work of tracing and verifying these addresses in numerous cases, the police helped a lot. Some policemen advised me against visiting certain locations – they were hot, risky spots. But I had to. I did it. In some cases, the accused were in police custody on account of a different incident. Accordingly, I visited the concerned police station and interviewed through the door or window of the lock-up. Face-to-face interviews often had unforeseen circumstances. Some accused at the interview time were under the influence of 'brown sugar' (adulterated version of heroin, a prohibited drug). Some of these encounters have left a deep impression on me and their recollection is often disturbing.

In a large number of cases tracing addresses did not help. On being suggested by others, I had to visit temples, gambling dens, bootlegging joints, or particular spots in the locality where such elements gather. At several places, I had to tell lies suiting to the situation in order to meet the accused. Had these people known the real purpose of my visit, they would not have come out? In a few slum areas, when I asked about a particular name and address from a local person, he would instantaneously suspect me to be a policeman. "Have you brought a warrant?" And I would play the game and would innocently ask, "What is a warrant?"

From Kalyan to Colaba and Dahisar to Churchgate, including congested slum pockets like Dharavi, Bhenganwadi, Pathanwadi, etc., there was no area in Mumbai in which I did not have an errand, labour and expense on transport notwithstanding.

Convincing the Respondent: Tracing the address and meeting the accused was not crossing over the hump. In quite a few cases I did meet the right person at the first attempt, but as he concealed his identity, I had to retrace. Being involved in numerous cases, he and his likes were not wholly unjustified in harbouring suspicion. On approach, typical barrage of questions would be: Where did I come from? Was I from the police? Was I from the court? Was I from the CID? Even when I gave them my true identity it hardly worked. At least in the beginning I had to be less truthful. "I am from social welfare department", or "… from the local school of social work". Based on the trial and error method in several cases, later I evolved a combination of diplomatic approach and slippery introduction to find my way through my respondents. Right from the beginning, I became aware that they looked more at my feet than at my face, in order to make out whether or not I was a policeman. Keeping long hair, using slipper, dressing somewhat shabbily helped. In a considerable number of cases it did yield results.

In some interviews, the respondent (the accused) or her/his relatives voluntarily referred to the charged offence and started explaining how they were not involved in it (providing their version of it). I immediately used to tell them that I am not interested in that part (whether they have committed the offence(s) or not) of the case. I will not be asking any questions on that issue. When I clarified this, in some cases I could see a relaxed look on the faces of the respondent and her/his relatives. Despite my clarification, if they narrated their version of the event, I showed interest in listening to it and did not note anything on the schedule. I explained to them that I was interested in knowing their experience with the police, court and advocates, if they have any, due to this event, and how this experience was impacting on them. In some cases this approach helped to convince the respondent and others.

Interviews and Interruptions: Successfully locating the address and convincing the accused did not mean a smooth interview. While interviewing the accused, members of the respondent's family and neighbours would assemble. This meant a report barrage of questions on my identity. This was followed by more questions. Some of the typical questions were: After filling the schedule, would it benefit the accused? If not, why should we cooperate? After fumbling some explanation, I would start the interview. In some cases, interview questions asked to the respondent would be often answered by the onlookers. Requests for allowing the respondent to speak were seldom acceded to. The gathering around us would so much affect the number of questions asked as it did the response pattern of the accused. I was hardly prepared for such unexpected developments in the field. Whenever possible, I tried to take the respondent to a nearby restaurant or to a place relatively free from disturbance. In some cases it was necessary to interview the accused in the presence of relatives or friends, so that s/he felt secure. In the majority of interviews paying attention to explanations offered by others was unavoidable. What is more, I had to respond to their questions in no way related to the study. Without this additional conversation, I would not have continued the interviews. Quite a few respondents were wiser. They would generously state, "You can fill in the form on your own. If somebody comes and asks us, we will tell them that we have filled it." A response of this type shows how the accused were not readily forthcoming for interviews.

The interview schedule included a Likert type of scale to understand anxiety levels of the accused in the criminal justice system. According to the scale, when I asked questions to the respondent (the accused), the response would be 'han', 'hun' or an unexpressive face, but no clear 'yes' or 'no'. In a few interviews I realised that, at least in some cases, I am unable to capture what I intended to through this data collecting method. The chosen data collecting method was a hindrance in understanding anxiety levels of the accused in the Indian context. Depending upon the interview and response pattern, I selectively skipped some questions from the schedule.

In a relatively good locality, according to the given address I went to a flat to interview one respondent. In the flat I saw three people – father, daughter and son – and I started introducing myself and the purpose of my visit. It appeared like a family dispute case. The three people angrily shouted at each other and started quarrelling. They picked whatever came to their hand (belt, iron box cord, etc.,) hitting one another and running around the flat. I was so scared, I thought they might hit me as well, I just wanted to run away from the place. When they calmed down, I did not speak of the interview, just left the flat and never returned. I have not been able to wipe out this disturbing and shocking scene from my memory.

As some of my respondents were in a far away prison, I undertook an overnight journey to interview one respondent. On showing the permission letter, I was allowed to interview the respondent in the presence of a prison officer who sat a few meters away but was able to hear and watch the interview. I did not like the officer's presence there. While interviewing, I was noting down responses in the schedule. The officer objected to it, though I had a clear permission to conduct interviews. I had to tear off the half filled interview schedule. I tried to remember most of the responses and filled the schedule after getting out of the prison.

Meeting the accused for the first time and interviewing him was easy and expeditious. After the first encounter, if the accused suggested some other day to complete the work, it was chancy to accept the suggestions. These types of respondents, unusual situations, interruptions and interference during interviews made me think about the accuracy of responses. Is the generated data reliable and valid? I did not have any methods to ensure this. I also wonder, was it necessary to persuade respondents for an interview in this way?

Helpful Community People and Respondents: These negative experiences should not mean that there were no pleasant encounters. In some cases, community people guided me to the exact places. Some people persuaded the accused to respond to questions freely as it was not harmful to her/him. This helped me in many ways. For example, I was looking for a few respondents in a slum area, but was not able to trace them. To meet these respondents, I was advised to first meet a person, who was a kind of group/community leader (gang leader). I met the person and clearly explained about myself and the purpose of interviewing. Once everything was clarified to his satisfaction, he assured me that he would arrange to get all the three boys for the interview. By the time I finished all the three interviews, it was very late night. They advised me not to go out as the area is very dangerous and made arrangement to spend the remainder of the night there itself. With great anxiety the night passed away and in the early morning I returned home. When my identity and credibility was clearly established and their doubts were cleared without having many queries, the accused willingly and confidently responded to the questions with hospitality thrown in. Accepting a cup of tea or a glass of soft drink often became a medium to establish a workable relationship.

Interview Timings: If one wants to venture into this kind of research, s/he should be prepared to work at any hour of the day. Working during night hours was the way of data collection. Most of the interviews began after 10 p.m. One of the interviews was over at 3 a.m. Everyday returning home at 1 or 2 a.m. was a routine matter.

Completion and Shortfalls: Despite these difficult experiences the task of data collection continued. Of the sampled 278 cases, 195 (70.1%) were contacted and 247 interviews (includes multi-accused cases) were completed. It was not possible to interview the remaining 83 (29.8%) cases due to non-cooperation, untraceability, change in residence and outstation address.

Data from Advocates : More than 500 advocates practising in 23 courts were approached to fill in the questionnaire. A majority of them refused to cooperate straightaway. Meeting advocates individually, and explaining to them the purpose of the study and requesting for their help or alternatively announcing in the bar-room and requesting them to help, were the approaches usually adopted. Some advocates perhaps thinking that the questionnaire had something beneficial for them would grab it, but would soon return it. Names of the advocates to whom questionnaire was circulated were noted down for reference and they were requested to return it within 10 days to me or to the secretary or president of the bar association. None of the filled questionnaires were returned in time. At the expiry of 10 days, a notice was put up at the bar-room requesting the return of the questionnaire. This however did not bring any significant result. Advocates are busy professionals – at least this is the impression all of them give.

Incidentally, advocates seemed to approach in a professional way. One advocate told me, "It will cost you Rs. 200." Another advocate added, "senior advocates will charge you in four figures." If my memory serves right, at least five of them dropped similar hints – which, I was not unfortunately in a position to catch. In one courtroom, an advocate took initiative and accepted the questionnaire. He promised that he would fill in and return it. After a few days when I reminded him, he had a disarming clarification to offer, "A friend of mine is also doing research on similar lines. I have given the questionnaire to him."

Another advocate advised to see me in the evening for completing the questionnaire. Accordingly I met him. We sat across the table. After initial conversation, he would read a question from the questionnaire and angrily and loudly explain to me how the question is wrong. For every question he was getting angry and shouting, and was not at all writing his responses to the questions. I lost interest in getting the questionnaire completed by him and was very keen to get out from there, but did not know how to abruptly end the meeting. Later I realised that the respondent may be under the influence of alcohol. Unwillingly I continued for a little more time, stopped reacting to his questions, appreciated his point of view and smoothly concluded the meeting (though to me it was an abrupt termination of the meeting). This was another scarey experience that cannot be easily forgotten.

On the other hand, when I met four advocates in their office, they gave sufficient time and discussed several issues in depth. Some advocates asked me to come to their office, but due to paucity of time it was not possible. Apparently, meeting advocates in their office and interviewing them, rather giving them a questionnaire, was more expeditious. They felt happy and proud to give interview rather than filling in forms. For instance, when I gave the questionnaire to one senior advocate, his reaction was: 'For the last 20 years, I have only signed on papers; everything else is done by my juniors." Another advocate said, "I am very bad in writing."

As per the plan, 230 questionnaires were circulated to advocates. After repeated reminders I did manage to collect 58 questionnaires personally and only one questionnaire was received by post. The return rate of the questionnaire was about 25 per cent.

Data from Police Prosecutors : Approaching and talking to police prosecutors was comparatively easy. But when it came to filling in the questionnaire they were evasive. Their typical defence was: "We are government servants, we cannot write anything unless it comes through proper channel." Efforts were made to convince them and 30 questionnaires were circulated. After several personal meetings, reminders and requests, only eight (27%) were returned. Police prosecutors who did not return the questionnaire were having good alibis. They had lost it. It had been misplaced. It would not be traced. No time to do this kind of work. These types of responses may also suggest that they are not interested in completing the questionnaire.

Learning from the Experiences

Overall, my field experiences suggest that collecting primary data and uncompiled secondary data from the criminal justice system (courts, the accused, advocates, prosecutors, prisons, police lock-ups) is not easy. Researchers need to really search for this type of data in the criminal justice system. They need to be tolerant, persuasive and to creatively think about alternative practical approaches. I am not sure whether every researcher faces these types of data collecting difficulties in such settings. However, in hindsight I feel that I would not have experienced the type of difficulties I did or would have experienced fewer difficulties, had I followed the following approaches.

1. I should have started data collecting work not only after obtaining necessary permission from respective authorities, but also after properly communicating the same at all offices where I needed to access the data.

2. Instead of selecting 23 sample courts, spread all over Mumbai, and selecting 10 to 12 cases from each court, I should have selected only two or three courts and selected a large number of cases from them.
3. I should have anticipated problems associated with interviewing sensitive respondents and their likely suspicion and refusal, and should have selected a bigger sample size allowing for high sample mortality.
4. I should have a given an honest and clear introduction of myself and my purpose of interview. If respondents exhibited any type of inhibition, I should have dropped them from the study and proceeded to the next one. I should not have devoted so much of time for tracing and convincing the accused.
5. I would avoid or be very careful in using psychological scales (developed in some other socio-cultural contexts) to understand attitudes and anxiety levels of the accused. If some questions were not working in the field, I would consistently drop them or appropriately revise them.
6. To collect data from advocates, first I would find out the most suitable time and location for them to complete the questionnaire and accordingly approach them. Certainly, I would not approach them during their work/busy hours. Alternatively, I should have collected a list of advocates' addresses from their association and mailed the questionnaire to them. If such a list was not available, I should have made a list of volunteer respondents with addresses from each court and mailed the questionnaire to them with a self-stamped and addressed return envelope.
7. To collect data from prosecutors, I should have despatched the questionnaire to them with the chief prosecutor's cover letter asking them to voluntarily complete the questionnaire.

Conclusion

In this paper, I have discussed the way I chose the research topic and research objectives, questions, design and instruments. I have reflectively presented my data collecting experiences and lessons learned from them while obtaining permission from criminal justice officials, pretesting, observing the court working, interviewing the accused, studying case progress and getting the questionnaires completed by advocates and prosecutors. The purpose of this exercise is to help myself think and learn about better data collecting methods and approaches in the criminal justice system in particular and social science research in general. The exercise has made me conscious about the research activity and the way I conduct research. I hope the paper would help other researchers gain similar insights.

References

1. Dhawan R.S. (1986). *Litigation Explosion in India*. Mumbai: MM Tripathi.
2. Dhawan R. S. and Kalpakam P. (1978). *The Supreme Court Under Strain: The Challenge of the Arrears*. New Delhi: Indian Law Institute.
3. Lee R. M. and Renzetti C. M. (1993). 'The problem of researching sensitive topics: An overview and introduction'. In Renzetti C.M. and Lee R.M. (ed). *Researching Sensitive Topics*. Newbury Park: Sage.
4. Mayur, R. (1986). 'Is there a Future in the Life of Mumbai?' In Mayur, R. and Vohra, P.R. (ed), *Mumbai by 2000 A.D.* Mumbai: Vohra.
5. Mukherjee S. K. and Gupta A. (1978). *Delay in the Administration of Justice*. Rome: United Nations Social Defence Research Institute.
6. Pawar M. (1993). *Justice processing sans justice: Delays and Plight of Defendants*. Mumbai: Tata Institute of Social Sciences.
7. Rajan V. N. and Khan M. Z. (1982). *Delay in the Disposal of Criminal Cases in the Sessions and Lower Courts in Delhi*. New Delhi: Institute of Criminology and Forensic Science.
8. Srinivas, M.N., Shah, A.M. and Ramaswamy, E.A. (1979). *The Field Worker and the Field: Problems and Challenges in Sociological Investigation*. Delhi: Oxford University Press.

Part III

Gathering Data from Rural and Indigenous Communities

7
Lakshmi Lingam

The Stranger with a Shoulder Bag: Reflections on Field Research

Introduction

In this paper, I would share my field experiences which moulded the research methodology, the research agenda and provided me greater insights into the life of women and villages than would have been possible otherwise (Lingam, 1988). The experiences and the lessons that are learnt in the process, might provide insights to new researchers, who are nervously getting set for fieldwork or are on the field or have returned from fieldwork with a heavy heart.

Objectives of the Study

The research study attempted to examine the relationship between agro-ecological differences and social structure, and its influence on women's role and position. For purposes of field research, two villages were selected from the Village and Town Directory, East Godavari District, Andhra Pradesh. One village represented a highly capitalist-oriented agricultural system and the other a drought-prone agricultural system. The villages are in the same district with one situated in the delta region and the other in the upland region.

After preliminary trips to the sample villages and other villages in Andhra Pradesh, I had set out on data collection with three sets of schedules: (1) Village schedule (2) Household schedule and (3) Women-specific schedule. The village schedule was specifically for the purposes of gathering information regarding the village infrastructure, land holding and land utlilisation patterns, crops, fertilizer and manure utlisation practices, livestock population, residential patterning, caste composition, etc. The household schedule was for the purposes of gathering information regarding the household composition, asset holdings, occupations, incomes, debts, and other related information as a background for the Women-specific Interview Schedule, which was developed after a thorough literature review. It attempted to gather pregnancy history, occupation, wages, sexual division of labour, control over resources and property, freedom of movement, participation in household decision-making, etc.

Fieldwork Experience: The First Calamity

I had commenced the fieldwork during the summer in the upland dry region. Several parts of India had faced drought conditions and the region under study was facing drought for the second recurrent year. The dry village chosen for the study fulfilled the scientific sampling specifications and practical considerations. It was five kilometres away from my relatives' village, Dharmavaram, which I made as my base. Within the time gap between my preliminary visits and my visit with my schedules and other paraphernalia, there was a fire accident in the village. The villagers would have beaten me up if I asked them any other questions apart from the fire accident and loss of property. I had to abandon the village which was chosen after painstaking examination of census information, because I could not have possibly changed my research topic to 'Women's role in disaster management'. I was back to square one without a sample village and a perpetual anxiety of being able to convince the Supervisor about the unforeseen calamity. My elder father-in-law with whom I was living suggested me another village five kilometres away. I made visits to that village with him and another relative and confirmed the selection of the village after looking into the census information, parts of which I had fortunately got photocopied. I moved into that village and occupied an empty hospital quarter.

Gaining Acceptance: The First Test

To gain acceptance and a tacit approval from the villagers it is essential to meet the village panchayat president, panchayat members, the village level government officials/workers, the hospital staff like the doctors, the Auxiliary Nurse Midwife (ANM), the health visitor, multipurpose health worker, the school teachers and identified leaders of the dominant caste, etc. Over and above this, gaining acceptance of the respondents depends on how the researcher builds the rapport, by chatting, by sharing personal information and being a good listener. The other important factors that matter are:

- The place of residence the researcher chooses to stay;
- The people with whom the researcher associates, and their local standing;
- The respect given by the researcher to the villagers in order to understand their view point and accommodate their sentiments; and
- The low profile that the researcher plays as one who has come to learn rather than pose as an authoritative figure and dole out advice or pass value judgements.

There is a high likelihood that the researcher develops a superiority complex, being more educated than many of the villagers and being a city dweller. The researcher should be cautious, otherwise this biased perception would reflect on all the observations and the so-called findings.

Initial Reactions of the Villagers

To a researcher who is facing the field situation with the specific objective of data collection, the field experiences seem similar to that of a new daughter-in-law in the mother-in-law's family. I was an 'insider' and 'outsider' at the same time.

To a researcher who is facing the field situation for the first time, there is a great obsession to fill the schedules and complete the data collection according to the research time schedule. However, to the community the researcher is an intruder and it takes a valid amount of time for them to be convinced or accustomed to the researcher's presence.

My presence in the village evoked different responses from different groups. In the drought village the men thought that I was a Government official who is on a visit to the village to gauge the situation of drought and its implications to people. When I explained that I was not a Government official, then they questioned me, 'What benefit is it going to give us?' This is the most difficult question, which brings into your mind the ethics of research, the question of reciprocity in research etc. I responded that it might bring some programmes to the village in future. The people told me that, I must recommend (1) an employment guarantee scheme for immediate relief and (2) provide irrigation as a permanent solution.

Perceptions of the Researcher by the Villagers

I stayed in a quarter in the village and got introduced to the village through the Auxiliary Nurse Midwife (ANM). She was a good worker and was respected by the village women. The women thought I was a new lady doctor/new ANM. When I went individually to their residences they wanted me to attend to their health problems. If I were as interested in health issues as I am now, I would have collected lot of data on health. Constraints on the research agenda and objectives arrived at the initial stages of research by a mature researcher leads to a loss of lot of valuable data. The youth thought that I was a Naxalite or a CID (Criminal Investigation Department) informer[1]. Reason being, a few days before I went to the village there was a threatening letter allegedly from the Naxalites to two landlord families. The police was alerted and the Kshatriyas who are the upper and the 'dominant' caste in the village felt threatened.

The second village where I worked is a rich irrigated village. A Kshatriya caste man from the village was a member of the Legislative Assembly. The village was large and dispersed. People were curious but there were no rumours. I had stayed as a guest

---

1. This village is close to the agency tract of East Godavari district which occasionally, is visited by Naxalites. The villagers call them 'Annallu' (brothers).

with a Kshatriya family whose economic position had deteriorated. The villagers respected the family for its generosity.

A single woman, in a simple cotton sari devoid of any jewellery and carrying a cotton shoulder bag attracted their attention. The upper caste middle class women enquired if I was going to start a sewing centre. In the irrigated village the interest that I had shown in understanding the work of women 'lacemakers', made them think that I have an interest in starting a business in lace. Some women also suggested that I start an export business in lace. The lower caste women work as agriculture labourers and a few families have women migrants to the Gulf. The women suggested that I must go to the Gulf to earn more money, because my salary (scholarship) is very low.

Any conversation would necessarily always have the following queries. Where do you come from? Where do you stay? What is your caste? Are you married? Do you have children? What is your salary? The men refer to a salaried job as 'nitya panta' which literally means 'regular harvest'. This speaks volumes about the uncertainty and risk levels in agriculture.

Experience of Filling the Interview Schedule

During the initial stage in the village, I made an attempt to fill out the interview schedule while simultaneously collecting the information from women. One woman was highly perturbed and underreported the number of children she had. I could sense that there is inconsistency in the information she is giving. A girl from the neighbouring house said, "Why are you bluffing? Sarkar (government) will know if you bluff!" I discontinued the interview but returned to her house with the ANM after a couple of days. All the women in the neighbourhood broke into laughter and said, "She thinks that Sarkar (government) will find out the number of children we have and throw bombs or take away some children." The women were laughing but I would not be surprised if they too nurture such feelings. The pressure to adopt family planning measures might be high in this village, because of the PHC (Primary Health Centre) being located there. I took the opportunity to speak to the women and told them the national importance of women's work and their situation in the village, society and economy. Within a short period there was a total reversal of this situation and many villagers wanted to be 'written down'. People have absorbed the Government procedure of filling out forms as a first step to get a scheme/loan, etc. This brought about some sampling procedure. I had selected every sixth or seventh household for the study. Some women would complain that they are being left out and they may get left out of the beneficiary programme. At times, I used to note down the family composition details for the satisfaction of the women. Therefore, an initial isolation was taken over by an overwhelming enthusiasm. People know fairly well about census enumeration and things got easier in some places where I could just say 'jenabha lekhalu' (population census) and cut down explanations to curious passers-by.

Meanwhile, I discovered that it was a better method to draw a genealogical chart and gather lots of information at the same time. I have noticed that women used to be excited seeing the symbols and seeking their meanings. I used to decode the information after returning at night. Therefore, I have totally interviewed 182 women but have gathered quantitative information for 550 households (approximately) regarding their occupation, place of work, residence, number of children, births, deaths, etc.

Observations and Important Findings

My freedom to move in the village gave me insights into the varying degree of freedom enjoyed by women among various castes. I used to walk on the village streets and visit all localities of the village, a typical right which only the lower caste women in the village enjoy. My discussions with upper caste women on these issues coupled with the observations on the variations of women's work across the caste groups gave me important insights into the seclusion practices and the sexual geography of the village (Lingam, 1990).

Upper caste women maintain seclusion regionally known as 'gosha'. Most of the upper caste houses have one main entrance and one side entrance. Men occupy the main entrance and main verandah of the house. Women occupy the inner compound and kitchen house, which is generally constructed, slightly away from the main house. Some of the middle caste women move around freely near their homestead, breastfeed their babies in the open, etc., but do not engage in agriculture work or wage labour. Among the lower castes, most of the women participate in agricultural work but avoid visiting the village market place. The women belonging to the 'untouchable' castes enjoy greater freedom of movement but the lowest social status in the village.

Therefore, attempts to analyse casual experiences and observations enabled me to gain great insights, which were much more thrilling than a prosaic activity of filling up an interview schedule.

Sampling: Practical Problems

For the purposes of sampling organised information is essential. In general, not all villages maintain organised records on various aspects of the village. In villages with more than 500 households there are difficulties in getting a household list, which would enable us in sampling. It is possible to get an electoral list, but it would enlist the names of eligible voters only. Working out exact households from the list is a cumbersome task. If the researcher wants a sample representation according to the class status or landholding status, it is essential to get a list of landholders. In fact, it is not impossible to get this information from the Village Accountant or Panchayat Office, but the village officials should be fully convinced about the purpose of taking the information. Because land is the only major asset that villagers have, they expect the officials to maintain confidentiality and secrecy in this regard. After considerable period of testing me, the Village Accountant (who incidentally, for me and significantly for him, belong to the same caste) gave the necessary records.

Even if this data is available there still are certain problems with this data. Considering the fact that land-ownership in rural areas is fragmented and scattered, it makes the task of drawing up a list from the ledgers to reflect land ownership per household difficult, rather almost impossible. Arriving at a consolidated figure of landholdings per farmer requires the verification of the entire ledger, which tantamounts to examining the record as many number of times as the number of farmers.

In spite of painstaking effort there would still be an error in the landholding classification, because of the subdivision of lands which appear in official records. Therefore, a household even with a joint operational landholdings of 35 to 40 acres would appear in medium farmer list with five acres.

Farmers owning lands in the neighbouring villages, but residing in this village escape this list. Similarly owners of lands in this village, or in regions where there is irrigation, especially in the case of the drought village, are active in money lending and are the chief providers of capital. Such households escape the class list pertaining to the sample village. Further, the percentage of landholders is small in relation to the total population, which means further efforts are required to select the sample of landless and non-agricultural occupation household.

In the case of my study, I found ward-wise sampling much more useful. I arrived at this method after noticing that the residential pattern in the village is on the caste hierarchy lines with the upper castes occupying the centre of the village. The middle caste groups' residences being closer to the upper caste residences followed by the lower castes living on the periphery. The panchayat demarcation of wards in the village for the purposes of elections represents the caste clusters. I had chosen to interview every seventh household with an occasional flexibility.

There is a conflict between the questions of priority to the researcher and the 'researched'.

The experience of collecting data from the drought village had shaken me from a slumber. I had set out with questions regarding the role of women in the household and in agriculture and the status they have in the household with regards to control over resources, decision-making, etc. I felt that the women redefined my focus by speaking to me about the drought and its implications in great length. During the first few days, I was in tears not being able to grapple with the several dimensions of the gender questions, not knowing where to start, how to go about it, how to look for meaningful linkages. Certain hostile reactions from some women, in between, would make me feel that I was going 'one step forward and two steps backward'. I had finally made a decision to give priority to what the women want to speak and then to get information on a common set of questions which can be analysed and utilised for comparisons. The same format of interviewing and data collection was followed in the second study village.

Being a lone researcher I used to long for academic discussion. I tried to sort this out in two ways:
- Maintaining field notes in the form of a diary used to communicate with the note booking, and
- Picking up observations that puzzled me and discussing it with different caste and class group of villagers in my casual visits.

This used to give different perceptions from each group's vantage point. I had incorporated this style of explaining reality in my thesis too which also explains the variations in class and caste interests.

Summing up

Data collection exercise should be handled with curiosity, enthusiasm and an open mind. Research objectives, agenda and questions should not curb your freedom to observe, question, absorb and assimilate the experiences. A steady shift from quantitative techniques to qualitative techniques of data collection in academic research in the recent past provides greater space to the researcher's innovation.

References

1. Lingam, Lakshmi, C. (1988). 'Women's Role in the Reproduction and Production Spheres of Wet and Dry Villages of East Godavari District, Andhra Pradesh.' Unpublished doctoral dissertation. Indian Institute of Technology, Mumbai.
2. Lingam, Lakshmi, C. (1990). 'Women and Space: The Articulation of Gender and Caste in the villages of Andhra Pradesh.' Paper presented at the XII World Congress of Sociology, 9-13 July, Madrid, Spain.

8
I.U.B. Reddy

An Approach for Data Collection in Tribal Areas

Introduction

Rural areas constitute the most important single factor in the development of India and there is hardly any need to justify its importance in Indian economy. Rural development has become the main plank of national development because an overwhelming majority (75%) of population lives in villages, who are still in the grip of destitution, mass poverty, and illiteracy. In order to transform the rural areas, many of the development programmes now in progress are focussed in rural areas, especially in developing tribal areas. Further, the accelerated growth of tribal areas has been accepted as a national objective in our five-year plans.

Developing tribal areas provide challenges to social scientists to undertake research studies because of their distinctive characteristics, which are yet to be exposed to the outside world and subjected to modern development. The welfare of people belonging to tribal and other economically weaker sections has been one of the major national concerns after independence, for which the constitution makes various specific provisions.

Accordingly, the five-year plans have stressed the importance of establishing a number of development projects in tribal areas, so as to accelerate the growth of national economy. A large number of areas, in which natural resources like water, forest, and minerals are available are located within some of the developing tribal areas in India. Undoubtedly, these areas provide ideal locations for implementing various developmental programmes. This in turn is expected to bring a faster socio-economic and cultural transformation to such areas. However, there is a deplorable lack of competent research on various aspects of the transformation that has taken place. This warrants involvement of social scientists to undertake studies of changing rural life. This will provide an opportunity for formulating need-based policies and programmes for planned development of backward tribal areas.

Against the above backdrop, the present article attempts to bring out various methodological issues and problems involved in carrying out research studies in tribal areas. The article illustrates such aspects of data collection with the help of a research study undertaken for the purpose of formulating a micro-level plan for Semiliguda block in Koraput district of Orissa.

Study Area

The Semiliguda block in Koraput district is situated in the extreme south-western part of Orissa and it presents a unique case for research. The block presents not only an ideal micro unit of a typically hilly, underdeveloped and tribal area, but also has several other points favouring its choice for this exercise. A series of far reaching changes have been initiated in this remote locality by the initiation of two major development projects, viz, the National Aluminium Company Limited (NALCO) and the Upper Kolab Multipurpose Irrigation Project. The establishment of NALCO Project has opened up this remote area to the mainstream of economic development. Similarly, the execution of Upper Kolab Project is going to inundate 10 per cent area of the block and has induced many potential structural changes in all the sectors of economy in the block. Because of these developments, the block has been subjected to very fast changes in the social, economic, and cultural milieu due to recent activities relating to these projects. It is a backward tribal region and about two-thirds of population constitute disadvantaged sections comprising tribal and scheduled castes. In and around the block, there exists an abundant stock of bauxite, limestone, clay, construction materials, etc., besides vast natural resources like forest, livestock, water and land resources. A portion of the block is delineated as the urban area of Sunabeda (township of Hindustan Aeronautics Limited) and placed under the jurisdiction of Notified Area Council (NAC) for its development, planning and management.

Thus, Semiliguda presents an ideal case for formulating micro-level plan. The plan preparation is also expected to serve another purpose of cumulative data building process while testing the efficiency and sensitivity of the plan in terms of reliability and implementability, the new sets of data inputs required are to be identified.

Methodology for Micro-level Plans

Formulation of any plan concerned with socio-economic development hinges on proper exploitation of natural resources. For micro-level planning purpose, a sound data base on natural and human resources as well as socio-economic attainments and infrastructural builds are essential to make the plan realistic and implementable. However, developmental problems of tribal areas pose many challenges to the policy makers, administrators and planners. Therefore, the simplest development strategy of a tribal region must aim at improving the living standards of people by enabling them to participate more effectively in the process of production.

Study of Existing Situation: In order to prepare a sound micro level plan, it is essential to collate the detailed information on various aspects of development parameters. In this context, the following dimensions are identified for such an exercise.

Natural Resources: Identifying the available natural resources and superimposing them on certain socio-economic characteristics will help in understanding the rural contrasts. The objective of any plan would be to attain the maximum possible results by exploitation of resources that are available in the region. In drawing up a plan, the first task is to discover by surveying its natural resources, what geographical advantages and economic possibilities it may have (Dhubhashi, 1984). The important natural resources that need to be assessed in the context of micro-level plan are land, water, forest and minerals. In this context, the information such as nature of topography and land forms, rainfall and its distribution, temperature and humidity, drainage pattern, geographical concentration of mineral deposits, terrain features, ground water occurrence and lithology, source(s) of surface water for various uses, details of natural vegetation, forest resources with available species and its role in the local economy, need to be collated from different sources. Though, certain information can be obtained from the Block Level Offices, a substantial information needs to be ascertained from topographic sheets, aerial photo interpretation and satellite imagery analysis. These sources are becoming more and more popular in the present research studies due to the difficulties in obtaining the ground level data and it has also become expensive and time consuming. Further, due to easy access to satellite imagery and also accuracy of information, these sources must be utilised for deriving the concentration of available natural resources.

Human Resources: Any attempt to prepare a development plan for a region and its population has to take a note of the demographic variations across villages over a period of time. The study of human resources as a process of socio-economic conditions of rural people would provide the basic framework for a meaningful study of rural life situation. The analysis of population changes in relation to the settlement pattern is necessary to find out whether it is possible to decipher the latent types and characteristics of villages. This deciphering helps not only in unfolding the contrasts in characteristics but also provides a much needed perspective for planning the region (Hanumappa, 1981). It is hoped that this will provide the basic framework for a meaningful micro-level planning.

The various parameters to be analysed under this section include, distribution of population by caste groups, occupational structure, participation rate, unemployment, literacy level, availability of various skills, migration pattern, training programmes, fertility and mortality, etc. This information can mostly be obtained from census and National Sample Survey reports. The study of these aspects form an important ingredient for plan formulation. Further, the data on fertility and mortality have proved to be extremely useful for planning health and medical services and are found to be capable of broad epidemiological interpretations (Raza, et al 1978).

Socio-economic Conditions: The study of existing socio-economic conditions occupy a paramount importance in the context of any plan formulation. Proper and planned development of tribal areas calls for systematic study of the socio-economic system and cultural pattern of the people. The data for socio-economic conditions may be most efficiently obtained through sample survey. Efforts should be made to choose an appropriate method of data collection for carrying out the survey. Depending upon the time and budget, the sample size can be decided. A sample of about five to ten per cent of population with due representation to different strata can be considered adequate for any field survey of this nature.

The survey should aim at collecting the details such as income, expenditure, indebtedness, employment pattern, value of assets, etc., on the economic side, and information such as literacy, caste groups, food habits, housing conditions, cultural differences, etc., on the social side. In a survey of this nature it has been observed that there are problems relating to concepts and definitions. Unwillingness of households to furnish correct information and lack of accuracy of these information are very common. Other practical problems experienced during the survey arose because the study area mostly consisted of hilly tracks and forests. The research staff often found difficulty in making arrangements for their housing, food, transport, etc. Difficulty in understanding the local dialect has retarded the progress of the survey to some extent and inaccessibility in the hilly and forested track posed serious restrictions to the survey.

The study of existing socio-economic conditions will help us in understanding the standard of living and this in turn will facilitate formulation of need-based strategies for the local people. The study of housing and environment occupies the most important place in the welfare of rural people. These are very important because the development potentials are influenced by the environment in which people reside. The important aspects to be covered include: settlement pattern, the condition and materials used for roof, wall and floor of the house, etc. In addition, observation of various aspects of house such as availability of windows, sufficient ventilation, facilities for bath, toilet, kitchen, outlet for smoke like chimney or smokeless *chullahas*, storage facilities, availability of separate cattle shed, drainage system, water-logging during rains, disposal of waste water and materials constitute an important aspect of housing and environment of rural people (Reddy, 1988). Further, the study of cultural and social organisation of people will provide the means for the researchers to assess the need for adopting differential policies at various stages of development.

Sectoral Dimensions: The purpose of micro-level planning would be more meaningful if the potentials of different sectors are analysed. The primary sector consists of agriculture, animal husbandry, forestry, fishery, etc. The factors of production for agriculture include soil and water resources, animal and manpower, and mechanical power. In addition inputs such as seeds, pesticides and implements are important components of agricultural development.

Agriculture forms the basis of rural economy and in case of tribal areas approximately 90 per cent of people are dependent on agriculture for their livelihood. Further, in Semiliguda block, the tribals are deeply associated with agriculture with their age-old cultivation practices. The shifting method of Podu is still practised by them. However, due to rugged and undulating topography, scanty irrigation facilities and general backwardness towards agriculture, the overall agricultural production is very poor. Though the resource potential of the block is favourable for the development of agriculture, the desired level of economy is not up to expectation.

The important information that needs to be collected under agriculture included: land classification and land use pattern, land holding size, form of tenure, area under various crops during different seasons, crop yield, crop management and crop rotation. Besides, information about sources of irrigation, net irrigated area, etc., need to be collected. The study of input consumption of seeds, fertilizers, agricultural implements, agricultural credit facilities, marketing as well as storage facilities would provide detailed understanding regarding the existing agricultural situation and this in turn will help in proposing a viable agricultural plan for sustainable development.

Agriculture and livestock are considered the two most important pillars of rural economy. They together contribute about three-fourths of our gross national product. While progress in agriculture has been achieved through increased production and productivity, very little effort is put towards developing the livestock sector. Therefore, in any plan, efforts should be made to strengthen the animal husbandry sector for balanced development of the primary sector. The data such as livestock population, existing veterinary services and study of problems associated with livestock development are essential. In addition, data on horticulture crops and fishery would complete the primary sector.

The most important statistics on agriculture have been almost continuously available through annual agricultural statistics with a time lag of four to ten years. The classification of area is provided by either Surveyor-General or can be obtained from village records. Further, in the block headquarters the Agricultural Extension Officer, should be able to provide most of the information needed. However, for land classification the satellite imageries available from National Remote Sensing Agency, Hyderabad, would provide more accurate details. The village level worker will be of most use for providing village-wise data and also discussions with her/him would be more helpful in drawing up the programmes for agricultural development.

There is an urgent need to strengthen the link between agriculture and industry in the rural areas to ensure all round development of the region. In tribal areas, the industrial development is principally aimed at changing the employment structure and income level of the people. In these areas, industries are not only few but are also characterised by old production means and restricted consumer demand. In order to overcome these impediments and to increase productivity in this sector, it is necessary to provide substantive jobs to the entrepreneurs as well as to the employees throughout the year. This calls for formulating a rational industrial plan which will infuse dynamism in the sector for better employment opportunities and higher income generation. Such plan will focus on what type of industry can best serve the needs of the region by using local resources, absorbing local labour, investing locally available financial assistance, building local entrepreneurship and nurturing local and tribal skills. Further, the plan should explore the possibilities of developing a wide range of ancillary products for establishing a more sound forward and backward linkage in the economy.

The information such as details of existing units, number of workers, per unit employment, capital investment, training facilities for entrepreneurship, flow of incentives, subsidies and loans are most essential in drawing up an industrial plan. The District Industrial Centre as well as Extension Officer at Block Headquarters will be able to provide the above information in this regard. However the difficulty in collecting the information will be that the officials may not be able to provide the time series data. In the absence of this information, it will be extremely difficult to forecast the future development of industries. Further, the information will also be available from the publications of (a) *Reserve Bank of India Bulletin* (monthly), (b) Annual Report of RBI, (c) Planning Commission publications, (d) State Statistical Abstract or District Statistical Handbooks, etc.

The important aspect to be focussed under sectoral dimensions is amenities and infrastructure. Provisions of social facilities irrespective of costs is very important for the development of tribal areas with a large number of unprivileged population. Under this section, education, health, transport, electricity, drinking water, communication, trade and commerce, banking, etc., should be considered. The welfare of people in any area is undoubtedly related to the availability of amenities and infrastructural facilities. These have a common utility in a society and have common demands. In an area where a large number of disadvantaged population live, the importance of provision of such facilities is paramount.

Under this section, the information such as number of educational institutions and accessibilities, enrolment and dropouts, student-teacher ratio, existing health facilities, common diseases, programmes of health improvement, drinking water sources need to be ascertained. These information can be obtained from District Educational Office and Health Centres located in the region. Again our experience shows that time series data is not maintained leading to difficulties in assessing the trends in improvement of these facilities.

Creation of adequate infrastructure is indispensable in any developmental efforts to achieve economic and social progress. Infrastructures play an important role in opening up of areas by breaking down the barriers of isolation, stagnation and making way for development of social services. They also help in mobilising various economic resources and infusing several production processes in any lagging region.

Under this section, information such as road length used by different organisations, bus services and commodity movement, problems of transportation, sources of power supply, existing facilities of post and telegraphs, financial institutions need to be collated. These data are scattered in respective offices located in the region and some details may be only ascertained by conducting survey or interacting with knowledgeable local people.

Institutions: The role of village institutions is well recognised for bringing desirable changes in the rural areas. The institutions such as Gram Panchayat, co-operatives, Youth Clubs, Mahila Mandals and Balwadis, etc., play a vital role for bringing desirable changes in the villages. For a meaningful study of rural areas, it is most essential to understand the working patterns of these institutions and their role and the nature and level of participation of local people in these activities. For this, it is required to have a detailed discussions with the respective institutions and its members.

Developmental Programmes: Of late, the government has introduced several rural development programmes in order to reach out to the remote villages and uplift their living conditions. The study would be incomplete without the assessment of the impact of these programmes, their functioning, suitability to the local people, evaluation of benefits and harms, etc. Therefore, there is every reason to undertake a study to assess the impact of these development programmes for the growth of tribal areas.

Drawing up Plan Proposal: Once the existing information has been collated, it is desirable to draw up a future plan for the next 10 years, in order to implement the proposals for bringing desirable changes.

The first important task is to forecast the population and its related parameters. These population estimates are mainly to foresee the population with reasonable amount of accuracy. The forecast methods such as Arithmetic method, Percentage increase method, Geometric method, Registrar-General method, are some of the methods that can be used for its projections. Similarly, age-sex composition, working population can also be estimated, as these are necessary to draw conclusions about various aspects of the plan. Under plan proposals the areas to be given emphasis are agricultural development policies, manpower development policies, industrial development policies, social service policies, and so on. At the time of drawing conclusion, we must keep in mind the government's priorities and demands and needs of the local population.

Difficulties in Data Collection

While undertaking the exercise of micro level plan, the author experienced the following difficulties.

- Since the area is not connected by adequate transport facilities, it is very difficult to reach the selected villages. As a result, considerable time has to be spent in walking and reaching the place of study.
- The local people are mostly tribal and speak their own dialect. Therefore, it is very difficult for an outsider to make out their feelings and reactions on most occasions. It is therefore suggested that for study of this type, people who know the local dialect should be taken as interpreters.

- Due to absence of formal education and understanding among the local people, it is very difficult to make them understand the importance of research studies and this adversely affected the eliciting of accurate information. This raises doubts on the accuracy of certain data collected.
- The time was short for taking up the study in an extensive manner and the field investigators were handicapped due to suspicions of local people. They suspected that the survey was perhaps intended for further damages. Therefore, it is essential to take into confidence the local people before undertaking any study. For this, it is suggested that the local leader, or Government officials residing in these areas should be approached first and in turn they should apprise the local people about the purpose of the study.
- The study included personal questions related to income and expenditure, habits, customs, etc. Therefore some exaggeration and concealment cannot be ruled out.
- One of the major problem faced by the researcher in this study was the location of study area, about 600 km away from the parent institution and it was extremely difficult to make frequent visits. Therefore, it is always advisable to choose the study area close to parent organisation. This will be helpful in organising the field study in better way and can also facilitate frequent visits for filling of gaps and collection of missing data.
- Another problem faced during the survey was unwillingness of the households to furnish correct information and lack of accuracy of these information. The area of survey was full of hilly tracks and forests, which contributed to the difficulties. The research team often found difficulties in making arrangements for their accommodation and food.
- As regards the schedules, not sufficient thought could be given for deciding upon the list of items to be included. It was anticipated that much information would be available at the block and other offices. However, it was found that a good deal of information was lacking. Thus additional resources were used for collecting the information from various other

sources. In this regard, it is suggested that pilot visit is most essential for any research study to ascertain the details of various aspects, before preparing the regular visits to the field area.
- The reluctance of various officials to provide the required data/information is another problem faced by the researcher. The officials do not want to take out responsibility and often state that such information/data is not available with them. Sometimes, though the information is scattered, they are not willing to collate the data for this purpose and they often said that time does not permit them to gather such data asked for.
- It is also observed that the Government officials do not take the research studies in the positive frame of mind. They are of the opinion that it will not be possible to implement the finding of the research studies and always tell that politicians decide the priorities which are required to be implemented. As such they show reluctance in cooperating with the research teams in providing the relevant data.
- Most often the officials require the permission of higher authorities for furnishing the details which are not available at district and state headquarters. As such, a considerable time is lost in obtaining the necessary permissions. Therefore, it is suggested, that whenever it is required to visit any offices, prior permission should be obtained and the dates of visits should be kept informed.
- It is also very difficult to convince the officials, especially lower cadre officials about the utility of research study. This is because of their low level of understanding and lack of progressive thinking. This had affected the data collection from secondary sources to a great extent.
- The most important time series data on inputs and outputs on various aspects from offices was totally missing and this did not permit the use of trend analysis for future estimations and forecasting.

- The information obtained through primary and secondary sources suffered from the sense of subjectivity. Besides, many of the socio-cultural attributes could not be expressed in quantitative terms as they are qualitative statements only.
- In agricultural sector the spatial land use pattern, distribution of land, soil types, etc., were not available from block offices and irrigation plan could not be made more realistic as the spatial distribution of water resources and command areas were not known.
- While proposing infrastructural facilities in the block, the cost involved for different facilities could not be provided in the absence of relevant information from the field.

Conclusion

If the missing information as well as the difficulties mentioned above in collection of data/carrying out field survey, were eliminated, the plan would have been more sensitive and down-to-earth. Identification of these information gaps and reinforcement of additional data can be made by assuring collection of field data and remotely-sensed data from time to time. An examination of data vacuum collected for the study suggests that the reinforcement of information to database is possible. Four major operations in data collection are essential. They are (a) the primary survey questionnaire should be finalised only after undertaking pilot survey, so as to facilitate incorporation of appropriate and relevant items; (b) whenever certain information are not available from the expected records/offices, additional sources need to be tapped; (c) the system of keeping information records in rural areas is generally weak in India and hence arrangements should be made for recording adequate micro-level information by various grassroots level agencies including Gram Panchayats, Cooperative Societies, Village administrative Officers, and so on; (d) The remotely-sensed information should be procured at regular intervals and they should be digitised, processed and examined for making the spatial changes overtime.

Acknowledgment

The article is heavily drawn from a larger research project titled "Test Application: Planning for the Development of Semiliguda Block", in which the author was associated at IIT, Kharagpur. The author gratefully acknowledges the financial assistance of Department of Science and Technology, New Delhi, for carrying out this project.

References

1. Dhubashi, P.R. (1984). "Grammar of Planning (Part IV)", *Yojana,* vol 28, no. 12, pp. 30-34.
2. Hanumappa, H.G. (1981). *Socio-Economic Inventory for Block Level Planning.* Shiny Publications, p. 10.
3. Raza, Moonis, et al (ed.), (1978). *Sources of Economic and Social Statistics of India*, Eureka Publication, p. 98.
4. Reddy, I.U.B., (1988): "Study of Rural Life: An Approach", *Rural India*, vol 51. no .10-11, 1988, pp. 206-209.

9

M. E. Thomas

Reflections on Collecting Data from a Rural Development District in Kerala

Beginning of the Search

My interest in the field of rural development policies and programmes grew out of my experience in working with 'Solidarity', a voluntary agency engaged in social action, education, building critical awareness among the tribal people in Wayanad district, Kerala. During my short stay with the agency, I was responsible for organising the grassroots level people through small groups, educating the tribal and rural population regarding their deplorable socioeconomic and exploitative conditions, gathering data to support their vulnerable and dehumanising situations and strongly advocating for their cause. I was also exposed to the problems confronting the tribal people and the rural poor both at the micro and macro levels. Endemic poverty, widespread illiteracy, deep-seated superstition, lack of employable skills, unemployment, lack of access to healthcare, housing and other infrastructure were some of the problems faced by the rural and tribal people.

To uplift the rural poor and the vulnerable population groups, massive nation-wide programmes were designed and implemented in the seventies with the help and support of national and international agencies. Major programmes among them include:

Integrated Rural Development Project (IRDP) (for the rural poor), Integrated Child Development Services (ICDS) (for women and children) and Integrated Tribal Development Project (ITDP) (for tribals). The assumption seems to be that those left behind in the process of development including the underprivileged, can be uplifted through designing and delivering some programmes without power transfer, beneficiary participation and equitable distribution. Has it been possible?

My exposure to the problems confronted by the tribals and the ways governmental and non-governmental agencies tried to solve them suggest that it has not. The realisation soon dawned on me that the condition of the tribals and the rural poor had not changed in any substantial manner despite concerted efforts and investment of resources from all concerned. This raised several questions.

- Can rural development programmes transform peoples' socioeconomic status?
- Are rural development programmes effective?
- How much of the resources invested in these programmes do reach the targeted beneficiaries?
- To what extent do development programmes achieve their goals and objectives?
- What are the implementation problems and bottlenecks?
- Do rural development programmes promote peoples' participation in the implementation process?

My curiosity for answers grew further and it led me to study the *Dynamics of Rural Development: A Critical Study of Two Development Blocks in Kerala.*

Objectives of the Study

My study was set against this backdrop with the following objectives:

- To identify felt needs of the communities in two development blocks in Kerala and also internal and external resources to meet these needs;
- To look into the policies and programmes conceived and implemented in recent years to develop the communities and bring about a speedy rural development;

- To inquire into the background, motivation and communication skills of the grassroots functionaries responsible for the implementation of rural development programmes;
- To examine the formal and informal modalities designed to involve rural people in programme planning and programme implementation of rural development programmes; and
- To ascertain the impact of development programmes on rural and tribal communities in quantitative and qualitative terms and to analyse structural and operational bottlenecks faced in the implementation of these programmes.

The research questions designed to achieve the above objectives included:
- Have IRDP, ITDP and ICDS programmes and policies been able to deliver goods or transform people's lives?
- What are the problems that prevent the achievement of policy and programme objectives?
- Have these policies and programmes been able to promote people's participation in the planning and implementation process?
- Do development functionaries have the required knowledge, skills and competence in providing the services to vulnerable populations?
- What roles do local leaders, elites and teachers play in planning and implementing these programmes?

In order to achieve these objectives and answer the above questions, rural development policies and programmes, programme implementation, the adequacy of the administrative apparatus, the nature and quality of people's participation and the impact these programmes have been able to make on rural and tribal communities, were examined. It was also thought that focusing on contrasting development areas may provide better insight into differential impact of programme performance. Since all areas in the country are covered by a variety of concurrent development programmes, attention was focused on three major programmes, namely, IRDP for rural poor, ITDP for tribal population groups and ICDS for women and children. Further, the points of view of both beneficiaries and non-beneficiaries of the programmes as also of opinion leaders on relevant issues have been ascertained.

Research Method and Sampling Design

The study followed explorative and descriptive research approaches, and employed a survey research design. Sampling for this study was drawn from Wayanad district in Kerala. The district covers three development blocks. Based on target fulfilment and utilisation information, a high performance block (Manathavady) and a low performance block (Sultan's Battery) were selected. With the help of official records in the two selected blocks, lists of beneficiaries of IRDP, ITDP and ICDS were prepared. These lists were organised village-wise so as to identify the receptivity of the village (receptivity is operationalised to include programme coverage and performance). From each development block one high receptivity village and one low receptivity village. i.e. four villages in all were selected. Subsequently, from the lists of beneficiaries from each village, 50 beneficiaries were randomly selected. From the selected villages, a purposive sample of non-beneficiaries (25 non-beneficiaries from each village) was drawn. Likewise, a sample of opinion leaders such as school teachers, elites, local politicians, religious leaders was drawn from these very villages. The fourth sample was that of development functionaries operating at the block level and below. Thus the sample of study had beneficiaries (N=200), non-beneficiaries (N=100), opinion leaders (N=50) and development functionaries (N=60).

Data Collection Instruments

Interview Schedules: To collect primary data for the study, four interview schedules in accordance with the objectives of the study were developed for (a) beneficiaries, (b) non-beneficiaries, (c) leaders/elites/teachers, and (d) development officials. Interview schedules for the beneficiaries had items designed to elicit information on their socio-economic aspects including personal and family background, perception of problems in the village, exposure to and participation in development programmes and perception of the programme impact. In addition, there were 28 programme-specific questions. The schedule for non-beneficiaries had similar items except for programme-specific questions, some of which were reframed to avoid the implications of beneficiary-status. There were 68 questions in this schedule. The schedule for the leaders, elites and teachers had 63 questions covering such areas as their view on development programmes and functionaries, their understanding of the duties and responsibilities of the functionaries, perception of the impact of the programmes on the people and the communities, their collaboration and participation with the officials in implementing development programmes. The schedule also had programme-specific items and questions on the perception of the targeted and their participation in the development programmes. On the other hand, the schedule for officials dealt with their personal and professional background, communication skills used by them, competence, motivation, job satisfaction and work ethics, programme implementation problems, programme-receptivity, target achievement and their view of the targeted populations and opinion leaders. There were 64 questions in this schedule covering the above areas. These were pretested, rendered in Malayalam (the native language of the state selected for the study), and standardised before being used for data collection.

Observation: An observation sheet was developed to gather information on the programme implementation process and important formal staff meetings at the district and block levels. The observation sheet included such items as the agenda for the meeting, the kind of development-related discussions in the meeting, the procedure of conducting meeting, community problems identified and solutions discussed to solve them, how people's participation was promoted, training needs of the officials identified and strategies adopted to meet them, etc.

Secondary Data Guidelines and Formats: Appropriate guidelines and formats were developed to collect all pertinent data required for the study. These formats included such items as listing of the names of rural development programmes for the rural poor, tribals and women and children, the length of time the programme was in service, target achievement rates, programme impact in terms of not reverting back to programme eligibility status, delivery problems and suggestions made for further improvement.

Description of the Study Area

Understanding the unique nature and characteristics of the study setting is élan vital for meaningful and successful data collection. This study was conducted in the district of Wayanad in Kerala which is one of the 14 districts in Kerala located in the northern part of the state bordering the states of Karnataka and Tamil Nadu. The district has three development blocks namely Kalpetta, Manathavady and Sultan's Battery. As stated earlier, the study was set in Manathavady and Sultan's Battery blocks. In the district, there are 48 revenue villages of which 12 are in Sultan's Battery block, 16 in Manathavady block and the rest in Kalpetta block. Of these villages, Thondernadu and Thrissilery from Manathavady block and Noolpuzha and Pulpally from Sultan's Battery block were the villages studied. Thus, village communities form an important level of analysis. Village communities in Kerala are dispersed (Miller, 1960). The population of these communities consists of Hindus, Muslims and Christians. In certain areas, scheduled castes and scheduled tribes in varying proportions also constitute substantial population groups.

All the villages had reserve and vested forest and grew mainly cash crops. Major cash crops include tea, coffee, pepper, ginger, cardamom, areca-nut, rubber, rice, turmeric and coconut. Villagers do come to the market in the evening not only to purchase things but also to have discussions with others on general and current topics of one's interest. Generally, people from one particular part of the village have an occasion to interact and interchange ideas. Trade union movements are quite strong in these village communities. Almost every trade including barbers to masons has a union and the members are strongly united for their rights. Most of these are politically motivated, but cases are not rare where a group has stood united without any political affiliations. This, of course, has added to the awareness factor of village population groups.

Collecting Data from Beneficiaries and Non-Beneficiaries

Primary data collection from the programme beneficiaries and non-beneficiaries at the village/block level was carried out. Beneficiaries were those who had received the services and benefits of IRDP, ITDP or ICDS for the last one year. Non-beneficiaries were those eligible for these programmes but were not currently receiving any kind of benefits and services in kind or cash. As mentioned before, 200 beneficiaries and 100 non-beneficiaries were interviewed. Before actual data collection was launched, four to six weeks were spent with development functionaries and villagers in order to gain familiarity with and generate support from prospective informants. I shadowed several development functionaries and officials while they visited the field and beneficiaries for follow-up visits. This also provided me with an opportunity to observe the interaction of development officials with beneficiaries and prospective beneficiaries. I also spent time in the evening in village markets and shopping areas where villagers would have casual gatherings. I attended as many meetings as possible just to get a sense of the problems and prospects of these village communities. This was one way to get to know the community and the people. Contacting and interviewing beneficiaries was hardly smooth. It was quite a problem to approach and interview beneficiaries who were spread over a large area, often in widely separated small hamlets. Living in the community brought me closer to the villagers as I was able to talk with a number of them in the evenings, listen to their conversations, stories, trials and tribulations of rural and tribal life. This made some of the respondents feel more comfortable to answer questions and provide valuable information for the study. There were a number of practical problems encountered by the researcher. As mentioned earlier, village communities in the study area were dispersed over a wide area and transportation was not available in some places. This made access to the homes of the identified beneficiary and non-beneficiary respondents very difficult. Sometimes, I had to walk for miles to reach a respondent's house but only to find that the family members were away. This was quite a discouraging and frustrating part of the data collection. Some of the beneficiaries were suspicious of me as they thought I was an investigator from the Rural Development Department conducting follow-up enquiries about the services provided. This was a rather big problem as some of the beneficiaries were used to selling the benefits they received in kind prematurely for short financial gains in order to meet their immediate needs. This has considerably affected the outcome of the programme in terms of its utility and benefits. Such suspicious approach to the researcher could have potentially affected the reliability of some of their responses, as the respondents were more likely to provide information to give a false impression of success of the programme. Although I tried to clarify my identity, I did not think it went too far.

Some part of the data collection took place during the monsoon (rainy) season and this was an added natural hurdle. Despite these difficulties and inconveniences, the data collection experience was positive and enriching. Some of the villagers went out of their way by substantially contributing their time and energy. There were times when the hospitality of some of the people in the community took me by surprise.

Yet another problem was the dialects used by the tribals. The study district had a sizeable tribal population (17.2%). Similarly, the proportion of tribals in the study villages was more than the district average. In fact, the data show that among beneficiaries, 53 per cent were tribals and the rest non-tribals. The main tribal groups among beneficiaries included Kurumars, Paniyas, Naiyickens, Adiyars, Uralis, Kurichiays and Kadars. Interviewing the tribals was further complicated by the fact that these different tribals spoke different dialects. This meant that I had to have additional help from people who could translate their dialect into Malayalam. Often, the researcher had to draw upon the courtesy of local leaders for better understanding of the tribal way of communication. Needless to state, using an interpreter who translates the information is like second hand information. Since I used village leaders and in some cases tribal chiefs as translators, it is conceivable that some of the respondents might have been obliged to provide information. This in turn might have affected the quality of the data. Sometimes data collected through a third party translation could also be incomplete and might very well be coloured by the subjective perception of the translator. I am sure this might have also occurred regarding the data collected from some beneficiaries of tribal groups. While the process of data collection was time-consuming and requires patience, it was both stimulating and insightful.

Collecting Data from Leaders, Officials and Teachers and Through Observation

Contacting and interviewing development functionaries were relatively easy as they had specified office and working hours. They were quite cooperative and helpful. From the two development blocks, 60 development functionaries from Block Development Officer (BDO) to VEO/Anganwadi Worker (AWW) were interviewed. In accordance with the sampling design, 50 opinion leaders (primary school teachers, elites, local politicians and religious leaders) were interviewed.

Some of the valuable information that enriched the study is the result of a meaningful and extensive data collected through observation and casual conversation with development functionaries and beneficiaries. For example, data collection experience brought home the adverse impact of top-to-bottom planning. From the interviews and conversation I had with a number of top level officials and development functionaries, it was clear that policies and programme planning always originated at the top level which in turn was received with indifference by people and grassroots level functionaries. Beneficiaries, non-beneficiaries and some officials reported number of instances for achieving the target by digging wells in forests where there is no water, constructing check dams on rivulets which did not have enough water, building community halls which people never use, granting cycle shops where there is no road. This demonstrates that development programmes howsoever well conceived at the apex level may lose its intrinsic value by the time they reach the grassroots. These were some of the responses I got from respondents and functionaries regarding questions on the implementation problems and bottlenecks. This researcher also had the opportunity to observe some of these things first hand while travelling in these communities to collect data. Many respondents including local leaders, and functionaries reported that the felt-needs of the community is not often given priority. It was also observed that a few tribals were beneficiaries of several programmes and grants at the same time. The glaring difference between target fulfilment and performance achievement is another reflection from the field that is still very vivid. "Many a time projects and schemes", stated a development functionary, "are handed down by higher-ups at short notice and are to be implemented in a short span of time. As a result, the functionaries can do justice neither to such projects nor to its beneficiaries. Thus, the purpose of such schemes is defeated." One of the beneficiaries shared with me that they receive the assistance in kind one day and dispose of the assets the second day. Amazingly, in order to achieve targets a few people were given assistance again and again. This led one of the officers to share with me that many development programmes achieve their targets more on paper and less at the grassroots. Field observations have also shown that the resources are thinly spread over a large number of persons rather than adequately assisting some of them who would have substantially improved their condition. Funds meant for development programmes were often diverted to other programmes and as reported by one of the functionaries, the fund granted for a community hall was utilised to construct a building to house the village office.

In addition, observation data were collected from formal meetings. These included Block-Level Coordinating Committee (BLCC), Block Development Committee (BDC), Panchayat Board Meetings, Monthly General Conference, area meetings of ICDS staff, staff meeting of ITDP and spot visits. I was able to attend one such meeting and collect data through observation. These meetings seldom went beyond routine matters and discussion of administrative memoranda, policies and target fulfilment. The meetings were more authoritative than being democratic and hence far from team-oriented in their approach. Further, the interaction between grassroots functionaries, BDO, CDPO (Child Development

Project Officer), VEO, AWW, and villagers was observed by shadowing the officials in the field. The officials were very friendly with people and supportive. However, they often lacked the development-oriented perspective these programmes require of them. The officials were not able to assess the progress objectively, suggest practical solutions to some of the problems beneficiaries posed, and in many cases, they did not have enough skills in developing the potentialities of the beneficiaries.

Collecting Data from Secondary Sources

Extensive review of literature on theoretical and empirical aspects of social policy, social development, social planning and also rural development was carried out. This is further supported by the data collected from specialised institutions undertaking research in the area of rural development and the information collected through interviews and consultations with experts at these research institutes. This was carried out partly during the pilot study and the remaining during the data collection period. The ideal time for collecting such information is before the instruments are developed so that the instruments would reflect the patterns of enquiry and the kind of tools used in similar areas. I spent considerable amount of time at the National Institute of Rural Development (NIRD), Hyderabad; Institute for Social and Economic Change (ISEC), Bangalore; Asian Institute for Rural Development (AIRD), Bangalore; Centre for Development Studies (CDS), Thiruvananthapuram and Tata Institute of Social Sciences (TISS), Mumbai. NIRD is a premier institute established to further research and training as well as to provide leadership in the area of rural development. Its library was particularly useful as it was also a premier research institution in rural development. Not only did this opportunity provide me with access to their libraries, but it also gave me a chance to consult with experts and researchers in this area. AIRD is a voluntary agency espousing the cause of developing communities. It also engages in educational and awareness generation activities for the development of the rural poor. CDS is a research-based centre promoting scholarly interests and exchange programmes in the area of development including rural development. TISS is the premier social work institute in the country, which offers Masters in social work in several specialisations including Urban and Rural Community Development. TISS also had very good collection of books on various aspects of rural and community development in India. During my stay at these institutions, I had the opportunity to consult with researchers and experts in these specialised agencies on issues relating to my topic and the broader policy and programmatic issues in the area of rural development. These discussions were very useful as it provided more insight into regional issues encountered in implementing IRDP, ITDP and ICDS. A large amount of data was also collected from central agencies such as the Ministries of Agriculture and Rural Development, Department of Women and Child Development. Agencies such as State Directorates of Development, Tribal Welfare, Agriculture and Rural Development were source of valuable information. Similarly, relevant data were also collected from the headquarters of selected districts and blocks. These data primarily included national, state, district and village level statistics on target achievement, resource allocation and investment, programme reach and coverage, etc. There were a few organisations whose functioning overlapped with rural development efforts, namely Commercial Banks, Revenue Department, etc. Besides, there were non-governmental organisations both secular and denominational that were actively involved in the development of rural people. The data and discussions focused on the rural development strategies and models adopted by the Indian government and how the model evolved from a historical perspective. These experiences of collecting secondary data and consultations with experts helped me clarify some of the issues I had and gave credence to my research agenda.

Field Reflections and Discussion

As I reflect (Atkinson and Shakespeare, 1993) on my data collection experience, what stands out is the lessons learned and insights gained from the realities of the field. Following are some of the important lessons learned and insights developed.

I felt overwhelmed by the number of dimensions covered by the study and that brought home the fact that the problem formulated was not sufficiently narrowed down to manageable size. To some extent, the study lacked depth and possibly focus due to this factor. Further, this has led me to spend a lot of time in collecting data as well as investment of resources.

I collected data from the beneficiaries of three major programmes, namely, IRDP, ITDP and ICDS. After having collected the data from these three different programme beneficiaries, I realised that it was not the best idea to study all three under one design. Although there are things in common between the three, they are different programmes with different objectives and different beneficiaries.

Using the same interview schedule for IRDP and ITDP beneficiaries did affect the quality of the data and the ability to compare results between the two to some extent. Clearly, tribals are a special group with distinct culture, values and belief systems. They may also have special meaning for concepts like development. For example, one of the tribal chiefs was assisted with a new tiled roof house as part of the ITDP project. When I interviewed him, I observed that the new house was used for the cows and he was living in the old thatched roof hut. When I asked about this, he stated that it was not healthy to live in the cemented floor house with tiled roof and he felt very unnatural to live in that new house. The chief also commented that the new house is good for cows and the cemented floor is easy to be cleaned when filled with cow-dung. I think trying to solve the tribal populations' problem using modernised solutions is perhaps not the answer. The solutions probably need to come from within these communities.

Using the same schedule for IRDP and ITDP beneficiaries was difficult for me, as I had to consciously make an effort to use the appropriate programme-specific jargon while interviewing the respective beneficiaries. There were a few occasions when I was confused between IRDP and ITDP-specific questions. This of course has caused interruptions and prevented the flow of the interview as I tried to correct myself at such occasions.

The interview schedules for beneficiaries and non-beneficiaries were long as they had programme-specific questions and it took a lot of time to complete. There were times when I could see that the respondent was bored and tired of answering questions. This was also true for me as I was also tired, particularly on those days when I had more interviews. While it was difficult for me in some cases to stop the respondent from giving me a socio-economic lecture about wide variety of topics, there were others who were rushing in great speed wanting to get it over. This too affected the quality of the data to some extent.

In retrospect, I think that using a guided interview schedule focusing on the policy and programme planning issues for the experts and researchers in the premier institutions I visited would have been extremely useful for the study. In the absence of such an instrument, my questions at times lacked direction and purpose. That was definitely a lost opportunity.

One instrument that would have been very helpful in studying the impact of development programmes was case progress report of selected programme beneficiaries. Since these programmes were different in nature and scope and since the success of the programmes depended much on the individual, such case progress studies would have added depth to the study. Tracking such individual cases would have given me qualitative information about the programme's success and failure that could never have been collected through other approaches including structured questions.

To assess the impact of these programmes, I had relied on a series of questions reflecting the subjective perception of progress made by beneficiaries. After data collection, I realised that this was not perhaps the best to assess the impact of these programmes. It would have been more appropriate and scientific to develop sub-scales on the impact of these programmes and test them for validity and reliability through pretesting samples. Such sub-scales for IRDP, ITDP and ICDS beneficiaries would have been very useful for this study although it would have required much more thought and time.

While collecting data, I realised that some of the questions for beneficiaries and non-beneficiaries were not framed in a way that would make meaningful sense to them. For example questions on community problems to tribals and some villagers were met with the response that they did not have any problems in their communities. The problems of the tribals as perceived by outside world are not really problems for them as I mentioned in the case of the tribal chief who used new tiled roof house for rearing cows. Most tribals and some rural people do not have the concept of annual income or how much they earn in a year. They do not put a price to the agricultural produce and the concept of saving money is nonexistent in many tribal communities. Similarly, I became increasingly aware that some questions needed more prefacing, much like a conversation, in order to avoid the monotony of a question and answer format. I think that a conversation-oriented and recorded focus group discussion (in small groups) is an appropriate tool to collect data from these respondents.

Finally, the polarisation between quantitative and qualitative data did not exist in the field as it did in academics. Some of the qualitative data that I collected can never be quantified as it would completely lose its meaning and significance in the quantification process. Recoding, categorising and regressing data, although, accepted in quantitative analysis, definitely represent summarised version of the original data. However, the sheer volume and size of the data collected brought home the importance of quantification for meaningful presentation. I do however think that both qualitative and quantitative data can be harmoniously used to uncover different dimensions of the study (Shaffir and Stebbins, 1991). While quantification allows for data reduction and summarising, qualitative analysis can often provide the depth and meaning to various dimensions of the problem under study. For example, some of the anecdotal stories that I described earlier can never be quantified. And these anecdotal stories powerfully communicate the flaws of developmental efforts and drive home a strong message to the reader about some of the implementation and delivery point problems. These are some of the things I would be cautious about, if I were to do the study all over again.

Conclusion

Unlike the ideal situations which I contemplated as a young researcher, particularly in the comforts of the classrooms, I unwittingly discovered that the field is extremely unique and it restructured my experience, modified my perceptual reality and provided richness and meaning to the problem under study. The experience I had was quite valuable and it helped me in designing more appropriate instruments and conducting better studies in my later years. In closing, I hope that this may be of use to beginning researchers interested in studying rural and tribal communities.

References

1. Atkinson D. and Shakespeare P. (1993). 'Introduction'. In Shakespeare P., Atkinson D. and French S. (ed), *Reflecting on Research Practice*. Buckingham: Open University.
2. Miller E. J. (1960). 'Village structure in North Kerala'. In Srinivas M. N. (ed), *India's Villages*. Mumbai: The Indian Society of Agricultural Economics.
3. Shaffir W. B. and Stebbins R.A. (1991). 'Introduction. In Shaffir W. B. and Stebbins R.A. (ed), *Experiencing Fieldwork*. Newbury Park: Sage.

PART IV

Gathering Data on and from Non-Government Organisations

10

Simon Combe

An 'Outsider's' Tale: Experiences of Collecting Data on Voluntary Agencies in India

Introduction

Since late 1984 I have been working on a series of interrelated research projects concerning the activities of voluntary agencies in rural India. These have ranged from developing a definition of the term 'voluntary agency' in the Indian context and a general overview of the indigenous grassroots level voluntary agency sector in rural India through to my current project which consists of a set of case studies of such voluntary agencies active in rural India. This paper is an account of my experiences in the collection of data in India. The paper examines the nature of the research project (the problem addressed, aim, method, conceptual framework, and findings); some factors of a general nature that in retrospect shaped my experiences in the collection of data; my experiences in the collection of data in India; and, some of the lessons I drew from these experiences.

The Project

In the context of increasing concern at the failure of the state to bring about any significant change in the level of development in rural India, an increasing number of people in recent years have become interested in the activities of the indigenous voluntary sector and the role it might play in the process of rural development. Some commentators have been extremely impressed by the sector, suggesting that it has a major role to play. Others have been less impressed, suggesting that it might well do more harm than good.

The Problem

Despite a large body of contributions on this sector and the debates concerning its role in the process of rural development, no widely shared understanding as to what 'voluntary agencies' were, had emerged. As a result, the debate had not been as productive as it could have been as contributors were arguing the merits and demerits of 'voluntary agencies' with often quite different perceptions.

The Aim

The primary aims of this project were to: first, suggest a definition of the term 'voluntary agency' that could be used by all participants in the debate concerning the role of voluntary agencies in the process of rural development in India[1], a definition that was not too inconsistent with how people involved in the debate had understood and/or defined the term (and thus was acceptable to the vast majority of them); and, second, demonstrate how this definition could help in the process of distinguishing voluntary agencies from other types of formations – similar yet different – active in the process of rural development in India.

Methods

In the light of the scope of the study, that is, the whole of India; the

---

1. While my own understandings of the key terms framing the study changed as the study progressed, the terms 'India' and 'definition' were eventually understood in the following ways: 'India' as those areas within the borders of the nation state of the Republic of India as stipulated in its Constitution on the 25th of November 1949; and, 'definition' as "a formal and concise statement of the meaning of a word" (following William T. Mcleod, ed), The Collins Paperback English Dictionary, Collins: London, 1986, p. 224).

lack of reliable or up to date details concerning the number and locations of voluntary agencies; and my own research background, it was decided that the study would rely primarily on the use of qualitative data, namely, documents; the memories and records of interviews and conversations; and the memories and records of observations.

Findings[2]

As noted above, the aim of the study was to develop, test and explain the application of a definition of the term 'voluntary agency'. The definition of the term underwent a large number of changes during the course of research as it was tested firstly against the understanding and/or definition of term by those who had contributed either to the material on the sector or the debates concerning its role in the process of rural development and secondly as a tool for facilitating the classifications of formations as 'voluntary agencies'. That having been said, the term 'voluntary agency' was eventually defined in the Indian context as being: "a non-state, non-party, non-profit, secular, formal, finite collectivity, providing personal services, to people, other than its own members".

Factors Shaping the Experience of Collecting Data

In retrospect a number of interconnected factors can be said to have had a significant role in shaping the experiences I had during the collection of data. These included, my own background; my status as an 'outsider'; the nature and source of my finances; my health; friends; and the places I used as bases for the collection of data.

Background

The first factor which shaped my experiences in the collection of data was my background. My undergraduate degree had been a Bachelor of Arts in which I had focused on Australian Social History. My major works dealt with the eugenics movement in

---

2. For an early version of the paper coming from this research see: Simon Combe "Towards a Definition of Voluntary Agencies" in R.K. Gupta & S.P. Srivastava (ed.), *Action Sociology and Dynamics of Rural Development*, Ajanta Publications: New Delhi, 1989, pp. 121-137.

Australia during the first part of this century and housing policy for the poor in Sydney during the 1920's. My interest in housing led me to do a Masters degree in Town and Country Planning in order to become an urban historian. However, due to a set of circumstances – largely governed by the fact that most of my close friends within the department were from developing countries – my interest shifted from Australia to developing countries and from history to the present.

In 1983 I travelled to Sri Lanka to do some preliminary work for a Masters dissertation on a comparison of state and non-state credit provision for housing for the rural poor. However, for a number of reasons – including the outbreak of hostilities in Sri Lanka in mid 1983; the difficulties I had in distinguishing between state and non-state credit; and the fact that I had along the way become much more interested in India – I abandoned the project in Sri Lanka and shifted my interest to India. During the course of 1984 I further shifted the focus of my study from a specific concern with credit for housing to development in general and from a comparison of state and non-state formations to a specific type of non-state formation: the voluntary agency.

As a result of all of this, when I arrived in India in March 1985 for an eight-month period of data collection I really had very little knowledge of the country I was coming to study. My academic background was that of history, town planning and regional development theory and there was hardly anyone in my department involved in looking at India or voluntary agencies who could have given me guidance. I had been introduced to the Vice Chancellor of Benares Hindu University in Varanasi at a conference in Australia and had also had an invitation to come and visit the National Institute of Rural Development (NIRD) in Hyderabad after I had written to them asking whether I could stay there for a while. I should note that I could have come to India along with a list of addresses of Indian field offices for Australian non-government organisations who were funding voluntary agencies in India, but after having had experience of having done this in Sri Lanka, decided against this as it had resulted in my getting a very one-sided view of the voluntary agency sector. Thus, armed with two articles on the voluntary agency sector in rural India and little else I commenced collecting data.

The 'Outsider'

Perhaps the most important factor shaping my experiences in the collection of data in India was my status as an 'outsider': that is, a foreigner. Being an 'outsider' was in many ways a mixed blessing. On the one hand, I found that I often had easy and immediate access to places and people that I do not think I would have got had I been an Indian student. Having once gained access, I often found that people were far more patient and showed far more latitude to me than I know Indian friends of mine researching similar topics received. Interviews lasted longer. Often I was invited home to meet families and taken around personally to meet other staff. While I hope that this reception was in part because I was pleasant and showed an interest in knowledge, activities and views of the person I was interviewing, undoubtedly an important factor often was my being a foreigner.

If there were pleasant outcomes flowing from the fact that I was an 'outsider', there were also unpleasant ones. People could be unhelpful, discouraging and in some cases quite hostile. On more than a number of occasions I was told, for example, that there was no point in my continuing my studies because as an 'outsider' I would never understand India. Another variant of this argument was that as I could not speak 'the language' I would never be able to understand what was going on fully.

However, in such situations I felt the need to defend myself and this I often did with the following arguments: that, as an outsider I was in the position to offer a fresh perspective; that some of the best contributions in Indian History, Sociology, Economics, etc., had come from non-Indians; that, anyway, being Indian had not stopped many people from producing very bad contributions; that, as an 'outsider' I did not come to the subject with the baggage of local caste, class, communalism of regional ties; that as most people whom I was studying spoke English; that I could not speak Hindi well did not really matter; and that anyway, as I was attempting to cover the whole of India having even a sound knowledge of one Indian language was not going to solve the problem.

Whether I necessarily agreed with all these arguments or not was not the point. The fact was that at times I needed to use them. The impact of this occasional branding as an 'outsider' along with the impenetrable barrier it supposedly placed between me and understanding the 'Indian reality' meant that it took me a long time before I started formally interviewing people or visiting individual agencies: and having started to do so, to feel confident enough of my understanding of what was going on, to ask the type of questions I wanted to ask.

Finance

A third factor shaping my experiences of collecting data was the extent and source of my funding. The funding of my research during this phase came almost totally out of my own pocket: and as I had been a student for most of the preceding years these funds were relatively small. This meant that I had to determine fairly carefully how I could best utilise my limited funds to maximum effect. It also meant that I could not hope to collect the data for all the phases of my research during the one trip to India but had to go back to Australia in order to earn more money so as to return and finish collecting data.

Although I had very limited funds, I decided to spend most of them on data. I had limited time in India and so really could not spend the time analysing the material at point of contact. This meant that I either had to purchase the item if available or photocopy the whole or parts of it. As a result, major portion of my funds went to the purchase of books, pamphlets, journals and photocopies. Much less was spent on food, transport and accommodation.

Certainly it affected my confidence and also made me painfully aware that any wasted day or mistake ate away at my very limited savings. And gradually as research went on, added to my growing debts, which in any case I had to settle.

Oddly enough the fact that I was funding my own research often generated quite a different response from the people I interacted with in India. One of the first questions I was often asked was in fact "where was my funding coming from". When I replied (self consciously) that it was coming from my own pocket, in most cases people were genuinely surprised and impressed that I "cared enough about my work or topic"

Health

A factor that shaped the whole range of activities associated with the collection of data during this project was the state of my health. Like many other researchers in new and strange environment I had problems with my health. For many researchers these problems are usually associated with food and water. This was not the case with me: the food and water have never troubled me in India. The main cause for my ill health was the time I had chosen to undertake my visit and the fact that having done so and having got sick I made no allowance for the situation and instead pushed myself harder to cope.

I had decided – quite consciously – that I would carry out the collection of data for my research during the height of the Indian summer and the monsoon. I had read many critiques of western researchers who only chose the cooler and more temperate months in which to go to 'the field'. I decided not to follow in their stead and set out for India at the beginning of the summer months.

Having arrived in India I headed to Varanasi from where, as I have noted above, I had received an invitation from the then Vice Chancellor of Benares Hindu University (BHU) to visit their Centre for Integrated Rural Development (CIRD). I therefore proceeded on a 40-hour train journey that ended up taking much longer and most of it in 40-45°C heat in a more than usually crowded carriage. Again, in normal circumstances this journey would not have been a problem. However like many other students undertaking their first major research trip overseas I had been working very hard before leaving Australia and as a result had arrived in India in a state of exhaustion. A state only aggravated by the trip to Varanasi.

However, not only did I arrive in Varanasi in a state of exhaustion but I also arrived to discover that the Vice Chancellor who had invited me to visit the University was about to leave. I managed to see him on his last day and was warmly welcomed and introduced to the head of the CIRD but when I went back the next day to check on the accommodation I was told that as there was no Vice Chancellor, no decision could be taken as to my accommodation. As a result, the only accommodation that I could find at short notice, at a price I could pay, and for the length of time I was staying in Varanasi, was near the railway station, some 10 km away from the university. From here I thus proceeded to commute daily, again often in 40°C heat, and often by foot.

As if these were not enough, my state of health was not helped by the fact that for much of the period there was no electricity – in part due to an extended strike. The supply of electricity in Varanasi being not good at the best of times, one night there had been a power cut. Unfortunately however this cut occurred during the telecast of a particularly, exciting important cricket match and 'spontaneously' hundreds of the citizens of the city rushed to the power station to protest at the interruption in the telecast of the match. Once at the power station, they proceeded to attack some of the power workers who, understandably, had then proceeded to go on strike. Again in normal circumstances this would have been fine except that as I was already sick I found that during the day I really need the fan to cool down – especially on the days I had walked to and from the university. The only time therefore when it was cool enough to work was at night, except that at night there was no light. The end result of all this was that by the time I left Varanasi I had lost well over 10 kg, the loss which in retrospect I could ill afford to make up.

The loss of weight had its impact in a number of ways. Firstly, I found that I was more vulnerable to colds and flues. Secondly, I was prone to exhaustion after only a few days of activity. Thirdly, as I became sicker and sicker and my work progressed more and more slowly, the more worried about the progress of my data collection, the more I pushed myself to work harder and harder. Finally, especially towards the end of my stay, I became increasingly irritable and impatient with situations that normally I would have coped with quite well.

Friends, if all this sounds like a horror story, well in fact most of the time it wasn't. The factor that made the difference and made data collection possible, and for the most part enjoyable was the support and company of friends. As I have noted above, I had come to India knowing nobody and having few contacts. However, wherever I went I found people who were friendly and supportive. In Varanasi these included for example the drivers, peons and students at CIRD and the family of a person I had met on the train trip from Mumbai. In Mumbai it included a Reader in History from the University of Sydney and one of his students, who were both doing research there in Bangalore, Chennai, Bhubaneswar, Kolkata, New Delhi and the other towns and cities in order to collect data. It included the people I met or friends and relatives of friends to whom I was directed who provided support and friendship. However, most of all, it was the staff and course participants of the NIRD in Hyderabad.

The importance of friends was that in addition to providing company by talking, playing cards and going to the movies, they continually showed an interest and enthusiasm in what I was doing – often bolstering my flagging state. In addition, they often recommended people whom I should speak to and suggested people with whom I could stay with in various towns and cities I visited. Later on during this period, as I was getting weaker and weaker, they also forced me to go to the doctors despite the fact that I was arguing that I was alright when clearly I wasn't. I think it is doubtful that I would have continued the collection of data had it not been for their help.

Friendships were not without their problems. Being an 'outsider', I found that I often became friends with a broad range of people at any one place – many of whom did not necessarily like each other. This meant that at times I had to be fairly diplomatic and careful about who I saw, for how long, and what I said. Secondly, maintaining friendships could take up a lot of time. For example, there were times when I really needed to work but instead was pressured into going to a wedding, a lunch, a movie that I really did not have time to go to but felt I had to go to if I was not to offend the person who was inviting me.

Finally, there were burdens I placed on friends that I really wished I did not have to. Research in India, like anywhere – especially for an 'outsider' not used to how things are done – has its frustrations: red tape, slow service, crowded buses, quarrelsome rickshaw drivers, etc. Occasionally, as a result of these frustrations, I'd burst into a fairly intense 'critique' of these aspects: 'critiques' I know invariably sounded like – and perhaps often were – a fairly intense critique of India itself. I was fairly careful to whom I gave these critiques – generally giving them only to close friends. However, they could be quite reactive and in retrospect it was not fair that I vented my frustrations on my friends: especially as they were also in retrospect often quite irrational (the critiques that is, not the friends!). In all cases the friendships survived, although one in the early monsoon months in Delhi – was sorely tested.

Bases

The final factor of a general nature that shaped the experiences of my collection of data were the bases I used for my research. By 'base' I mean the places where I was attached and/or stayed for any significant period of time. During the collection of data for this project I had three main bases – the CIRD at the BHU in Varanasi where I spent a month at the beginning of my research; the NIRD in Hyderabad where I spent the largest portion of the rest of my stay in India; and the International Guest House at the Pusa Institute in New Delhi where I stayed for a month. As bases, each of these were quite different in terms of what they had to offer and what subsequently I managed to get out of them.

The first place at which I was based was the CIRD at the BHU in Varanasi. As a Centre it had a small but acceptable library; a helpful support staff; and was involved in a variety of research projects related to rural development. One such project was concerned with the encouragement of the household production of traditional medicines. Whilst the research being undertaken at the Centre was no doubt fairly good, as a base the Centre proved a disappointment as I had to commute 10 km daily to reach there.

Later I was to discover that one of the major places involved in the study of voluntary agencies – the Gandhian Institute of Studies was in Varanasi, as were the headquarters of a number of important voluntary agencies active in eastern Uttar Pradesh. Of course, the fact that I did not discover this until I had left Varanasi was my own fault. Had I done enough preliminary work on my topic I would have known this. However it did not help that I had chosen a base on the basis of the fact that they were prepared to have me there as opposed to what they had to offer me in terms of my research.

The International Hostel at the Pusa Institute (IARI), New Delhi was a different type of base. At Pusa I was not attached to any centre or department and so was not looking or expecting much help in that respect. Its attractions as a base were that I had a number of friends living in one of the adjacent student hostels and it was cheaper than staying in a hotel. Besides it offered a room with a desk and a bookshelf.

As it turned out, it served the purpose well. It was comfortable; the food cheap; and I had lots of people with whom I could talk to at the end of the day. Furthermore, once the students at the hostel found out what I was studying they proved an invaluable source of background information about some of the organisations and people I was visiting. In addition they recommended other places I should visit and passed on clippings of newspaper and journal articles they felt I might find interesting. The hostels themselves were some 2 km away from the main gates. Thus in order to get to the places I had to visit, I had to travel first to the gates and then generally catch two buses – all of which took a couple of hours there and back every day. This was to prove very wearying in the middle of the monsoon especially when I was not well.

The NIRD in Hyderabad, where I stayed longest was also a long way from the centre of Hyderabad but had far more advantages than disadvantages. The Institute is the main Government training and research centre for rural development in India. As a base it offered both good accommodation in the form of two hostels; research facilities in the form of a very good library; attachment to a faculty that was interested and involved in research on voluntary agencies in rural India; and a stimulating environment in the form of the constant stream of course participants and conference delegates from all over India, from government and non-government organisations, and from secretaries of departments down to village level workers. It provided a place where I could be contacted and from where I could go forth into the field and return without much problem. Finally, it provided a stable environment with a constant group of friends. As in the case of the importance of friends, I doubt I would have achieved even half of what I did in the end had it not been for the fact that I was able to stay at the NIRD.

Experiences of Collecting Data

Documents

The primary form of data collected were documents. The reasons for this were two-fold. Firstly, given the state of my knowledge about the voluntary agency sector in India when I started it was felt that it would be best to read as much as possible about the sector before starting to interview people or visiting agencies. Secondly, as the aim of the study was to examine the understanding and/or definitions of the term 'voluntary agency' throughout India, it was felt that the quickest and most efficient way of doing this would be by collecting and analysing the documentary material on the agencies rather than trying to systematically visit or interview people from agencies of all types within the sector, from all over India.

Whilst the extent and types of documents in which information relevant to the research questions was unknown at the beginning of this phase, by the end of it information had been located in books; journals and newspaper articles; newspaper reports; pamphlets, posters and other propaganda; annual reports of organisations; unpublished papers and reports; private papers; and films, videos and audio cassettes. The 'authors' of these documents included researchers; journalists; politicians; public servants; the members, executives, and staff of voluntary agencies and non-government libraries; other non-state/non-party formations; and the staff and members of non-indigenous government and non-government, national and international organisations. The documents were located in government and non-government libraries and documentation centres; bookshops; government and political party offices; the offices of voluntary agencies and other non-state/non-party organisations; the offices of non-indigenous donor organisations and the homes and offices of friends and acquaintances. These were located through the use of such tools as abstracts; bibliographies; indexes; catalogues of publishing houses; friends; and, a bibliography I produced myself in order to prompt people to suggest documents I had not yet located.

As noted above, I had arrived in India with only a couple of articles on the voluntary agency sector. The collection of data was initially very slow, and in the first three weeks I found very little. As noted above, the staff of the CIRD at BHU were convinced that I did not have much of a topic and were unable to suggest any material. However, all it took was the gift of a special issue of the journal *Yojana* on the role of voluntary agencies to 'get the ball rolling'. The issue, in addition to providing some 20 articles on the sector suggested the names of authors which I should follow up and the organisations I should visit.

Once in Hyderabad, staying at the NIRD, the collection of documents received a further boost. First of all there was a department which was directly concerned with the activities of voluntary agencies and the names of some of the key articles produced on the subject. Secondly, the library and documentation centre at the Institute had references filed under the heading 'voluntary agency' in their card catalogue and newspaper files. Finally, many of the participants in the courses at the institute from voluntary agencies had brought with them copies of pamphlets, annual reports, etc., produced by their organisations, material they were only too happy to show or give me.

There was however a limit to the amount of material the staff of the Faculty of Human Resources Development, the library and course participants at the Institute could provide and as a result I had to go out to collect additional data. This involved my travelling throughout India to the major cities and visiting various organisations which I thought might prove to be good sources of books, articles, unpublished papers and reports, etc. I got the names of these organisations from either friends or references in the various documents I had already seen or collected. In some respects it was a fairly inefficient use of time. The collection of documents in each new city involved travelling to get there; time spent in settling in; and time spent in locating the various organisations I wanted to visit, which were usually spread throughout the city. It could also prove fairly unsuccessful in that some of the organisations of which I had high hopes would be able to be good sources of material offered very little. On the other hand, as an approach it could also prove very fruitful. Organisations which seemed fairly unpromising could end up delivering a wealth of material. Material, furthermore, I doubt I would have located had I not gone there in person.

As noted above one of the tools I used in order to locate documents was a bibliography I prepared and distributed to people who I met while collecting data. It was actually from the course participants and conference delegates at NIRD that I originally got the idea for the first time of these bibliographies. They would often ask me what I had found so far and I would give them my card box to look at and make suggestions of material I had missed. Eventually these cards were used to compile a bibliography which was then typed up and handed out. In addition to trying to prompt people into suggesting material which I had not yet located I also used it to help me gain the confidence of people I was meeting by demonstrating that I was a serious student.

The collection of various types of documents was not without its problems or frustrations. The sheer physical effort of travelling from institution to institution and from city to city was very wearying. Secondly, as noted above, as I was time bound and thus often had to photocopy documents – by far the most consistently frustrating task I encountered in India! Finally, the bibliography I had produced often failed to produce the kind of response I was hoping for. This was especially so in the case of senior people within the voluntary agency sector who would often suggest nothing and literally throw it into a pile of papers on their table.

Memories and Transcripts of Interviews and Conversations

Supplementing documents as a type of data collected during this project were the memories and transcripts of interviews and conversations. These took a number of forms; formal/informal; brief/extended; structured and unstructured. Among the types of people contacted were members, leaders, staff and clients of voluntary agencies; social scientists; state and central government officials; politicians; members, leaders and staff of other non-state/non-party formations; and staff of non-indigenous funding agencies. People were interviewed/conversed within a variety of locations including offices; private homes; conference and workshop venues; parks; restaurants; cars and trains. The topics covered included the general questions on the role of voluntary agencies in rural development; the significance of government overtures to the voluntary sector within the draft of the Seventh Five-Year Plan; and, the critiques of the sector by the Communist Party of India (Marxist).

It took sometime to begin interviewing people. This was because at first I really had little idea as to who I should interview or what I should ask. It was therefore not until the third or fourth month that I started to make appointments with people to discuss aspects of the voluntary sector in a more systematic way. Initially my location at the NIRD was a great help. In addition to the fact that a large number of people involved with the voluntary agency sector came to the Institute as course participants, many of the leaders of the sector and leading commentators on the sector came as guest lecturers and conference participants. In such cases arranging a meeting was simply a matter of contacting them directly or asking a member of the staff of the Institute to introduce me. Many of these people invited me to come and visit them in their own cities and introduced me to other people they felt I should speak to.

Whilst on a number of occasions I tried to contact people by phone or by writing to them I generally found that in the case of the latter, I did not get a reply, and in the former, if I could actually get through to their offices, I could not get past their secretaries – many of whom guarded their 'charges' very carefully. Generally, however, I found that if I presented myself at the office of the person I wanted to speak to and managed to speak to them in person, I had little trouble in arranging a time to meet.

Whereas I was generally happy with the documentary data I collected, I was not very happy with either the quality or quantity of the data gathered through interviews and conversations. Among the reasons for this were the types of people I spoke to; the subjects covered by the conversations and interviews; the manner in which they were recorded; and the problems arising from the fact that I decided to be straightforward about my own position on the debate concerning the role of voluntary agencies.

Whilst I ended up speaking to a larger number of people than I expected, there were many types of people I should have spoken to but didn't. Part of the problem was that I tended to rely on meeting people who came by circumstance or to whom I was introduced by people I had met through earlier contacts. I was much more reticent about contacting people with whom I had no link. In part this was due to a certain degree of shyness born of the fact that I was an 'outsider' and a new comer both to the study of India and voluntary agencies. In part it was also due to some fairly discouraging encounters.

With respect to the contents of the conversations and interviews, I often found that a lot of time was actually spent discussing what I was doing and the nature of my research project. When finally I was able to move the conversation around to some of the issues I wanted to discuss there was often little time left to go into much detail and the interview/conversation would end with not much having been achieved.

As to how these meetings were 'recorded', whilst in the case of conversations I generally made quick notes in a pad afterwards if something of interest came up. In the case of interviews, I tried to be much more systematic: either jotting down key words to represent the flow of what was being said or stopping the conversation to write down a comment in more detail. In the case of conversations, I relied too much on my memory and because I was not regular enough in noting down information that I found useful or informative, much of what I learnt was lost. In the case of interviews, I simply found that my note taking failed to capture what had been said during the interview. The key words often seemed meaningless even a couple of hours after the interview. I had brought along to India a tape recorder but never felt that I was in a situation where I could use it.

Finally, the quality of the material of some of the conversations and interviews were clearly affected by my decision, if asked, to be fairly straightforward about my views concerning the debate on the role of voluntary agencies in rural development. I had debated this question with myself and had decided that if I did have an opinion on the debate it was only fair that – if asked – I gave it. Whilst in many cases this proved to be no problem and the people with whom I was talking to were quite pleased that I was prepared to be honest about what I thought. On a number of occasions people strongly objected to my views and meetings could be abruptly terminated or be marked by poor replies to questions. This might not have been so much of a problem as these people were clearly in a minority. However, there were also people who were in a position to provide particularly interesting and useful information.

Memories and Records of Observations

The final type of data collected during the exploratory phase of research consisted of the memories and records of observations. These included observations of voluntary agencies and the other types of formations that commonly dealt with them. These people, groups and organisations were observed "in the field" that is in their project villages; their offices; and at conferences and workshops. The observations were both structured and unstructured; participant and non-participant; and took place in eight states and the Union Territory of New Delhi.

As noted above, I had the opportunity to observe voluntary agencies in a variety of settings and contexts, however it was relatively late in my stay that I began to actually observe them on their 'own ground': that is to observe them involved in activities associated with the primary activity of providing services to people in rural areas. The reasons for the delay in actually visiting voluntary agencies were similar to those accounting for the delay in interviewing people, namely: shyness; consciousness of 'outsider' status; and a desire to make sure I knew a fair bit about the voluntary sector in general and the voluntary agency I was visiting in particular, before I went to visit them.

The 'role' played while observing agencies and other formations differed according to the situation. In the case of workshops, conferences and training programmes in which I was able to observe, for example, the staff of voluntary agencies, I also participated. When I visited the voluntary agencies my role was more of a non-participant observer. For the most part observations were short term. Agencies would be visited for a day or two and then perhaps visited again a month or so later. Again it should be noted that I was primarily concerned with what people in the formations I visited actually understood themselves to be and thus not interested so much in getting a detailed understanding of the sector. Therefore I thought it best that I try to visit as many agencies as possible rather than concentrate on only a few ones. In most cases when visiting an agency, I would be assigned a guide who would sit down and talk to me about the agency and then show me around the headquarters explaining how the organisation worked. Then, depending on the time available, I might be taken out to visit one of the field offices to observe an activity or project organised by the agency.

I did however spend a couple of extended periods with voluntary agencies when I was in effect a guest of the agency and lived with staff members, supposedly observing their day-to-day activities. The most lengthy of these involved a 10-day tour with a large and very prominent voluntary agency in Andhra Pradesh, an agency involved primarily with tribal and scheduled caste communities. The agency had its very well appointed headquarters in Hyderabad and field offices set up in various other parts of the state. Before actually starting my period with the agency, I had gone to the main office to speak to some of the senior personnel and to look through some of the annual reports and evaluation studies produced by the agency and/or funding organisations. I then went back to commence a 10-day trip to have a look at the activities of the organisations throughout the state. Travel was by jeep and accommodation was arranged at the field offices and on occasions at the homes and offices of village level workers employed by the organisation. My main guide was one of the upcoming middle level workers of the organisation and he would take me to the various places I was to stay, introduce me to the staff and then go on with his own work in the area, coming back to pick me up in a day or two in order to move onto the next location.

Overall the attention I got was very good. I was well housed and well-fed. People were friendly and the programme so designed that I managed to see a variety of activities in different contexts. The field visit however was not without its problems. The organisation had had many foreign visitors before. However most of these foreigners had been from donor organisations and so what I got was the 'donor observation tour'. This experience was rather like being on a roller coaster ride with one 'thrill' after another. I went from one successful medical centre to a well-managed annual village meeting to an opening of a 'gobar' gas plant, etc. As I was on what had been a tightly scheduled trip and the fact that I was after all a guest of the agency made it difficult to suggest that we stay on in one place a little bit longer or that I be allowed to observe a normal day in the life of an average village level worker.

Another problem was that again, although I was very well looked after, there was nowhere I could get away to reflect on what I had observed. People from the agency were constantly around trying to keep me occupied. On a couple of occasions I tried to sit down and note down what I had seen during the day. People would try to read what I had written over my shoulder or engage me in conversation. In the end, whilst I was grateful for the experience and for the hospitality provided by the agency, I was not very happy with the data produced by the observations. Whilst at the end of the trip I had some idea of what was being done, I really had not been able to observe how: and whilst I had observed successful projects, I had not been in a position to observe unsuccessful ones.

Lessons Learned

The lessons learned from this experience can be divided into those relating to the general factors shaping the experience of collecting data and those related to the actual experience of collecting specific types of data.

General Factors

I think, in retrospect, that I came to India underprepared. My knowledge of India was poor; I had almost no contacts; and only a vague idea of what I wanted to look at. Had I not received the invitation from NIRD, I might well have found myself totally at sea: not really knowing where to go; what to look at; or, what to do. On the other hand, the decision to distance myself from the foreign donor agencies was in retrospect correct. The experiences I had when I was visiting voluntary agencies and was assumed to be a donor representative leads me to believe that I was much better off having not made my first connection with these agencies when arriving in India and thus, possibly, deciding to use one of them as a base for my field work.

With respect to the extent and source of my finances, as in the case of my status as an outsider, I think there is little I could have done. In many ways I am glad I did not come to India with vast amounts of money as it meant that I ended up staying in such places as student hostels and with friends – places where I ultimately came to feel much more at home in India. Something I do not think would have happened had I stayed in expensive hotels or international student hostels.

However, with respect to deciding to spend much of my funds on data, while this seemed the best, and in fact the only decision I now have my doubts. There were times when I was particularly unwell. I think I should have taken myself away to somewhere quiet and cool and rested, but did not because of the expenses. Likewise, I should have spent the money on posting all the material I was collecting by post back to Australia. This again I did not do because of the expenses involved – and admittedly, in part, the nightmare it could be trying to post things from India – gambling on the possibility that I would be able to carry it back with me without being charged excess baggage. While this was a gamble that paid off, it meant that I spent much of my time in India carrying well over 50 kg of books, journals and other assorted printing matter on my back. This did nothing for my state of health and only slowed me down. This meant that I had less time in which to work: the supposed reason I was collecting this literature at place of contact in the first place!

With respect to my health there were things I should have avoided. Clearly, I should not have done things like walk long distances in the middle of the day especially when I was unwell in the first place. Having become sick, I should have recognised the fact and gone off to somewhere cool and quiet to recuperate rather than staying on and putting more pressure on myself. Since that time I have generally been much more careful about pacing my work when in India and have been much more relaxed. On few occasions I have been unwell, I tried to make sure that I was better before getting on with my work, although the continued limitations of time and money when in India have not always made this easy.

Each time I go back to India the importance of establishing good friendships while collecting data has become more and more obvious. Clearly there are some problems. Maintaining friendships can take time away from research and there are always problems that your friends may not get along.

As in the case of friendships, the importance of having a good base was clearly demonstrated by my experience. The main lesson to be learned was that in choosing a base I needed to be mindful of whether the people at the place I was staying were interested or concerned with my interests, and if not, not rely too much on them with respect to my work. Location is also an important factor. I think in retrospect that I should not have for example continued to stay at the International Hostel at the Pusa Institute despite the many advantages it had to offer. In the end it was simply too far away from where I had to do most of my work, and in a situation where I had only a limited amount of time to spend in New Delhi, far too much time and energy was wasted on travelling.

The Experience of Data Collection

For gaining the experience of collecting documentary types of data, it was all right to choose to travel personally to the various organisations throughout India. Whilst it meant that much time and energy was spent in travelling, by the end of my experience in India, I had a much better understanding of the resources available for social science research in India in general and for the study of voluntary agencies in particular. In the end, the majority of documents I collected came from Mumbai, New Delhi and Hyderabad. However, there were a number of important and highly useful documents I do not think I would have got had I not gone to the places I discovered them in person.

The use of the bibliography[3] I produced in order to help gain people's confidence in the seriousness of my study and to serve as a prompt for them to suggest documents that I had not collected before, as noted above, was problematic. I was naive to expect people working on similar subjects to be encouraging or helpful by suggesting material I should look at. On the other hand, when it served its purpose it worked very well. As a method I still continue to use it although the days when I would give a copy to every second person (I am now on my fifth edition) have ended.

As for interviews and conversations, I should have been much more assertive than I was in seeking out people with whom I had no link to interview. Although I managed to speak to a lot of people, I relied far too much on the introductions of friends and other people I met along the way. For all my doubts about the state of my knowledge, by the time I started interviewing people in a more systematic way, I knew more than enough to 'perform' in the interview.

With respect to the question of interview content, I found that as time went on I managed to ensure that less and less time was spent in discussing matters of a general nature and my own work and more and more time discussing the voluntary agency sector.

---

3. Simon Combe. *Voluntary Agencies and their Role in Rural Development: A Bibliography.* Sydney: Macarthur Institute of Higher Education.1986.

One problem was that the discussions of general questions were often very informative and useful in understanding the positions taken by the person involved on issues specific to the voluntary agency sector. Likewise, I found that if they had a fairly clear idea of what it was that I was trying to do, often they were far more likely to address the questions I wanted to ask or to volunteer answers to questions I had forgotten to ask. In the end I think the ideal solution is to have at least two meetings: one in which you get to know the person whom you want to get information from and when you can discuss issues of a more general nature and the objects of your research, and a second in which you concentrate on the specific questions flowing from your research.

With respect to recording interviews, I think in retrospect that I should not have been so reticent about asking people whether I could tape interviews or at least spend more time thinking about how I would take notes during the interviews. In the end whilst I learnt many things from these meetings, relatively little was recorded or stayed in the (conscious) memory for later use. With respect to giving people an idea of my views in the debates concerning the role of voluntary agencies, I was right to divulge these views but at times I should have been more careful in how I expressed them to certain people.

Finally, with respect to the experiences associated with observing voluntary agencies, I think I should have, again, been far more assertive in asking the leaders of agencies whether I could come to observe their activities instead of observing them in situations not related to the primary activities of providing services or of observing only those agencies in the field to whose leaders I could get a personal introduction. The other great lesson I learnt from my experiences in observing agencies in the field was that if possible I should ensure that I had a bit of autonomy, that is, I should try not to be 'tied' to the agency night and day; and that I should try to be in a position where I had a certain degree of control in what I was to see.

Conclusion

The question I am asked most often in India - after the one about the supposed practice of contract marriage in Australia[4], is "What do you think of India". A potentially contentious question at the best of times, I normally find myself falling back on a variant of a line from the poem by A.A.Milne:

> "*When she was good, she was very very good,*
>
> *and when she was bad, she was horrid.*"[5]

At times things could get so bad that I wondered why I bothered continuing. However at the next moment everything was fine and I wondered why I ever thought things were bad. The important thing I kept on reminding myself was that this was the first time I had undertaken research in India; that I was doing it under rather unusual circumstances; and that if things did not go well all the time, or I was not always happy with the quality or quantity of the data I was collecting, that was to be expected.

By the time I left I had answered the questions I had wanted to answer; I had collected a large number of documents on the sector which I could use in other research projects; I had visited a large number of organisations; and had spoken to most of the major

---

4. According to my questioners 'contract marriage' was a form of marriage rampant in Australia involving a practice whereby the two contracting partners agreed to live together for a period of two years for the purpose purely of sex. No love was to be involved, and the contract could be either terminated or extended after the two-year period. Almost every second person I met in India had read about and were understandably curious about the nature of its actual practice. It was invariably my sad duty to inform them that it was the fanciful invention of some Indian journalist rather than a reflection of what actually went on in Australia ... or in Sydney at least.

5. The full stanza of the poem is:
    There was a little girl who had a little curl,
     right in the middle of her forrid.
    When she was good, she was very very good,
     and when she was bad, she was horrid.

contributors to the debate on the role of voluntary agencies in rural development. Most of all, despite the bad experiences, I had – to use another old line – fallen madly in love with India and its people. A love affair which continues to stand the test of time!

11

SWAPAN GARAIN

The Research Climate in NGOs: My Experience in Data Collection

Introduction

There are a range of factors drawing the change to performance, objectives-based ways of operating. As the pressure for accountability increases, generally including the demands of funding bodies and increasing levels of education among consumers and staff, non-governmental organisations (NGOs) are gradually realising the importance of assessing its performance in order to be responsive to the needs of the target groups. In the absence of skilled staff to undertake evaluation studies, NGOs are turning to social scientists for it. Organisational researchers who have developed expertise in studying highly structured organisations (e.g., commercial firms, government organisations, etc.) and the social scientists who have been concentrating on individuals and groups in societal context are taking interest in studying not-for-profit, flexible NGOs. While applying the research knowledge and skills developed and learnt in the context of highly formal organisations, organisational researchers are continuously experiencing different situations requiring adaptation and/or modification of skills and knowledge base. This paper aims at highlighting the difficulties faced by the organisational researcher in studying NGOs and the steps taken to cope with such difficulties.

A Study of Perceived Organisational Effectiveness of NGOs

During the post independence era, hundreds of organisations in both at the government and non-government sectors have come into existence with the aim of raising the standard of living of the disadvantaged, deprived and the poor. In the pre-independence period, self satisfaction, commitment to welfare and service orientation were some of the motivations of the promoters of NGOs in India. In the 1950s, welfare orientation was the dominating factor in the activities of NGOs, and they began to concentrate on schemes of the Indian Planning Commission for the poor and the disadvantaged. Subsequently, they have realised the need to plan with the participation of the target groups in order to achieve greater effectiveness. As a result, a definite trend towards independent functioning of NGOs has been noticed. As a direct implication, NGOs have begun to diversify their sources of funds rather than being dependent on government grants. Along with governmental efforts for promoting NGOs, the flow of foreign funding has helped the growth of the NGO sector in terms of the number of organisations, the range of programmes, and the size of project areas. Since the late sixties and early seventies, professionals with training in management, medicine, engineering, law and social work have started entering the NGO sector in a big way. Thus there is a trend towards institutionalisation in NGOs. The entry of trained personnel and consequent institutionalisation has led to the introduction of performance standards to raise staff efficiency and effectiveness of the organisations. The impact of experimentation on, and promotion of alternative models of development in different fields has resulted in a remarkable change in the allocation of funds to NGOs by the government, bilateral and multilateral development aid agencies, and by a large number of foreign non-governmental funding agencies. The increased resources have enabled a steady growth in the activities of the NGO sector. Professionals have brought with them the different value system and the style of functioning which are often in conflict with the existing practices in the NGOs, and sometimes with the orientations of the promoters and office bearers of NGOs. However, despite the general opinion, there has been a growing concern by the policy makers and the chief executives (usually professionally trained persons) of NGOs about the effectiveness of organisations. In this context, it is being felt that the background-related factors, job characteristics and commitment of the programme staff may play important roles towards perceiving organisational effectiveness.

The main thrust of the government and the NGO activities (as reflected in different government documents) is to spread the growth of the NGO sector, and thereby promote private voluntary initiatives to work with the people. This objective will not be met unless a systematic effort is made for human resource development in the NGO sector. The problem of performance and commitment of human service professionals is becoming a critical factor in the NGO sector in the changing context. The present study aims at taking a comprehensive look at particular organisational aspects of the NGOs in India. The appropriate cultural, structural, managerial and psychological aspects determine the creation of a favourable environment for the functionaries to work in. An in-depth understanding and appreciation of the organisational processes in the NGO sector will require assessment of NGOs in a total perspective. The present study took a holistic view in understanding organisational behaviour in the NGO sector.

A review of the theoretical and empirical literature on the organisational effectiveness reflected a lack of consensus of the meaning of concepts among the researchers. The four univariate models of organisational effectiveness, most commonly cited, namely, the rational goal, the open system, the human relations and the internal process models were found to be inadequate in taking a holistic view of organisations for performance evaluation. However, it was found that the competing values model, succeeded in developing a multidimensional model of organisational effectiveness in integrating the four different models of effectiveness mentioned above, into one model. But the basic assumptions of competing values model were not in conformity with the assumed special characteristics of NGOs, for example, constituency preference (e.g. organisational members, target groups, etc.), flexibility or absence of rigid organisational structure, irregular flow of funds, use of volunteers, project/programme-based approach towards development functioning, community/target group participation, etc. Besides, a major limitation of such research (i.e., in organisational effectiveness) in the context of the Indian situation, both in the commercial organisations and in the NGOs was observed. Subsequently, a conceptual framework was developed in order to evolve a methodology for the generation of required data and to provide a structure for the analysis of perceived organisational effectiveness (POE) in NGOs in India.

The main purpose of this study was to explore the dynamics of NGOs' behaviour and effectiveness in the Indian context. The objectives of the study were:
- to examine and evolve appropriate methodological tools to collect and analyse data on perceived organisational effectiveness in NGOs in India;
- to generate primary data from selected NGOs in India and to make a comparative analysis of the NGOs from the two states, namely West Bengal and Maharashtra;
- to understand perceived organisational effectiveness, job characteristics and commitment with respect to the background of the programme staff;
- to study the differences in perceived organisational effectiveness, job characteristics and commitment by the grade of the staff and size of NGOs in the two states;
- to study the relative importance of job characteristics, organisational commitment, job involvement and work involvement in explaining variance for perceived organisational effectiveness of the programme staff.

In the absence of an appropriate inventory for assessing effectiveness of NGOs, a set of instruments was developed and/or adapted for taking an organisational behaviour perspective of NGOs. Validity and reliability were checked for all the instruments for the NGOs in a manner discussed below.

Considering the objectives of the study, a set of research questions were formulated. In view of the exploratory nature of the study, the development of a set of hypothesis was not undertaken.Formulations of research questions aimed at serving as guidelines for analysis of the data. In order to make a comparative analysis of NGOs, primary data were collected from NGOs of different sizes from two Indian states, namely, West Bengal and Maharashtra. The sample size consisted of 504 programme staff from 22 NGOs from the two states.

The study indicated that:
- NGOs from two different states (West Bengal and Maharashtra) were not different in terms of POE, and job characteristics of programme staff;
- Organisational commitment, job involvement and work involvement differed significantly in the two states;
- POE and job characteristics showed significant difference across the size of NGOs, and commitment variables reported statistically insignificant differences;
- There were similarities in terms of the staff having certain backgrounds, reporting some levels of POE, job characteristics, organisational commitment, job involvement, and work involvement; and
- For a given set of variables, a set of corresponding variables (predictors) of importance was identified.

Development and Standardisation of Instruments

The nature of my study necessitated the use of a set of standardised instruments. Given my five years of training in Social Work and lack of previous experience in independent research work, I was in fact feeling incapacitated. I had some previous experience in interviewing respondents and filling schedules in organised settings (i.e., industries and government administration). The question of standardised instruments led to a lot of apprehensions about my own research capability. But I was determined to use this opportunity to develop my skills. I began with a survey of available instruments to measure the key constructs of my study, namely,

POE, job characteristics (JC), organisational commitment (OC), job involvement (JI) and work involvement (WI). In the course of literature review, I came across widely used instruments to measure the last three constructs (i.e., OC, JI and WI). Although they have been developed and standardised for highly structured organisations in developed countries, I came across literature testing their reliability and validity in Indian situations in the large industrial organisations. Considering the operationalisation of the said constructs in my study, I found it convincing to check their validity and reliability in NGOs and then use them in my study. I could not find readily available instruments to measure POE and JCs. As regards job characteristics, I found my operationalisation of the construct in consonance with an instrument that was developed for the scientists and engineers. I found it appropriate to use this instrument as a basis for developing one for NGOs. But my efforts for POE came to a dead end. Nothing seemed to have been done at the empirical level. A large number of available theoretical models confused me all the more in regards to their appropriateness to NGOs. Keeping aside their relevance to NGOs, I took interest in studying the effectiveness approaches, namely, rational goal, internal process, human relations, open system and the competing values approach. I also examined the methodological part of different evaluation studies. Another question that was creating discomfort in my mind was the issue of integrating different instruments for my study. In the absence of an available assessment inventory, it became a challenge for me to not only develop and/or standardise a set of instruments, but also prepare a package for evaluating NGOs.

How can the NGOs be evaluated? What are the criteria one needs to consider for evaluating NGOs? Who should be the respondents? What should be the best method for collecting data for evaluating NGOs? With many more questions, I entered the field. At this point, I had the single objective of developing an instrument to evaluate NGOs. I visited a couple of NGOs, stayed with them and interacted with the Chief Executive Officer (CEO) and the project leaders. I had number of informal and unstructured discussions/interviews with NGO leaders. Many a time, I met them at odd hours in the office, tea-shop or home. As it is a culture in NGOs to take the guest for a visit to successful projects, I took the opportunity to enquire about the success criteria of such projects. Often I used to record our interaction using a small tape recorder with permission. Before going to bed everyday, I used to note down the important points. In the first phase, I interacted with 11 NGO leaders. Then I came back and analysed the data in the form of recorded interactions and the points noted in my diary. I could broadly classify nine areas for evaluating NGOs. Armed with interview guidelines based on the identified nine broad areas for evaluation, I began my second phase of interaction with the NGO leaders. At this stage, I went for semi-structured and formal interviews with the CEO and project leaders of the same NGOs. The idea of including project leaders was guided by the importance of widening the base of getting feedback. With the help of interview guide, I could stimulate the respondents to throw light on all the criteria identified in the first phase for evaluating NGOs. The data were recorded in the same manner as in the first phase. At the end of the second phase of field work, I returned and analysed the data. The data helped me to reorganise the criteria for evaluation and also to sharpen their focus.

At the third stage, the list of criteria was given to a group of nine item writers: three field practitioners, three social work educators and three management educators. A set of 100 items was generated. After deleting the overlapping items, 48 items were retained for collecting field data from the programme staff working in NGOs.

On the basis of data collected from 100 respondents, item analysis was done. Considering high item-total correlation, it was decided to go ahead with the data collection. This instrument to measure POE of NGOs was standardised on the basis of 493 programme staff from 22 NGOs. The final instrument with 28 items has shown acceptable level of reliability and validity. Validity was checked by way of face validity and factorial validity. Chronbach's alpha based on item variance, correlation's matrix and item-item total correlation were calculated for checking reliability. Factorial validity was used to identify the dimensions of the instrument.

Development and standardisation of POE instrument raised my level of confidence, both in terms of my acceptability in the NGOs and in terms of my research skills. I had stepped into most of the NGOs with my own initiatives. I felt at home everywhere. This interaction with the NGOs' leaders opened the way for my data collection in these NGOs. After collecting data on the items of POE instruments, I was again unclear about the type of analysis needed for standardisation. My inquisitive mind led to spending long hours, day after day, on working on computers. I worked on my own on every possible combination to get the best factorial structure for the instrument. It was an equally challenging experience like collecting field data.

While the job characteristics scale was developed and standardised for the purpose of this study, reliability and validity of the other three instruments (viz. organisational commitment, job involvement and work involvement) were checked. Factorial validity and Chronbach's reliability of all the five instruments used in this study were above accepted level.

The present study has shown a set of patterns in reporting the findings of the study. This reflects the integration of the five instruments in measuring performance of NGOs.

Data Collection Process

Collecting data from NGOs poses several challenges to researchers. This is partly due to the existing research climate in NGOs, as discussed elsewhere in this paper. Attributes of NGOs as organisations set limits in the data collection process. Step by step account of my experience may be examined in terms of identifying the universe of the study, the preliminary inquiry, personal contact, data collection sessions and the recording of data.

Universe

In order to retain a comparative nature of my study, I proposed to collect data from government and non-government organisations in the state of West Bengal. This would have resulted in two different types of organisations operating in the state of West Bengal forming my universe. Government organisations were found to be very large and having bureaucratic set up, whereas NGOs were small and flexible. Due to a non-cooperative attitude on the part of government organisations, I had to drop those organisations from my study. Besides, I found that there were a few government development organisations operating in the state. However, it would not have been technically advisable to compare NGOs and government organisations even if they agreed to participate in the study.

Considering the comparative nature of the objectives of the study, I explored other areas for comparison. Comparison of NGOs working in two states was found to be feasible and suitable to my requirements. Considering my familiarity with the NGO sector, language, logistics, financial and time constraints, I decided to collect data from West Bengal and Maharashtra. Thus, all the NGOs engaged in development activities in the sates of West Bengal and in Maharashtra formed my universe.

Identifying the NGOs operating in the target area was a challenge to the researcher. Unlike developed countries, India does not have a complete database of NGOs either with the government or at the NGO sector. Database of NGOs are maintained by different government bodies as well as the NGOs to suit their own purposes. Registrar under the State Societies Registration Act of 1860, being the registering authority for giving legal status to majority of the organisations, I approached the office of the Registrar. My experience was very discouraging. Retrieving information from the Registrar's office was a difficult task. Besides, almost all types of organisations may get registered under this Act. As a result, database at the Registrar's office may be considered as a 'garbage pit without the services of rag pickers'. A wide variety of organisations carrying out various types of activities were found to be registered with the office of Registrar under the Societies Registration Act. For example, sports associations, libraries, charitable agencies and educational institutions along with NGOs were found to be registered under the said Act. Classifying thousands of organisations and identifying NGOs engaged in development activities, from the Registrar's office could be an independent large research project. Being disappointed with the information base at Registrar's office, I began exploring other sources. My exploration led to identification of more than a dozen databases, namely, different ministries at the state level (e.g., Rural Development, Social Welfare, Human Resource Development, etc.), autonomous government-sponsored organisations (e.g., Council for Advancement of People's Action and Rural Technology; Central Social Welfare Board, etc.), funding NGOs, networking NGOs, etc. At each of the above sources, I found information only on those NGOs which are in touch with them. Thus, a comprehensive database was not available to get a complete listing of NGOs operating in both the states. Then I looked into my own card-catalogue database developed over the years. As part of another sponsored project, I was in the process of computerising the database. I took this opportunity to speed up the process. I explored every possible source of information/database to update and add to my computerised database. Besides, the above mentioned sources, I scrutinised the available directories and also banked upon personal contacts. Thus, I developed a comprehensive database with information on large number of NGOs and this formed my universe. In this context it may be noted that one will never get a complete list of NGOs due to two major reasons: (a) mandatory registration under one authority is not existing, (b) new NGOs are coming into existence every day. This comprehensive list developed by me for the purpose was used for collecting preliminary information about the NGOs.

Preliminary Enquiry

I prepared a proforma to collect first-hand and basic preliminary data about NGOs operating in the two states. This was considered necessary as the information available in different sources had different reference years. Given the project-based functioning of majority of the NGOs, the basic data (annual budget, staff strength, number of projects/schemes, project area, etc.) keep changing. In the proforma, a column on the willingness of the CEO to participate in the research study was included. I sent the two-page proforma with a cover letter explaining the purpose of collecting basic information and of the proposed research project to all the NGOs included in my comprehensive list. Within a period of two months more than 100 NGOs from West Bengal and Maharashtra had returned the filled-in proforma. While matching the basic data of the NGOs with the organisational level controlled factors, initially 24 NGOs, 12 each from West Bengal and Maharashtra were picked up as per the requirements of the study.

Personal Contact

I personally visited all the shortlisted NGOs to discuss with the CEO concerned about my research project. While some CEOs were receptive to such empirical work, majority of the CEOs approached had asked/remarked in an unexpected way. I was not prepared for such questions. Why do you want to take up a research on NGOs? How/why did you select our NGO? How much money are you getting for this research? How is it going to help our organisation? Although some of the questions initially put me in an uncomfortable situation, those questions enlightened me and moderated the perspectives of my study. I also prepared well for interacting/facing with the CEOs next time.

During the first contact with the CEO, I had twin objectives: to explain the purpose of the study and to clarify the nature of assistance/data needed. I made it clear that the participation of the staff was voluntary and the individual as well as organisational level data would be kept strictly confidential and the data identifying individual NGOs would not be published without written permission from the CEO concerned. Most of the CEOs felt relieved knowing that I would not see/ask for any files and finance-related papers.

Data Collection Sessions

Once the CEO of the NGO agreed to cooperate and participate in my research project, I requested her/him to identify/designate an official who would coordinate the data collection in the organisation. In most cases, CEO herself/himself had delegated the responsibility to one of the staff members to assist me in collecting data, before I requested him for it. In some cases, CEO took up the responsibility in coordinating the data collection work.

Once I got to know the designated coordinator to help in my work, I had detailed discussion with her/him about the purpose of the study, type of data to be collected, the eligible respondents and the data collection procedure. In order to identify the eligible respondents, I made a list of all the staff (with name, designation, nature of work and number of years in service) working in the organisation. Given the reasonably small staff strength in the NGOs, I could get most of the information from the CEO or his immediate subordinate. A complete list of the staff in the organisation helped to systematically delete the names of those staff members who were not eligible. The support staff (administrative support, workshop personnel, etc.) and those who had no interaction with the target groups were outside the purview of this study. In the design stage, I had decided to select the sample size through random sampling from the list of eligible staff members. Given the small number of staff working in NGOs, it was not practicable to reduce the respondent size further through sampling. Thus, it was decided to approach and involve all the eligible staff in the sample.

A note on the details of the research project was circulated by the CEO or the project leader a week prior to the forthcoming staff meeting. In the staff meeting, I got an opportunity to brief the staff about the research project and clarify their doubts. Then a tentative schedule for data collection in small groups was determined. The staff members were grouped according to the projects/departments they belonged to. The concerned staff members were reminded about the data collection date on the previous day. The data collection sessions were conducted usually after lunch hours so that the staff could attend to their target groups in the morning hours. Although the sessions were mostly held in the office premises, in some cases, they were conducted at the project site and sometimes in the evening hours. Since most of the staff members were usually operating from different centres/villages, some sessions were conducted on the day they gathered for weekly/fortnightly staff meetings.

In the data collection sessions, the research coordinator designated from the NGO introduced me to the staff members. With a small briefing about the objectives of my study, I distributed one page explanatory note to the respondents giving the procedure for responding to the questionnaire. My presence in the session was useful in clearing their doubts. Then I distributed a set of questionnaires to each of the respondents who needed to assume different roles for answering different sections of the questionnaires. I briefed the respondents about the beginning of each section, about the nature of role they needed to assume (e.g., informing about the agency in general, about his or her own job only and his or her personal attitude towards the job). While collecting filled-in questionnaires from the respondents, I checked whether each item had been responded to. In case an item was left blank, I requested the respondent to attend to the case. Thus all the filled-in questionnaires were usable.

The respondents took two to three hours to respond to a 20-page questionnaire. English speaking respondents took less time in answering to English questionnaires. The field level staff responding to either Marathi or Bengali version of the questionnaire took the maximum time. At times, I had to clarify some questions with examples. This could be due to their lack of wider exposure, absence of opportunity to reflect and review their own work, and unfamiliarity to research/evaluation work.

In NGOs in which the CEO took personal interest and/or herself/himself coordinated data collection work, I was satisfied with the data collection process. Where a project leader was in-charge of the coordination of data collection work, I also had cooperation of the staff. In both the cases, the response rate of the staff in participating in the study was high.

However, in many organisations data collection sessions did not go smoothly. In most NGOs, CEO gave permission and it was left for on me to do the rest. Here, I found the staff indifferent to the research study. Getting a common time to conduct the session was difficult. In order to cope with the problem, I met the staff individually, explained about the study and the procedures for responding to the questionnaires and passed on the questionnaire with a request to hand over the filled-in questionnaires in the office of the CEO next day. But, I had to meet each staff again and again over a period of one to two weeks to get back the filled-in schedule.

In such cases, questionnaire return rate was very poor. Five organisations from West Bengal and three organisations from Maharashtra had to be excluded from the study due to non-cooperation of the staff. This was partly due to indifferent attitude on the part of CEO. From my base in Mumbai, I visited some organisations up to five times to collect the data. As some individual staff members were non-cooperative, the CEO, though enthusiastic, advised me to forget receiving back the questionnaires from such individuals.

Five NGOs approached me to conduct staff development sessions during data collection visits. Conducting staff development sessions was a rewarding experience. I enjoyed contributing my bit in making the organisations effective. This had a positive impact in getting cooperation from the staff in my research.

In examining my data collection experience, I would say that NGO staff from Maharashtra were in general more cooperative than those from West Bengal. Due to my personal contact, some CEOs from West Bengal took interest in my work, and came forward to help me, but the staff were indifferent. In case of Maharashtra, I found the NGOs in general were more receptive, except the ones with politically oriented promoters. With regard to size of NGOs, I found the small ones were more willing to participate in the research and less suspicious than the large NGOs in both the states. Large NGOs usually had many professionally trained staff and some of them were trained social workers, but their responses were mixed. One large NGO with a missionary background had a well-trained Director with about 20 trained social workers on staff. But, I found the people from top to bottom to be indifferent and some were suspicious of research work.

Two types of data were collected and recorded for the purpose of this study. Individual level data and organisational level data. Individual staff members responded to a set of questionnaire in a five point Likert scale besides providing personal background information. Organisational level data were collected by mailing a proforma to collect preliminary information about the organisation.

A Few Surprises while Collecting Data in NGOs, Despite NGO Experience

Being an insider, I was not new to the NGO sector. I began my career in the NGO sector. My first job in a funding agency had given me an opportunity to work closely with a large number of NGOs operating in different parts of the country. Some of them were operating in Maharashtra and West Bengal as well. Besides, I have been teaching NGO management related topics to postgraduate social work students and as such I am familiar with the issues being debated or faced by the NGO sector. I often accompany groups of students for rural camps and study tours organised in collaboration with NGOs. Before starting my research work, I had undertaken an extensive tour of NGOs operating in different districts of West Bengal. A British lady engaged in action research on NGOs in West Bengal had in fact introduced me to the NGO sector in West Bengal. At present, I am on the Managing Committee/Advisory Board of a couple of NGOs operating in both the states. Being familiar to many NGOs and/or its CEOs was an advantage in getting their cooperation. Sometimes, this informal relationship resulted in CEO giving less priority to appointment with me or getting my work done. It was not a question of deliberate non-cooperation but an incidental delay affecting my schedule of data collection. One of my friends heading an NGO in Maharashtra resigned during my data collection and I could not complete my data collection work in that agency. Subsequently, I had to drop that agency from my list. In some of the NGOs, my former students/friends were working at the supervisory level. Some of them clearly told me that most of the staff from their organisations would not cooperate with such studies in spite of CEOs approval. This orientation helped me to play my approach or drop the organisation instead of visiting again and again to pursue the staff. The possible reasons for non-cooperative attitudes are apathy to anything non-routine/unusual, fear of getting caught for giving opinion contrary to agency's stand, etc.

While visiting an NGO, I was accompanied by a foreigner. The Project Director reacted in a lighter way in Bengali, yet at the first instance he asked "What is this British lady doing here?" Fortunately, the British lady had an earlier encounter with him and did not take offence. She explained to him in Bengali that she was working in the NGO sector in West Bengal for the last twelve years. In another instance the CEO knowing that I am teaching at the post-graduate level said, "It is your age to study and not to teach!"

Initially I used to get very irritated with the CEOs who used to give lectures on NGOs and the need for research, and finally used to become indifferent to my research work. In a couple of instances, I found the CEOs using different approaches to avoid participation in my research project rather than clearly stating their position. Most usual method used was to delay the fixing of schedule for data collection sessions. In some cases, I had to follow the CEO's advice/instruction to leave behind questionnaires to be filled up by the staff at leisure. I could never get back the filled-in schedules on the first appointed date. In one case, the Project Director admitted to have lost the whole packet of filled-in questionnaires and it never reached me. Instead, I was asked to supply another set of blank questionnaires. I dropped this NGO from my list. In case of six organisations, I did not get back any/adequate number of questionnaires for consideration for the study and I had to drop those NGOs.

I never had any difficulty in approaching any organisation. In most cases, I could find either a friend/student working in the NGO or a common friend knowing the CEO or some staff of the NGO. Knowing even a grassroots level staff was of help to get acceptance from the CEO. My exposure to the NGO sector helped me to understand the anxiety of the CEO in participating in an external research study, the possible doubts/questions regarding the research project, or their expectations from me. My familiarity to NGO sector was of great help in avoiding many embarrassing situations and as such facilitated my data collection.

Facilitating Factors
My Village Background: I have been born and brought up in a village. Till I completed my graduation and moved to Mumbai, I

had been engaged in every type of work that a poor village illiterate boy was expected to perform. In this research project, I have studied rural NGOs. My rural background made me feel at home while staying in the villages for collecting data. Open air toilets, bathing in the pond and sleeping in the courtyard with the staff in the village helped in getting easy acceptance among the staff. This resulted in their interest in taking part in my research project. At times for second or third visit to the same NGO, I arrived without any prior notice as I could not stick to my schedule due to logistic problems. Since I could accommodate all circumstances, unscheduled arrival was rather welcomed.

Association with Premier Institutions: My association with two reputed institutions became known to all the NGOs during the first interaction with the CEOs. I have been a faculty member in one institute and a research scholar in another institute. As a recognition to my representation of the institutions, the CEOs and the staff from the NGOs often came forward with a helping hand. A faculty of such a reputed institute visiting and staying in their organisations was regarded by many NGOs as a step towards developing networking. Of the 22 NGOs, five approached me to address their staff.

Visit to Project Sites: Although the nature of my research design did not require visit to the site or talk to the target groups, in most of the NGOs, the CEOs arranged for my visits to some successful projects. In some cases, I was taken to other projects in order to get my feedback to enhance their effectiveness. Considering this ground reality of visiting project areas, I arranged data collecting sessions at the site itself instead of waiting for the next staff meeting at the office. I found that the field staff were more comfortable while responding to questionnaires at the site.

Constraints

Availability of Time: Throughout the course of my research work, I was holding full-time faculty position at an institute of post-graduate training and research. Since I was offering six full subjects and supervising field work of social work students throughout the year, I was not in a position to take time off to go to the field during the semester. I could only visit during the weekend and semester breaks. I planned my visits in consultation with the NGO executives to make best use of it for collecting the data.

Translation of the Questionnaire: Since majority of the staff of rural NGOs speak only their mother tongue/provincial language, it had become essential to translate the questionnaire into the two languages of the two states (i.e., Bengali for West Bengal and Marathi for Maharashtra). Although Bengali was my mother tongue, I found myself incapacitated in fully translating the questionnaires. And I did not have confidence in Marathi. Translating to simple language is a skilled job and it needs concentration and patience on the part of the translator. I struggled for a couple of months to find the right persons. My Bengali speaking students prepared the first draft and the same was refined by a literary expert from an NGO in West Bengal. One of my former students did the major work in translating into Marathi. Both Marathi and Bengali versions of the English questionnaire were refined by a number of people before getting feedback from NGO functionaries. I had to pay special attention to prevent distortion of the statement while translating. Besides, I had to be present during data collection for clarifying the language/meaning of a statement if necessary.

Administrative Apathy: Initially, as stated earlier, I had planned to study government and non-government organisations in the state of West Bengal. I had identified two government run comprehensive area development authorities. On the basis of preliminary enquiry and correspondence, I personally approached the CEO of one of the organisations. On my second visit, he issued an official circular introducing me and my research project to the middle level executives at the head office and the project directors. In spite of the official circular, officers at the head office as well as the project director refused to cooperate in the pretext of official secrecy, under the Official Secrets Act. Their political affiliation and 'no-work' culture of the organisation in general were clearly visible. Since the chief minister was the honorable chairman of the organisation, his approval in my project was sought by the officers. Considering non-cooperative attitudes of all the officers I interacted with, I did not think that a permission letter from the chief minister would change their attitude and result in their interest and cooperation in my research project. In the other organisation, I could not even personally interact with the CEO on a number of occasions. Everyone else in the organisation directed me to see the CEO. I had no choice but to drop the idea of collecting data from government development organisations.

Non-availability of Documents in NGOs: Initially I had planned to analyse some of the reports and periodical reviews of activities of NGOs. This analysis of documents could supplement the findings based on primary data in preparing my report. I found that some of the NGOs do not even prepare an annual report. Certain NGOs did not have a ready list of programme for staffs with their background. In order to prepare the list of eligible staff for participation in my study, I had to make the list by asking information from the project heads. Recordings and documentation are found to be in general the neglected area in NGOs.

Travelling: Collecting data from organisations operating in rural areas is indeed a difficult task. The organisations that took part in my study were located in different districts in the state. In order to reach out to the NGOs often operating in inaccessible terrain, I used all types of available mode of transport like train, bus, truck, boat, cycle-rickshaw and cycles, besides walking. At times, I walked six to eight kilometres to reach the site. Waiting for the transport was a common problem. Sometimes NGO staff was to reach me by bicycle or to give me company to walk to the nearest transport points, which were a few kilometres away. In spite of physical strain to reach out to the NGOs, I used to enjoy travelling and interacting with the staff.

Financial Consideration: During the days of my data collection, I had not received any contingency grant (I received a small grant for data analysis and stationery at a later stage of my research work). I used my personal income for data collection work. Except on a few occasions, most of the NGOs took care of my hospitality and that was of great relief.

Lack of Collegial and Supportive Atmosphere in My Employing Institute: Unfortunately, I did not have a good collegial and supportive environment at my workplace. Cooperation and understanding from colleagues would have greatly helped me. From the stage of conceptualising the problem and developing the instruments, I had been receiving technical guidance from one of my senior colleagues. At the crucial stage of statistical standardisation of the instruments, this crucial guidance did not come through. This was a crisis situation for me. But, soon I overcame my over-dependence and began to learn the techniques on my own.

Improving Research Climate in NGOs : Some Observations

Since the seventies, professionals trained in different disciplines like social work, medicine, engineering, law, management, etc., are entering the NGO sector in a large way. This has led to two classes of manpower in the existing NGOs, namely, promoters and managers/executives. The entry of professionals has led to the systematisation of the functioning of projects, NGOs and a trend towards institutionalisation. Professionalisation and institutionalisation are the two factors which will contribute towards a favourable research climate in NGOs in the long run. I have found during the data collection that the NGOs having an in-built system of recording, reporting and monitoring activities are more open to researchers, than otherwise. Besides, such a system is found to be contributing towards efficiency of the staff and effectiveness of the organisation. A culture of promoting in-built systems of evaluating NGO projects is another area requiring attention. I have found that the CEO appoints consultant to prepare an evaluation report as per the requirements of funding agencies. This dependency on outside consultants reflects the non-availability of skilled staff in NGOs to undertake evaluation work. I am of the opinion that the research and evaluation skills of the existing programme staff can be improved through appropriate training and subsequent opportunities for the staff to carry out such assignments. NGO staff's participation in evaluation work will help them to overcome the fear of facing criticism and will eventually improve the research climate in NGOs. Participatory evaluation research, I have experienced, will ultimately improve staff efficiency and organisational effectiveness.

Conclusion

I have independently and single-handedly worked on every aspects of the data collection process. This valuable experience has helped me understand the research climate in NGOs and the dynamics of NGO management. Further research may focus on longitudinal studies using perceived organisational effectiveness instrument (POEI) on the same set of NGOs. This will explore the merits and demerits of POEI in the context of NGOs in a changing/dynamic task environment. I hope the experiences I have presented here may help NGO researchers prepare better for data collection on NGOs and collect high quality data.

Part V
Making Sense of the Available Data

12
JOSEPH M. CHANDY

Social Research Using Computerised Data Sets

Introduction

Secondary Analysis in Social Research

This article is an attempt to narrate some experiences related to working with a computerised database in the study of a group of teenagers who were children of problem drinkers. When we think about social science research, the classical and usual picture that comes to mind is that of a researcher who constructs a questionnaire that covers the research questions of his/her study and then identifies a sample and goes to the field and collects data. This scene is fast changing and soon may be a thing of the past. A major influence for this is the fact that independent data collection is becoming increasingly difficult and prohibitively expensive and time consuming and therefore, a desire to find alternative ways to answer the research questions is intense in the minds of researchers.

Further, the following developments in the recent past have paved the way for a change in the traditional approach to data collection and analysis in social science research and for a renewed emphasis on what is traditionally called the 'secondary analysis'.

The advent of computer-based analysis in social research makes it easily possible for social researchers to share the data with one another, instead of going through the tedious process of generating fresh data, without, at the same time, compromising the quality of answers to the research questions.

Many agencies, especially service agencies like hospitals, educational institutions, and criminal justice institutions, routinely computerise information about their clients. In the United States, as part of the reporting requirements for the programmes under Title XX of the Social Securities Act, many agencies have developed Management Information System (MIS) whereby they collect, store and process client data. These MISs provide enormous amount of detailed and readily available data for the researcher to analyse and answer his/her research questions. Further, these data sets provide huge numbers of cases thereby enhancing the potential for advanced statistical procedures, which may be limited when fresh data are collected by an individual researcher, since he/she is often limited in resources and thereby in the sample size.

Beginning in the 1960s, we are witnessing another unprecedented phenomenon in social research; the advent of various networks of Data Archives. Each of these agencies would administer and collect data sets from various parts of the United States and other countries.[1] These data will be copied on magnetic tapes and they are shelved as books in a conventional library and are available for loan or purchase, together with the accompanying documentation. Many archives furnish technical assistance in the use of the data files. Some may even perform data tabulations and other statistical assistance.

These Data Archives include many Universities in the United States which construct their own data sets on important areas of interest. For example, the Adolescent Health Program of University of Minnesota constructed a model data set for information about various issues of teenagers in Minnesota. The study which is the subject of this article is based on this data base. Later these same researchers were invited by other States to construct similar data sets in those states. These data sets are available for analysis.

---

1. Here are two examples of such Data Archives: (a) Inter-University Consortium for Political and Social Research at Michigan, and (b) Rand Corporation Data Facility in California.

The essential condition for these approaches to data analysis is the availability of high technical and highly sophisticated resources in terms of computers and softwares. Secondly, it demands that the social researcher of the future be very well conversant in the use of mainframe computers and statistical packages and other data analysis softwares.

Advantages

Before going any further, I would also like to point out some of the advantages and disadvantages of this approach. Secondary analysis is much cheaper and faster than doing original surveys. With the data already collected, the expenses are mainly those of purchasing the data set, making it computer-ready and compatible with the system, and buying computer time. The researcher can independently complete the research, without even the help of an ancillary staff. If the original survey was done by experienced professionals, or the data sets are created and maintained without coding mistakes and other measurement problems, we may benefit enormously from these advantages.

Many of the data collection problems can be circumvented in secondary analysis. Data archives furnish a large quantity of machine-readable data. Further, large samples or even nationally representative samples will be available to the researcher, which is often difficult, if not impossible, for an individual researcher.

Further, secondary analysis offers the researchers an opportunity to build on what is already available and also design complex studies including trend analysis.

However, there are disadvantages too. A serious problem is that of validity. The second researcher has no assurance that the data collected by the original researcher will be appropriate to the questions he/she wants to answer. Sometimes the second researcher may think that he/she would have asked the questions differently, or would have added a few more relevant questions. Therefore, the main concern of the second researcher should be whether the question that was asked, provides a valid measure for the variable he/she wants to answer.

Objectives of the Present Study

The research that is mentioned in this paper was undertaken at the School of Social Work, University of Minnesota. I became interested in what is known as 'Resiliency research'. Some of the pioneers in resiliency research also come from the University of Minnesota. This approach is basically concerned with the so called 'at risk' or vulnerable populations. Some examples of the vulnerable populations include children of schizophrenics, children of divorce, or children who were victims of sexual abuse. These authors concentrate on those factors that make some of these vulnerable people beat the odds and develop and function normally, in spite of their vulnerability. They argue that if these prospective factors that promote resiliency in vulnerable persons can be identified, then that will lead to devising effective prevention programmes. The present situation is that there is a disproportional fixation among human professionals towards treatment, rather than prevention, although the word prevention was in the professional jargon right from the sixties.

As part of a course on Adolescent health, I became interested in the children of alcoholics, who form a vulnerable population. I was brought up in a village in Kerala, where alcoholism is prevalent to such an extent that there were sixteen liquor shops in my village, compared to only twelve provision stores. I was very much interested to know how far alcoholism of the parents influence the social and psychological functioning of children.

Therefore, the research questions that I wanted to study for my dissertation were the following:

- Are the children of alcohol abusers really a vulnerable group, who are at risk of social and psychological malfunctioning?
- What are the social and psychological outcomes for the children of alcohol abusers? Are they significantly different from general population?
- What are the factors that make some children of alcoholics resilient and develop normally and function efficiently in society?

I had originally planned to come to India and collect my data that answer these questions. I was a bit concerned with the cost and time involved in such an undertaking. However, things changed in a very desirable direction unexpectedly. As part of a course on Adolescent health, I had written a paper on the cultural definitions of alcoholism. The Professor, Dr Robert Blum, liked the paper very much, and consequently he invited me to use a data base, which he, as the project director, had just completed in Minnesota. This could save me at least nine months and about US$4000. I thought this is a good offer, although I felt very uncomfortable with the prospect of working with the huge data set, since I did not have much experience or training in it.

The Database

The database mentioned above was constructed from the Adolescent Health Survey which was conducted in Minnesota during the school year 1986-87 and in which over 34,000 public school students in grades 7-12 participated. The survey was a joint venture of the Adolescent Health Programme of the University of Minnesota, and Minnesota Department of Health and the Minnesota Department of Education. This project was designed to create a state-wide data base of health status indicators, risk factors and adolescent health concerns.

The Adolescent Health Survey used a comprehensive instrument developed by a team of educators, health professionals and social scientists from Minnesota and across the USA and had questions on physical health, school performance, substance use, nutrition and eating behaviours, sexual behaviour and attitudes, risk-taking, anti-social behaviours, mental health and relationships with family and friends. Many of the individual items and sets of items had been used and validated in previous research. Other items of the questionnaire were pretested and revised, and the final version was pretested on over 1000 adolescents prior to the state-wide administration.

Completed questionnaires were digitised through electronic scanning and written to a tape which is presently available through the Health Sciences Computing Services of the University of Minnesota, using CYBER NOS/VE system.

Population of the Survey: The population consisted of all students, grades 7 through 12, enrolled in Minnesota public schools in the 1986-87 school year. Private schools were not included. The survey intended to derive a sample that adequately represented schools of all sizes.

Sampling Methods: The sampling frame consisted of lists of school districts provided by the Minnesota Department of Education.

The sample was selected by a stratified clustered design. All districts were first stratified by district enrolment. Districts were then randomly drawn from within the district groupings. When a district declined to participate in the survey, it was replaced by an additional district. Thus, approximately 50 per cent of the original districts and 70 per cent of the students who were enrolled in the participating schools participated in the survey.

Sample Size of the Survey: The sample size was decided to be at least 5000 students per grade with a total sample size of 30,000.

However, the final sample size of the survey was 34,710 unweighted cases and 34,706 weighted cases. The statistical weight was intended to correct for disproportionate sampling by district size and by geographical population distribution. Consequently, the weighted sample is representative of the population of public school students in Minnesota. The standard error is estimated at about three percent.

Thus, the database I was about to work with was a huge one by any standard, having more than 700 variables. The immediate concern for me was to learn NOS/VE language and the SPSS-X statistical package. Although, I had some experience in using mainframe computers after coming to the University of Minnesota, I never had independently used NOS/VE nor the SPSS-X. It seemed overwhelming and sometimes I felt that I had taken up an endeavour that was beyond my capacity and my training. I was asked to get a manual for SPSS-X. Its sight itself was not encouraging – having more than 1000 pages of 1/4 demi size! The computer centre of the university periodically offers short courses on these packages and I took one for NOS/VE. It gave me only a very general idea about the system. They seemed to assume that every one learns about computers by actually using them. But for students like me with absolutely no background in the use of computers, this was indeed frightening.

The major factor here was to understand the logic of how the computers function and once that was understood, then working with the computers became easy and comfortable. Gradually, after spending many frustrating hours before the computers, my fears evaporated and I became confident to use the mainframe.

At this time, the IBM was offering 40 per cent discount on personal computers to the university students and faculty. I decided to avail of this opportunity and purchased a computer, so that I could work at home conveniently. I also bought another instrument called modem, which allowed me to get connected to the university computer from my home through telephone lines. This gave me immense flexibility since I could work on my data as and when it was convenient for me and I had no need to schedule appointments with anyone. With this I was set for my analysis of the data.

The Sample of the Study

Once the data base was at my disposal, my immediate concern was whether I can answer my research questions. First of all, I needed to identify a sample of children of alcoholics. The data set did not contain any information about medical diagnosis of parental alcoholism. However, I was able to identify a reasonably reliable sample of teenagers whose the parents, either one or both, habitually drink. This I could by combining the following three questions of the original questionnaire.

1. Within the last five years, have one or both of your parents ever had problems because of drinking or drugs?
   Yes ☐   No ☐   I don't know ☐

2. How often does your mother or the female guardian use the following (without a doctor telling her to):
   Please mark 1, 2, 3, 4, 5, 6 or 7* in the box provided.
   - Cigarettes ☐
   - Chewing tobacco/snuff ☐
   - Beer/wine ☐
   - Hard liquor (rum/whisky/mixed drinks) ☐
   - Marijuana ☐
   - Cocaine (coke/toot/snow) ☐
3. How often does your father/male guardian use the following (without a doctor telling him to):
   Please mark 1, 2, 3, 4, 5, 6 or 7* in the box provided.
   - Cigarettes ☐
   - Chewing tobacco/snuff ☐
   - Beer/wine ☐
   - Hard liquor (rum/whisky/mixed drinks) ☐
   - Marijuana ☐
   - Cocaine (coke/toot/snow) ☐

A student who answered 'yes' to the first question and '6' (daily) to hard liquor of either 2nd or 3rd question was included in the sample. This combination of questions was expected to give a very conservative measure of parental alcohol abuse. It showed that at least one of the parents of the teenagers in the sample used hard liquor daily and there were problems in the family during the last five years due to drinking or drugs. Was it a valid measurement of parental alcohol abuse? I have sufficient reasons to believe that it was.

These children were considered vulnerable due to parental alcohol abuse. Out of the 34,000 teenagers of the database, there were 838 teenagers that fulfilled these conditions and they were accepted for my sample. This sample was sufficiently large for me to use the complex statistical procedures that were necessary for my study.

---

* 1 = Never, 2 = Over a year ago, 3 = Less than monthly, 4 = About monthly 5 = About weekly, 6 = Daily, 7 = Don't know.

The database had information about the social and psychological outcomes that were of interest to me such as abuse of alcohol and other chemicals by these teenagers, their school performance, their risk of getting pregnant, their risk of eating disorders symptoms and their risk of suicide. In identifying the protective factors that made some of them resilient, the major statistical procedures I used were Discriminant Analysis and Logistic Regression. I could identify seven categories of independent variables to be used in the Discriminant Modes, namely Physical, Socioeconomic Status, Family supportiveness, Family stress, School supportiveness, Peer supportiveness, and Attitudinal positives. Overall, the data set was very useful to answer my research questions.

What are the major difficulties I faced in this process? I did not have to undergo the frustrating difficulties of data collection such as identifying, meeting and interviewing the respondents which many of my colleagues have painfully narrated. I also did not have to go through the tedious process of coding data entry. Funding is usually another serious concern in this context, although I had no difficulty regarding this. The computer centre defrayed almost all the cost of the computer time since I was a student.

However, my frustrations and difficulties were of a different nature as stated here.

Data Manipulation

The fearful fact, I came to understand after my sample was pulled out from the database, was that I was the only person who knew the most about this sample in the data base. This meant there was a tremendous limit to another person's assistance to me. The database was already available in the SPSS-X system files. This was a major help, since I would straightaway start using my SPSS-X programmes. It took a lot of energy and time to learn the system and make it suitable for me to manipulate the data the way I wanted. The staff of Adolescent Health Programme were especially helpful in setting up my data for my analysis.

Statistical Procedures

The Statistical Clinic of the School of Statistics was very helpful in understanding the procedures I wanted to use with my data. But I had to write my own SPSS-X programmes, which often was very difficult and time-consuming. The major contradiction I found here was that the people in the statistical clinic were very conversant with the theoretical aspects of the statistical procedures, but were not very familiar with the SPSS-X and its various options; but, those in the Computer Centre knew how to write SPSS-X programmes, but did not know much about the theoretical implications of statistical procedures. This means that I had to commute between these two groups of consultants and then integrate what I got from them into programmes that will give me the desired results. It was not an easy process.

For example, I wanted to find out the Odds Ratios for the discriminating variables of my modes. The SPSS-X output does not give this information, although we can compute them manually. However, another software package, BMDP, produces this output as part of Logistic Regression. This resulted in me having to take the variables of interest from SPSS-X files in a form readable by BMDP and then use BMDP. This meant that I had to get myself familiar with the BMDP manual, also having more than 1000 pages.

What are the things I missed in this form of research? Definitely the thrill of meeting the respondents in the field and the opportunity to observe them and take notes that are qualitative, and could enhance the richness of my report. Probably, I also missed the fresh air of the field work, since I was fully confined to the four walls of my study room.

Conclusion

In the future, more and more social researchers will be using computerised data sets and perhaps, this may even become the mainstream research approach. As social researchers, we should appreciate the fact that in social research, the range of possibilities of observation in order to find answers to questions of social life is immense and no method is inherently superior to another. As Babbie

(1986) says: "There is no single method of getting information that unlocks all puzzles. Yet there is no limit to the ways you can find out about things. And more powerfully, you can zero in on an issue from several independent directions, gaining an even greater mastery of it."

Reference

1. Babbie, E. (1986). *The Practice of Social Research*, Belmont: Wadsworth Publishing Co.

PART VI
Conclusion

13

MANOHAR PAWAR

Learning from Data Collecting Methods and Experiences: Moving Closer to Reality

"As every researcher knows, there is more to doing research than is dreamt of in philosophies of science, and texts in methodology offer answers to only a fraction of the problems one encounters. The best laid research plans run up against unforeseen contingencies in the collection and analysis of data; the data one collects may prove to have little to do with the hypotheses one sets out to test; unexpected findings inspire new ideas. No matter how carefully one plans in advance, research is designed in the course of its execution. The finished monograph is the result of hundreds of decisions, large and small, made while the research is underway and our standard texts do not give us procedures and techniques for making these decisions. ... Social research being what it is, we can never escape the necessity to improvise, the surprise of the unexpected, our dependence on inspiration ... It is possible, after all, to reflect on one's difficulties and inspirations and see how they could be handled more rationally the next time around. In short, one can be methodical about matters that earlier had been left to chance and improvisation and thus cut down the area of guess work (Becker, 1965).

Introduction

The main aim of this concluding chapter is to address the following four questions:
- What can we learn from the researchers' data collecting experiences presented in this book?
- What are the main difficulties which are likely to obstruct understanding field reality?
- How can we overcome these difficulties?
- How can we improve our data collecting knowledge and skills so that we can understand the field realities and research issues better?

The ten data collecting experiences presented in this volume clearly show that every researcher had experienced some difficulties, challenges and unexpected surprises in their data collection process. In hindsight, they also have recognised some shortcomings in their data collecting instruments and in the way of administering them. These experiences help us realise that the process of collecting data is not smooth. Researchers may encounter problems and difficulties in the field as every time, the nature of setting, the research problem, the researcher, the researched, the time of research and prevailing social conditions may differ. Thus an analysis and awareness of these difficulties may help researchers use the chosen data collecting methods effectively, anticipate field problems and difficulties, and accordingly plan to overcome them. It is also important to note that despite a number of field difficulties, unexpected surprises and sudden changes, the researchers were able to 'successfully complete' the data collection work. Respondents and communities have extended cooperation and provided needed information with warm hospitality. Such positive experiences should hearten both new and experienced researchers to venture into the field to satisfy their curious minds and answer their research questions. Researchers must be driven by curiosity, like the curiosity of a child. Their inquisitive mind should be cultivated and always open.

Difficulties and Possible Approaches

The analysis of field difficulties experienced by researchers and some approaches they followed to deal with them shows that field difficulties may emanate from three 'R' factors or a combination of the three factors. These are: (1) the researcher, (2) the research problem, and (3) the researched. Although all the three factors are important and these can affect each other, in a way the main actor appears to be the researcher.

The Researcher

The researcher is the one who initiates the research process-identification of the problem, research design, setting and respondents, and interaction among them. The researcher's thinking, feeling and doing can cause and resolve difficulties. For example, while narrating field experiences, many researchers have expressed that in the field they felt nervous, anxious, incapacitated, irritated, uncomfortable, overwhelmed, beyond their capacity, frightened, frustrated, tired and at times less confident. This psychological inner state of researchers may be due to their own personality factors, their level of understanding of what they were doing, entry into an unknown field, the nature of setting and respondents' and communities' reactions. However, it is important to be aware of this state in the field and raise questions: Why do researchers enter into this state? To what extent this state affects their data collecting process (that is their observation ability, interviewing ability, responding ability, note taking ability)? To what extent does this state block researchers' efforts to understand field realities? How can researchers overcome these contextual feelings?

On the other hand, the researchers' experiences also suggest that when they become conscious of their own state and issues in the field, they undertook additional reading, they become better informed about the issue, they practised more, tried to become better acquainted with the field and drew on more professional skills. A number of researchers have stated in relation to their field experiences that they felt comfortable and confident, they were assertive and flexible in interviews, they demonstrated warmth, empathy, friendliness and pleasantness and they showed interest in what the respondents had to tell and allowed additional questions and discussion which were no way connected to their instruments and research problem. Importantly, they were also able to establish their credibility. Do these approaches take researchers closer to reality? Anecdotal evidence suggests that these approaches were one step closer towards understanding issues in the field.

Such field experiences seem to suggest that researchers need to concentrate on their competence, attitude and action to collect high quality data from the field. Researchers can enhance their competence by acquiring knowledge and necessary field information in advance, by looking at field requirements, by practising and developing needed skills, by anticipating problems and by preparing possible remedies. Field experiences suggest that it is very important for researchers to feel comfortable and confident in the field by enhancing their competence. Equally important is the researchers' attitude towards the research problem, the field, respondents and communities. Researchers need to introspect about their attitudes and perceptions and see whether they are impeding the way of their data collecting work. Belief in ethical research practice, respect towards respondents irrespective of their background, status, cooperation and noncooperation, respect toward respondents' communities and conditions, awareness of and freedom from one's own prejudices and preconceived notions about the field will help develop conducive attitudes which are likely to facilitate a better data collection process. Researchers also need to be conscious of their actions in the field, that is, the way they behave in the field and whether such behaviour is blocking the collection of realistic information. The way of presenting themselves to respondents (see also Shaffir, 1991), informing them about the research work and purpose, joining community activities, asking questions, noting observations, using intermediaries, etc., do matter and affect the data collecting process. Researchers having any attractive item with them may distract respondents. Researchers as insiders may omit some important data as they are part of it and may take the information for granted, and researchers as outsiders may include some unnecessary data as they may find everything useful at face value. If researchers develop a good level of competence, develop appropriate attitudes and take right actions in the field they are more likely to obtain rich, reliable and valid data that may in turn take them closer to reality.

The Research Problem

The second source of field difficulties is the research problem. Certain problems researchers encounter in the field are due to the nature of the research problem and the decision researchers make to collect data in a particular setting. For example, some research problems involve sensitive issues such as bankruptcy, the accused in the criminal justice system, ethnicity, the development of children, etc., (Lee and Renzetti, 1993). The researchers' experiences have demonstrated that respondents or communities may feel threatened and insecure because of the sensitivity of the issue. While tracing genealogies of families, information on women may not be available in some cultures. In some regions and towns it may not be possible to locate the universe of the community. Census reports may not have a particular type of information. A complete up to date and accessible list of non-government organisations (NGOs) may not be available. At times researchers may not have access to needed data or organisations. Information may not be well recorded and kept. It may not be, where it is supposed to be, well recorded and preserved. Some NGOs may not have a good record and documentation of their work. These are real problems in the field and are beyond the control of the researchers. When such problems are encountered by researchers, first, they should not get perturbed, second, they should clearly study the problem and third, they should look at possible alternatives. Once they analyse the possible alternatives, the most appropriate alternative can be chosen and changes introduced in the data collection strategies.

As stated earlier, difficulties may also arise due to the nature of setting and lack of information about the setting. The researchers' experiences have showed that their respondents were widely dispersed, they had to walk long distances to access some communities which were located in hilly and remote areas and they had to make do with inadequate food and accommodation arrangements. Some interviews were conducted at odd hours. Some of these difficulties were not only experienced in rural and remote areas, but also in large urban centres such as Mumbai, Bangalore and Calcutta due to unclear addresses and road maps. Unlike many developed countries, telephone facilities and telephonic appointments may not be feasible in some parts of developing countries. Many researchers seem to have dealt with these difficulties through trial and error and have experienced exhaustion, tiredness and tears. This type of experience is likely to affect researchers' physical and mental ability, at least initially and temporarily, and may weaken the data collecting process. Several creative approaches need to be explored to prevent and deal with such difficulties. Thorough pilot study should certainly signal such potential problems. Researchers need to anticipate and plan well, including logistics, to cope with some of the realistic difficulties in the field. Careful use of local guides/volunteers and resources may reduce some of the problems. When research is undertaken in rural and remote communities and tribal areas, researchers must learn to live happily with limited facilities and without the so-called luxuries of urban life. The pace of research work needs to be organised in such a way that it takes care of physical exhaustion.

The Researched

As stated earlier, the third category of difficulties may emerge from the researched, that is respondents and communities. Researchers in the field often need to pass many tests of respondents and communities. The main and most common difficulties experienced by the researchers were as follows. One of the common problems experienced by researchers is making entry into the community and gaining acceptance. How should the researcher enter the community and access respondents and gain acceptance? Gaining entry is an important hurdle which every researcher must overcome. The researchers' experiences show how the researcher makes entry in the field really matters. If the researcher is introduced by health officials, respondents/community may perceive the researcher as medical officer/doctor. If the researcher is introduced through government revenue officials, respondents/community may think that the researcher is collecting some information for the government. If the researcher is introduced through community political leader, this approach may be perceived from a political perspective. If the researcher enters on her/his own, her/his legitimacy may be questioned by the community gatekeepers. If the researcher enters through a friend/relative in the community, respondents/community may think that our neighbour's friend/relative is doing some writing work or study, yet, some others may question the researcher's presence. If the researcher is introduced by influential people in the community, respondents may accept the researcher on the face value and respond in a desired way. If the researcher is introduced through an NGO or a donor agency, respondents/community may think that the researcher may introduce some new programmes and services. These type of perceptions of respondents/community may colour their responses, at least initially. Thus researchers need to be conscious of how they are going to make an entry and how they will access respondents and they need to make an assessment about likely implications on the quality of data. It is not practical to recommend a particular entry approach as each entry approach has its own advantages and disadvantages, and each may appear as a right approach depending upon the context. At times a combination of approaches may be needed. However, it is practical for researchers to make a list of all the entry options and analyse the likely consequences of each approach on the data. This will help them identify an approach/approaches with minimum consequences on the data and to develop systematic plans to overcome those consequences. This is an initial problem and it must be overcome by researchers. Many researchers do overcome this hurdle successfully. Another approach is to exclude the coloured data once the incoming data pattern is established and the researcher confidently feels that initial data was coloured.

Once researchers make successful entry, they need to gain acceptance from respondents and communities. Without respondents'/communities' acceptance researchers may not be able to collect data. Gaining acceptance becomes an issue because respondents and communities have many questions about the new person (researcher) who has entered the community. In addition to questions, in the absence of clear communication they also have their own perceptions about the researcher. Thus it is hardly surprising that many researchers have reported respondents'/ communities' suspicions about the researcher. Is the new person (researcher) from Criminal Investigation Department (CID)? Is s/he collecting some secret information? These and similar questions and suspicions continue to exist in the minds of respondents, particularly those who come under sensitive categories (bankrupts, drug addicts, child abuse cases, etc.,) and those who are involved in some kind of wrong doing (receiving some development benefits in cash or kind and disposing them for immediate gain or the accused, etc.), if simple, clear and consistent information is not passed on to them. Most of the respondents in rural communities, particularly in developing societies will be unfamiliar with the academic world, its language and trappings. They may be curious and their interest and concerns may be expressed in straightforward questions such as:

- Who is this new person?
- Why has s/he come?
- Where has s/he come from?
- What does s/he want?
- What research is s/he talking about?
- Why is s/he asking these questions?
- Why is s/he observing certain events?
- What do I get from it?
- How is the community going to benefit from it?
- Is it going to harm me in any way?
- Who is supporting or funding this research?

Researchers need to be prepared with simple, straight and honest answers to such questions. Many researchers have some anxiety and uncertainty about whether they will be able to successfully collect data or not. Some researchers may also be under the pressure to collect data by any means. This type of anxiety, uncertainty and pressure may lead researchers to use some short cuts such as giving cursory introduction about themselves as well as their research, providing false answers to the questions, hiding information or giving different information to different people. If researchers do not provide simple, straight and honest information to respondents, they are less likely to get reliable and valid data from them. If researchers are true to what they are doing and share the same with respondents by demonstrating some of their good attributes (warmth, friendliness, etc., discussed above), they are likely to gain acceptance of respondents and communities. I believe establishing rapport and building trust are all part of the process of gaining acceptance. Researchers should also avoid defensive arguments, after all they are not in the field to debate and win it, though their research and findings might result in some debates that are beneficial to respondents and communities. This approach may take a little more time, may require researchers to repeat the same answer often, but it will help them gain acceptance and thereby move closer to reality.

Before starting data collection work, it is crucial to resolve ethical dilemmas, issues and approaches related to the research so that research respondents' rights to relevant information and confidentiality and their right to refuse participation in the project and their right to withdraw anytime from the project, are ensured and protected. In some developed societies, as part of ethical requirements, each respondent is given an informed consent letter and form. The letter generally addresses all the above questions, respondents' rights and also directs them to appropriate authorities, if they are not satisfied or if they want to complain. Respondents also need to sign an informed consent form and return it to the researcher. I am not sure whether this approach (signing the form) will work in developing societies, particularly if the researched are not literate and not exposed to research. There may be other culturally appropriate ways of ensuring informed consent. Taking respondents' signatures on the informed consent form may cause further suspicion and reluctance. Wherever possible and practical, this approach may be tried. However, informed consent letter is a good practice. It can be read over to respondents and copy may be given to them. It may also help the researcher establish her/his credibility.

After making an effective entry and gaining acceptance, researchers' data collection begins either through interview (structured, semi-structured, unstructured, informal, in-depth), questionnaire or observation, or a combination of these or any other data collecting methods. The researchers' experiences indicate several problems during the data collecting process. I have identified the following important difficulties for discussion.

Interviews

Location of the interview can be problematic both for the researcher and the researched, depending upon where and how it was arranged. For example, I thought of interviewing the accused at the court premises when s/he comes to attend the case at the court. This plan simply did not work and in hindsight I think that it was not the right location for the interview. Location of the interview should be such that it offers privacy to the respondent and the respondent feels comfortable to respond to the researcher's questions. In fact, the location of the interview must be chosen by the respondent, whether it is her/his own residence, nearby restaurant, park, or temple/church or a location suggested by the researcher. The researcher should also be alert enough to observe whether free and frank responses are affected due to the location of the interview, and move to appropriate location.

Due to sensitivity of the issue dealt with and probed in interviews, some respondents may feel threatened, identified, stigmatised and incriminated (see also Lee & Renzetti, 1993). As long as such feelings exist, respondents are less likely to offer free, frank and honest responses. Although it is hard to provide foolproof hints to overcome this problem, researchers must try to free respondents from such feelings. Efforts to overcome this problem might include ensuring direct contact with the respondent, rather than using a second person or intermediary to approach the respondent, strictly maintaining confidentiality, suppressing actual names, exploring the respondent's version of the events, opinions, etc., and avoiding using anything, e.g. tape recorder, which the respondent particularly finds threatening and choosing the location according to the convenience of the respondent. Carefully discussing the processes the researcher wants to use such devices as note taking or tape recording and the experience of the location at the commencement of the interview may allay fears or identify an acceptable approach.

Many researchers have experienced unwillingness, refusal and non-cooperation of and difficulty in convincing respondents for an interview. Some researchers, due to the pressure of data collection, seem to coerce respondents in different ways for an interview. This approach is not good and it will not help researchers to collect accurate and valid data. Despite the above discussed 'gaining acceptance' approaches, some respondents may not come forward for an interview. In such a situation, researchers should simply and politely thank them, withdraw from the interview, and go to the next respondent.

Another difficulty in research interviews is that when the respondent agrees an interview and the interview begins, members of the family and neighbours surround the researcher and the respondent, curiously watch or interfere in the interview process by adding their responses or suggesting responses to the respondent or diverting the respondent. This is a real interference and it is likely to affect the quality of interviews. Depending upon the context, sometimes family members' presence is needed so that the respondent feels comfortable and secured to give interview. Researchers have to carefully read the situation and see what the respondent desires and accordingly involve the respondent in keeping unnecessary people away from the interview. In case of siblings, some researchers have interviewed the other sibling simply to pacify her/him and excluded the data as it was not part of the sample. In some community, members show extra curiosity and interest in the interview and ask 'why not me also for the same interview?' (thinking that they might receive some services in cash or kind). Some researchers interview such additional people to satisfy them so that they will not further interfere and throw the completed schedule later. I am not sure whether these are right, and ethically appropriate approaches. Depending upon the context, researchers' prudence should guide them to deal with the situation. However, researchers should anticipate such interruptions and prepare well to minimise them so that a smooth interview is conducted and high quality data are obtained.

While interviewing some researchers have experienced two types of difficult situations. In the first situation, some respondents wanted to finish the interview quickly (not interested in having long and detailed interview) and some respondents needed specific questions to which 'to the point' answers could be provided (in case of unstructured, in depth qualitative interviews). In such cases, although the respondent has agreed to give an interview, he/she wants to get over it quickly. Researchers need to quickly look at the reasons behind such urgency. Is the time not suitable? Whether respondent has pressure to urgently attend to another important task. Whether the respondent is a busy professional who does not have time. Or is the respondent really not interested in the interview and indifferent to it? If the answer is 'yes' to the last question, researchers can do little about it except excluding the interview. On the other hand, if the respondent desired to get over the interview due to other reasons, researchers can propose and determine a mutually convenient time and venue for the interview, if practical. If not, researchers must try to obtain as much data as possible within the given opportunity. To avoid such situations, one researcher targeted talkative and not very busy respondents, but this approach may not help in all the contexts. In such situations, some respondents went on narrating and talking and it was difficult for some researchers to change the direction of the interview and bring it to the point according to the data requirements. Where and how to stop a talkative respondent is a sensitive issue. Researchers are often conscious of hurting the respondent, if they intervene and ask the respondent to stop the 'story' and come to the researcher's questions. Thus sometimes researchers may feel that they are losing direction in the interview and not able to obtain required data. In the second situation, researchers should not lose their confidence, they should become good listeners and show interest in what the respondent is narrating irrespective of whether it is related to the required data or not. Consciously allow respondents express whatever they are interested in expressing to the researcher. Give priority to what they want to say. Researchers may also recognise that they are providing an opportunity to ventilate. This may help researchers understand respondent's perceptions, expectations and motivations. Based on this understanding, researchers may clarify, if need be, and bring the interview back to the required point. Researchers also need to develop effective skills of sensitive intervening and directing the interview. To one researcher, tracing genealogies of families on paper had helped to counter unconfined narrations. Researchers need to creatively think of similar techniques depending upon the context. It is important to note that sometimes useful information comes before or after the interview and some researchers seem to have an ethical dilemma of including it in the data (French, 1993). In my view, such information may be included in the data if it is taking the researcher closer to a valid understanding of the issue.

Not knowing the local language has been a major difficulty experienced by some researchers. I think this is the biggest block to any researcher. Without understanding the local language, how do you move closer to reality? Perhaps, the other sensory perceptions (observation, non-verbal communication, etc.) may become doubly active to understand what is happening. Those researchers who knew local languages were also handicapped as they were not aware of local (tribal) dialects. This type of difficulty should not stop researchers undertaking research in such areas. Use of village leaders or tribal chiefs as translators or interpreters may influence responses and result in obtaining one-sided picture, not the real one. Researchers need to prepare and plan well to work with the language problem. They need to learn and develop local basic vocabulary. Most importantly, they need to identify, train and employ neutral interpreters (who neither take the side of the researcher nor the researched) who do not affect respondents and their responses.

After interviews, in hindsight, some researchers have admitted that they covered many dimensions and their interview schedule lacked depth, long interviews were tiring for both the researcher and the researched; some respondents found the interview process exhaustive and time consuming, and insufficient thought was given for deciding upon the list of items in the schedule. These difficulties emanate from data collecting instruments. Well-trained researchers and well-planned research can take care of such issues by designing and testing the instrument in such way that prevents these difficulties. There is no point in covering too many dimensions, without going in depth into any one particular issue. By pretesting, the optimum length of interviews should be estimated. If the interview takes long time, breaks should be planned at appropriate stages of the interview. In-depth/long interviews may be conducted in two to three separate sessions. If particular items of the interview do not work, the researcher should be flexible enough to consistently drop them from the schedule. To dovetail well with the current research culture, researchers prepare their data collecting instruments according to the positivistic framework. However, this methodological rigidity does not always work in the field. According to field realities and the changing nature of the research problem, researchers need to be flexible and open to introduce necessary modifications in their data collecting instruments and strategies. One should not compromise on the process of understanding reality through methodological restrictions (that is research design and instruments).

The data collecting experiences show that some researchers had experienced difficulties in recording semi or unstructured or informal interviews. In some interviews tape recorder invoked resistance, whereas in other interviews it facilitated. Some shorthand notes taken during the interview were found not useful. A researcher was not regular enough in noting down information that was found useful and informative. Many of these problems can be prevented by the researchers by planning, practising and by being alert and systematic. Tape recorder should not be used in interviews if it makes the respondent conscious and inhibits her/his responses. On the other hand, it may be used if it facilitates a good interview. Researchers need to take appropriate decisions depending on the field context. Although tape recording may appear easy, transcribing it later is a time consuming and an expensive process. Over-reliance on electronic gadgets is not recommended as they may not work when you need it most. With enthusiasm researchers may record interviews, but they may not find time to go back to them. These cautions need to be considered to make use of the tape recorder most effectively. The other alternatives are shorthand notes and memory. If the shorthand note method is also objected, the only tool the researcher is left with is her/his memory. When these alternatives are used, researchers must expand their notes and transcribe their memory in writing regularly immediately after interviews. Delay would fade memory and thus the collected data as well. If the researcher is from the same community (insider), s/he should be aware that too much familiarity with the issue may result in not recording certain obvious information and should avoid such omissions.

Finally, if researchers experience so many difficulties while collecting data, the most important difficulty is how to make sure accurate data is collected and how to ensure that the collected data is accurate. Some researchers have found it difficult to substantiate their impressions. Some have noticed exaggeration and concealment of personal data. It was also reported that when people did not understand about research, it adversely affected eliciting accurate information from respondents and data suffered from the lack of objectivity. As researchers, this is a 'big question' for all of us. Are we able to transfer the realities of the respondents in the field, 'the truth', in our data and to what extent? And how can we achieve this? Some of the approaches discussed above are aimed at facilitating the collection of accurate data. To examine the accuracy of collected data researchers may look at patterns in the data and inconsistencies and gaps from such patterns. One researcher has attempted to check the validity of data through the plausible pattern (face validity), testimony of multiple witnesses and official records. Another researcher cross checked the oral history data with written documents where available. These and similar approaches may be tried to check the accuracy of the collected data.

Questionnaires

Constructing a good questionnaire and collecting data through it require relatively sophisticated skills and literate respondents. In some settings (a group of students in schools or a group of trainees) it may be easy to collect data through questionnaires, whereas in other settings it may be somewhat difficult. A researcher has experienced difficulties in bringing together a group of NGO workers at a particular time to group-administer the questionnaire. Similarly, I have experienced difficulties in collecting data through questionnaires from public prosecutors and advocates. At any rate, one of the limitations of the questionnaire method is that its return rates vary and are often low. Our experience suggests that in case of a questionnaire, administering, completing and collecting it in one session will yield better return rates than giving a questionnaire to respondents and asking them to return it later. In spite of reminders and visits, researchers may not receive completed questionnaires. If questionnaire respondents are located in government or non-government or business organisations, the organisation head's cover letter asking the respective employees to cooperate with the survey may facilitate the data collection process. If organisations delay responses and do not provide time blocks for data collection, despite repeated approaches, it is likely that such organisations may not be interested in the researcher's project. If the expected respondents are busy professionals such as medical practitioners, lawyers, engineers, managers, etc., it is better not to approach them at their work locations (hospitals, courts, offices). Researchers may first find out the most suitable time for such professionals to complete the questionnaire and accordingly approach them.

Observation

Observation is a very powerful method to understand field realities, if properly employed. A number of researchers have used this method to collect data. Although their experience suggests no specific problem in using this method, researchers were conscious of an ethical issue. The researcher, as a requirement of the research method and to understand the reality as it is, does not inform the observed – s/he, parents, family gathering, group, actors in a particular event – about their being observed by the researcher for the purpose of a given study. Is this approach ethical? This is a debatable question and there may not be a conclusive answer to it. One way of overcoming this ethical dilemma is to get the research design and data collecting instruments approved by respective organisations' ethics committees, if they exist. In many developed societies, universities and research organisations/departments have well constituted ethics committees which periodically review research applications submitted by researchers and provide ethics clearance to research projects. If such committees and ethical guidelines do not exist, researchers should examine whether their observation approaches have any short term and long term harmful effects on the observed. If the answer is positive, that should guide ethical researchers to make appropriate decisions. Another important issue related to observation method is that some researchers who did not record their observation data regularly (preferably on the same day) had significantly lost the observation data. Thus regularity, consistency (observing, note taking, recording, etc.,) and timely follow up (of further observations and interviews) in whatever one does in the field are indispensable. Researchers also have noted that planned and arranged observations (e.g. planned visits to successful projects) provide only a partial picture of the phenomenon. Researchers must have some autonomy in observing so that they can get an adequate picture of the phenomenon being observed. The researchers' experiences show that sometimes meaningful data may be collected through casual experiences, observations and conversations. Researchers may not be able to capture such meaningful data when they approach respondents with questionnaire/interview schedule in a formal way.

Data from Government Organisations (GOs)

Researchers have experienced a lot of delay in obtaining permission from GOs to collect data. Thus research projects requiring permission/approvals from GOs and NGOs, and ethics committees may anticipate unreasonable delays in obtaining permission for data collection. The permission process should be started well in advance. If the research topic is sensitive and securing permission is doubtful, the researcher may start work on the topic only after obtaining the permission; project timing can be seriously jeopardised if permission is not sought early.

Some government documents such as court cases are written in shorthand (abbreviated) form and researchers may not be able to follow the handwriting of clerks. A thorough study of files and development of a glossary may help decipher government documents. Our experience also shows that some officials may not provide needed documents at the requested time. A most serious problem faced by one researcher was the reluctance of various officials to provide the required data/information. The researcher also experienced that government officials were not willing to collate data and they did not take research studies in a positive frame. Researchers have also experienced reluctance of officials in cooperating with research projects. It may also be very difficult to convince lower level officials about the usefulness of research. Some important information such as time series data and agriculture related data may not be available at block offices. Sometimes researchers may be able to access a huge amount of government data, but may not be able to easily identify needed data from it. Researchers who intend to collect data from government offices must be aware of these issues and prepare well to deal with them. Each researcher's approach may differ. I tried to establish rapport and friendly relation with some officials and it helped me most of the time to get case-files from them. If a particular information is not available from government offices, researchers must tap additional resources.

Other Insights

While one researcher found it difficult to express social and cultural attributes in quantitative terms, another researcher's field experiences suggested that it is possible to meaningfully blend qualitative and quantitative data.

The time/period of data collection need to be determined in such way that it is suitable and appropriate to respondents, communities and the researcher. Adverse weather conditions should be avoided to ensure a better quality data collection (unless such a condition is the requirement of data collection).

Depending upon the nature of the research problem and type of respondents, sample mortality rates vary. When the research topic addresses sensitive issues sample dropouts are highly likely. By looking at relevant data, researchers need to anticipate and estimate such dropouts and accordingly plan the sample size for the study.

In the field, some researchers desperately desired academic discussion with similar researchers which was not available. As a substitute, one researcher started keeping field notes and maintaining a diary. When researchers enter isolated fields, sometimes they reach a stage where they long for research discussions with peers – a kind of debriefing, clarifying and confirming. Researchers may consciously plan such opportunities. Modern communication technologies (E-mail, Internet chat, etc.,) may also be used to achieve this purpose, if they are accessible.

A few researchers who collected data without any financial support and by spending their own money appeared to have financial pressures and difficulties. Field data collection is often resource intensive. To ensure a smooth data collection process, researchers must make appropriate resource plans and mobilise adequate financial support in advance.

An equally important area is the researcher's own health. Researchers must give attention to keep good health in the field so that they can fully concentrate on data collection work.

The above discussed field difficulties and possible approaches essentially flow from the researchers' data collecting experiences presented in this book. This is not a comprehensive list of field difficulties. The suggested possible approaches may work for some researchers and may not for others. Thus they are not perfect remedies. Other researchers might have experienced some other difficulties and tried innovative approaches to deal with them. I hope that an exercise of this nature may stimulate such researchers to write and disseminate their field experiences to the research community so that we all can contribute towards developing better data collecting knowledge and skills.

In Search of Better Data Collecting Knowledge and Skills

Having discussed field experiences and difficulties, and learning from them, now I will try to address the last question: How can we improve our data collecting knowledge and skills so that we can understand the field realities and research issues better? My answer to this question would be very broad and general, though a fundamental one. The answer essentially lies in critically questioning the positivistic framework that we often follow while conducting social science research. In the introduction chapter, I have argued that social science researchers need to go beyond the framework of positivism to challenge some of its outcomes in social sciences and discover new research methods. This would require a major shift in the way we think, conceive and prepare research proposals and conduct research. At this point of time, such a thinking and practice may not gain acceptance from rigid social scientists whose thinking may not go beyond positivism and from large funding research bodies such as the Australian Research Council and the Indian Council of Social Science Research. Such new thinking and likely resistance from believers in positivism will result in a transition period of professional insecurity (see Kuhn, 1962, 1974). Increasing failure of positivism in social science research will lead to greater search for new research methods. When we start looking for new research methods, we will find them and that, I believe, may enhance our data collecting knowledge and skills. Meanwhile, the following practical approach may be considered.

In any research there are two equally important connected segments. These are (1) substantial content of the study, the issue, the topic or the research problem (what I call the reality) and (2) the procedure(s), that is the research method(s) (Creswell, 1998) to study the issue, the topic or the research problem. Sometimes, researchers may be preoccupied with either of them. There is a possibility that a researcher may plunge into methodological sophistication and unnecessary procedural and technical details (under the influence of positivism) to such an extent that the substantial content of the study distorts or evaporates. In contrast, a researcher may deeply immerse her/himself into the field realities without following the needed procedures and thus may lose direction in the field, and the purpose of being there. The substantial content of the study may also be greatly affected when a researcher does not recognise changing field realities and contexts and rigidly sticks to research procedures decided on the 'armchair'. As stated, while both are important, imbalance between them or the inappropriate use of procedures or methods to study the research problem may compromise on the objectives of the study and distort the reality.

It is logical to think and expect that data collecting methods we use to collect data about the research problem, should lead to the same findings, since the reality under study is one or the facets of the reality are the same. However, there are many research studies which suggest contrary findings on the same issue because research and data collecting methods were different. This phenomenon in research suggests that research and data collecting methods and the researcher have potential to colour the reality. With passage of time and other changes, same methods may yield different results on the same problem under study. If research methodology and research methods and positivism are distorting reality and creating hurdles to getting closer to it, at least in social sciences, why do we need to follow such a method? That is why, I am arguing and proposing that, perhaps, there is a need to explore alternative research methodology. In the introduction chapter, I have suggested a pluralistic approach to collecting data as it cuts across methodological dichotomies and differences (e.g.., positivistic and subjectivistic; qualitative and quantitative) and concentrates on understanding the reality. This is only an initial thought and requires further refinement.

We have another very good example towards this direction. Flyvbjerg (2001) in his book, *Making Social Science Matter: Why Social Inquiry Fails and How it Can Succeed Again*, persuasively argues that social sciences should not follow the path of the natural sciences research method, which I have often referred as positivism. According to Flyvbjerg (2001) the social sciences are strongest where the natural sciences are weakest, but they are not able to build on their strengths as they are caught up in a losing fight, because they have accepted terms (natural sciences method) that are self-defeating (p. 3). Based on a thorough analysis of relevant literature, Flyvbjerg (2001) suggests a phronetic social science approach (should not be seen as methodological imperative, but a cautionary indicator of direction, p. 129) for conducting research in social sciences. The phronetic social science approach essentially involves reflective (see Schon, 1983) and reflexive (see Steier, 1991; Usher, 1997) analysis and discussion of values and interests. The phronetic approach is guided by four questions:

- Where are we going?
- Is this desirable?
- What should be done?
- Who gains who loses; by which mechanisms of power?

While addressing the four questions, the phronetic researcher concentrates on values and power, remains close to the phenomenon studied (without necessarily "going native" or the project becoming simple action research), emphasises little things (knowledge of details), looks at practice before discourse, studies cases in contexts, focuses on asking "how" and doing narrative, joins actors and structures and encourages dialogue with multiple voices (for details see Chapter 9, in Flyvbjerg, 2001). The objective of the phronetic approach is to carry out analyses and interpretations of the status of values and interests in society aimed at social commentary and social action (see Flyvbjerg, 2001, p. 60).

These approaches give rise to the hope that better data collecting knowledge can be acquired and skills can be developed. To achieve this, new and experienced social science researchers need to:

- critically look at positivism and how it has hindered the potential of social science research;
- be conscious of doing research by following the framework of positivism like robots;
- thoroughly study available research and data collecting methods and be aware of their strengths, weaknesses and skills required to use them;
- employ reflective and reflexive methods;
- think and develop new approaches to conducting social science research and contribute to refining the existing ones; and
- regularly practice effective research and data collecting methods.

References

1. Becker H. S. (1965). "Review of Sociologists at Work". *American Sociological Review*, 30, 602-603.
2. Creswell J. W. (1998). *Qualitative and Research Design: Choosing among the Five Traditions*. California: Sage.
3. Flyvbjerg B. (2001). *Making Social science Matter: Why Social Inquiry Fails and How It Can Succeed Again*. Cambridge: Cambridge University Press.
4. French S. (1993). 'Telling'. In Shakespeare P., Atkinson D. and French S. (ed), *Reflecting on Research Practice: Issues in Health and Social Welfare*. Buckingham: Open University Press.
5. Kuhn T. (1962, 1974). *The Structure of Scientific Revolutions* (2nd edn). Chicago: University of Chicago Press.
6. Lee R. M. and Renzetti C. M. (1993). 'The problem of researching sensitive topics: An overview and introduction'. In Renzetti C. M. and Lee R. M. (ed). *Researching Sensitive Topics*. Newbury Park: Sage.
7. Schon D. (1983). *The Reflective Practitioner*. New York: Basic Books.
8. Shaffir W. B. (1991). 'Managing a convincing self-presentation: Some personal reflections on entering the field'. In Shaffir W. B. and Stebbins R.A. (ed), *Experiencing Fieldwork: An Inside View of Qualitative Research*. Newbury Park: Sage.
9. Steier F. (1991). 'Introduction: Research as reflexivity, self-reflexivity as social process'. In Steier F. (ed), *Research and Reflexivity*. London : Sage.
10. Usher R. (1997). 'Telling a story about research and research as story telling: Postmodern approaches to social research'. In McKenzie G., Powell J. and Usher R. (ed), *Understanding Social Research: Perspectives on Methodology and Practice*. London: The Falmer Press.

Note on Contributors

Joseph M. Chandy was the Director of the Department of Social Work at California State University, Bakersfield and had taught social policy and research. He had received his MA in social work from Tata Institute of Social Sciences, Mumbai, and PhD from the University of Minnesota, Twin Cities. Previously he had taught in social work programmes at University of North Dakota, University of Missouri-Columbia and University of Mumbai. His research interests were resiliency factors of at-risk children, effectiveness of social welfare programmes and health care issues.

Simon Combe is currently teaching and undertaking research in North-East China. He previously taught subjects related to agriculture, rural development and social research at the School of Agriculture and Rural Development, University of Western Sydney and Development and Asian studies at the Macarthur Institute of Higher Education – both in Sydney, Australia. After receiving his honors degree in History from the University of New South Wales, Sydney, he received his MTCP (Town and Country Planning) and Ph.D. from the University of Sydney where his research focused on the definition, nature and role of the indigenous grassroots voluntary agencies in rural India. His current research is focusing on the possibilities and limitations of participation in urban social welfare programmes.

Dr. Swapan Garain is the Professor and Chairperson of the Centre for Development of Corporate Citizenship at SP Jain Institute of Management and Research, Mumbai, India. He taught at the Tata Institute of Social Sciences (TISS), Mumbai, for 16 years. As a Senior Fellow at Johns Hopkins University, he worked on NGOs in Cyberspace Fundraising. Dr Garain holds Bachelor of Social Work (Hons) from Visva Bharati University, Masters in Social Work from TISS, Doctorate in Management Studies from Mumbai University and Diploma in Management from IGNOU. He has published a book and a number of papers. His recent research, teaching and consultancy have been in the area of corporate social responsibility, application of ICT in social sector, social entrepreneurship, structural and behavioural aspects of management of NGOs, philanthropy, rehabilitation and resettlement of project-affected persons and micro-enterprises. He is a member of the Steering Committee on Voluntary Sector constituted by the Planning Commission, Government of India and Group Advisor to IndianNGOs.com. He has helped setting up of a number of NGOs. He serves on various committees and boards of a number of non-profit organisations, associations, chamber of commerce, and of the government. He is the Founder Director of Interactive Karma India, a not-for-profit initiative of US-based NRIs for leveraging information communication technology for the social sector in India. Dr. Garain may be contacted at: eutsa@hotmail.com.

Dr. (Ms.) Ranu Jain is a Reader in the Unit for Research in Sociology of Education, Tata Institute of Social Sciences, Mumbai, India. Her Ph.D. dissertation is on boundary fixation and maintenance processes of ethnic groups. Since then she is pursuing her interest on the related phenomena like, communalism, minority majority issues, plural society and polity, and culture and education. She has conducted a number of research and action projects and has published several papers on the related issues. At present, she is pursuing a study to understand the process of hegemony building in India as well as the possibility of multi-culturalism in the era of cultural nationalism in India.

Rajani M. Konantambigi has a Ph.D. in Social Sciences (Child Psychology) from the Tata Institute of Social Sciences, Mumbai. She is currently a Reader at the Unit for Child and Youth Research at the same Institute. She is involved in the childcare and elementary education, research and practice issues besides implementation of a field action and research project on non-formal education for tribal children at Betul district, Madhya Pradesh, India. Socialisation and child rearing, and qualitative research methodology are her other areas of interest. She has been awarded the Rockfeller Foundation's Team Residency Fellowship, for a month at Bellagio, Italy, to edit a book on Daycare Provision For Children in India: Problems and Prospects.

Dr. Lakshmi Lingam is a Reader in the Women's Studies Unit, at the Tata Institute of Social Sciences, Mumbai, India. She is currently the Co-ordinator, Centre for Health Studies, TISS, and was the General Secretary of the Indian Association for Women's Studies for the term 2000-2002. Prior to joining the TISS, she pursued her doctoral research titled 'Women's roles in the production and reproduction spheres of wet and dry villages of East Godavari district, Andhra Pradesh', at the Indian Institute of Technology, Mumbai. She has published several papers on the following subjects – women-headed households, girl child, sex selective abortions, women's studies, reproductive rights, occupational health, women's health, migration and development. She has been widely acclaimed for her book *Understanding Women's Health Issues: A Reader* (1988), published by Kali for Women, New Delhi and her contributions to the VHAI & WHO's National Country Profile on Women's Health in India. She has been teaching the course, 'Status and Health of Women' to Masters in Social Work and Masters in Health Administration students for over a decade. Presently, she is engaged in a research project that attempts to assess the impact of Structural Adjustment Policies at the household level.

M.E. Thomas Dr. Madhavappallil Thomas, MSW, Ph.D., LCSW, is Assistant Professor of Social Work at the Department of Social Work, California State University, Bakersfield where he is currently teaching social policy, community development and social work administration in the Master of Social Work programme. Earlier he was Assistant Professor of Human Development at Eckerd College, Florida, USA. He has researched the impact of development programmes on children, women, rural poor and tribal population groups and has worked closely with a study funded by World Health Organisation on systems approach to family planning. While practising social work in the US, he has researched and developed a profile of at-risk adolescents based on their family interaction and its implication for treatment. Recently, he has completed (Co-PI) an Immunisation Evaluation Research Study for the Bakersfield Immunisation Coalition. Currently he is involved in programme evaluation and examining the effectiveness of urban revitalisation on the marginalised poor and the homeless. He has published several papers in journals related to social welfare programmes and policies.

Manohar Pawar has an MSW and Ph.D., is a Senior Lecturer in Social Work, School of Humanities and Social Sciences, and a key researcher of the Centre for Rural Social Research, Charles Sturt University, Wagga Wagga, Australia. Earlier he has taught at La Trobe University, Melbourne, and the Tata Institute of Social Sciences (TISS), Mumbai, India. Pawar has received a Quality of Life Award 2001, from the Association of Commonwealth Universities and Research Excellence Award 2001, from the Faculty of Arts, Charles Sturt University. He has completed a number of funded research projects and published several books and refereed journal articles. Some of his own and coauthored published titles are: *Community Informal Care and Welfare Systems* (2002, Vista); *Job Network and Employment Services in Wagga Wagga* (2001, Bobby Graham); *Towards Poverty Alleviation in Rural Australia* (2000, CRSR); *Social Development Content in Social Work Education* (1997, RSDC); and *Justice Processing Sans Justice* (1993, TISS). Pawar's current areas of interest include international social development, social work and social policy, social work education, NGOs and community development, criminal justice and evaluation research.

Martin Ryan is a Senior Lecturer in the School of Social Work and Social Policy at La Trobe University, Melbourne, Australia, where he teaches social work research and community work. Prior to entering academia, he worked as a financial counsellor and as a social worker in oncology and palliative care. His doctoral research was on consumer bankruptcy, and he has also conducted research on the skill and knowledge development of social workers, professional expertise, palliative care social work, social worker/nurse collaboration and a number of areas of social work education. He is the author of *The Last Resort: A Study of Consumer Bankrupts* (1995), *Social Work and Debt Problems* (1997) and *Professional Expertise: Practice, Theory and Education for Working in Uncertainty* (2000) (with Jan Fook and Linette Hawkins).

I. U. B. Reddy is a resettlement specialist in the Social Development division of the World Bank in New Delhi. He was previously on the staff of the Unit for Urban Studies, Tata Institute of Social Sciences, Mumbai. Dr. Reddy obtained his Masters and Ph.D. degrees in regional planning from the Indian Institute of Technology, Kharagpur (India) and an additional Masters degree in Sociology from Sri Venkateswara University, Tirupathi (India). His research interest is in displacement and resettlement issues, urban problems, and regional development, and he has authored two books on displacement and resettlement.